EXCEPT-AFRICA

EXCEPT-AFRICA

Remaking Development, Rethinking Power

EMERY ROE

Transaction Publishers

New Brunswick (U.S.A.) and London (U.K.)

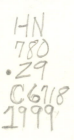

This book is printed on acid-free paper that meets the American National Standard for Permanence of Paper for Printed Library Materials.

Library of Congress Catalog Number: 98-40494
ISBN: 1–56000–399–5
Printed in the United States of America

Library of Congress Cataloging-in-Publication Data

Roe, Emery.
    Except-Africa : remaking development, rethinking power / Emery
Roe.
        p. cm.
    Includes bibliographical references (p.) and index.
    ISBN 1-56000-399-5 (alk. paper)
    1. Rural development—Africa, Sub-Saharan. 2. Rural deveopment—
Political aspects—Africa, Sub-Saharan. I. Title.
HN780.Z9C6718   1998
307.1'412'0967—dc21   98–40494
                                                        CIP

Contents

Dedicated to

Brian Egner, Tom and Roberta Worrick, and Gary Childers

Preface and Acknowledgments

This is my first real book on Africa; it is also my last. I've wanted to write this one for some time, as each chapter has a special claim on my attention. The introduction and chapter 1, which deal with development narratives, reflect my most cited work.[1] Chapter 2 developed a model of triangulation that I extended into a book on sustainable development.[2] Chapter 3 sums up twenty-five years of my thinking about sub-Saharan livestock development while making what I feel to be a major contribution to the study of pastoralism. Chapter 4 on expatriate advisors and land reform is the finest piece I have written and personally the most satisfying. I've been told that the article on which chapter 5 is based helped inaugurate a "boom and bust budgeting" literature, while chapter 6 on decentralization in Zimbabwe presents the results of my last fieldwork. Finally, the conclusion is based on an interchange between my critics and myself over what I consider to be the hollow center of African studies—its obsession with power and power politics. While the interchange has had no impact on the field, the topic remains central to my work on highly complex policy issues. Briefly put, the principal consequence of complexity is surprise, not power. I hope the reader will share the excitement that originally propelled the writing of these chapters and the satisfaction that comes with seeing old issues in a new and, I believe, more tractable light.

Beyond this book, I have little more to say. *Except-Africa* develops the widest array of counternarratives yet assembled to the pernicious development narratives that drive so much of contemporary understanding of African rural development and politics. This book is the first concerted effort of its kind, and these counternarratives provide a basis for reconstituting contemporary understandings of rural sub-Saharan Africa, particularly those in the media and Western popular opinion. This reconstitution is, however, an exercise I shall not be undertaking. A major argument of *Except-Africa* is that technical experts, such as myself, have used our expertise to assert rights as "stakeholders" in the land and resources of an Africa we do not live in and in which we really do not have a personal daily stake. I no longer am comfortable with being that "stakeholder." *Except-Africa* should be read less as the recommendations of a technical expert than as a summing-up by someone whose position now is that of bearing witness to rural people in Africa who are their own counternarratives.

***

This book is dedicated to four remarkable persons. Roberta Worrick—whose painting is copied on this book's cover and is better known as the author Maria Thomas—used to say we should never have been in Africa. She and her husband died in a airplane crash in Ethiopia before I thought to ask her just who did she mean by "we." Tom Worrick, the best official in the U.S. Agency for International Development (USAID) I've ever known in the field, was on his last posting before retiring. Gary Childers and I became friends when serving as Peace Corps volunteers in the same village. Royalties for this book will be sent to a fund in his memory, which, in case you wish to contribute as well, is the Whidbey AIDS Support Fund, P.O. Box 248, Langley, WA 98260. Last, there is Brian Egner, who was the first. My first boss, the godfather of my son, my good friend—you deserve your own book, but this will have to do.

***

Most of *Except-Africa* represents substantially revised journal articles. The following appear with the permission of Elsevier Science:

Introduction	"Postscript: Except-Africa" to a special section around my "Development Narratives" article, in *World Development*, vol. 26, no. 6 (1995).
Chapter 1	"Development Narratives, Or Making the Best of Blueprint Development," in *World Development*, vol. 19, no. 4 (1991).
Chapter 4	Emery Roe, "Public Service, Rural Development and Careers in Public Management: A Case Study of Expatriate Advising and African Land Reform," in *World Development*, vol. 21, no. 3 (1993).
Chapter 6	"More Than the Politics of Decentralization: Local Government Reform, District Development and Public Administration in Zimbabwe, in *World Development*, vol. 23, no. 5 (1995).

I thank Duke University Press for permission to use portions of previous material in chapter 1 and the conclusion, which originally appeared in *Narra-*

tive Policy Analysis (Duke University Press, Durham and London, 1994) and in "Against Power, For the Politics of Complexity," in *Transition* 62 (1994) as well as "The Sharp Edge of the Sword: Reply to My Critics," in *Transition* 64 (1994). Kluwer Academic Publishers has granted permission for use in chapter 2 of "New Frameworks for a Very Old Tragedy of the Commons and an Aging Common Property Resource Management," *Agriculture and Human Values*, vol. 11, no. 1 (1994). Chapter 5 is based on an article which originally appeared with Eddy Omolehinwa, "Boom and Bust Budgeting: Repetitive Budgetary Processes in Nigeria, Kenya and Ghana," *Public Budgeting and Finance*, vol. 9, no. 2 (1989). I thank the *PB&F* managing editor for permission to use this material. Different versions of chapter 3 are forthcoming with Lynn Huntsinger and Keith Labnow as "High Reliability Pastoralism," in *Journal of Arid Environments*, and as "High-Reliability Pastoralism Versus Risk-Averse Pastoralism," in *The Journal of Environment and Development*. Finally, elements of several of chapters (particularly chapter 2 and the conclusion) are drawn from my *Taking Complexity Seriously* (1998). Let me also again thank each of those acknowledged in the original articles without whose help this book would not have seen the light of day, especially Louise Fortmann and Scott Fortmann-Roe.

Notes

1. For example, see Melissa Leach and Robin Mearns, eds. (1996), *The Lie of the Land: Challenging Received Wisdom in the African Environment*, International African Institute in association with James Currey and Heinemann, Oxford and Portsmouth, NH. See also Des Gasper and Raymond Apthorpe (1996), "Introduction: Discourse Analysis and Policy Discourse," *The European Journal of Development Research*, vol. 8, no. 1. The most detailed presentation of the narrative analytical approach used in *Except-Africa* can be found in Emery Roe (1994), *Narrative Policy Analysis*, Duke University Press, Durham and London.
2. Emery Roe (1998), *Taking Complexity Seriously: Policy Analysis, Triangulation, and Sustainable Development*, Kluwer, Boston/London/Dordrecht

Introduction

Except-Africa and
Its Counternarratives

Preliminaries

The starting point of *Except-Africa* is its recurring theme: "There can be no development without alternatives." The proposition can be defended by appeal to any number of fields: philosophy (dialectics), psychology (gestalt), politics (pluralism), semiotics (definition through contraposition), history (contemporary), and more. But like all good foundations, this one is ultimately arbitrary. I certainly do not pretend I could defend the proposition to the satisfaction of all readers or even most of them. This book is for those who already glimpse the sense of what the proposition is all about and are willing to see what kind of twist I give to it.

More formally: there can be no development without counternarrative. It borders on a commonplace to say that the problems of African rural development are increasingly complex—that is, they are more numerous, interrelated, and varied than ever before. Because African rural development is genuinely complex, it is saturated with development scenarios deployed to stabilize decision making in the face of that complexity. In their simplest form, development narratives are the rules of thumb, arguments, "war stories" and other scenarios about rural development that enable decision makers to take decisions, be the decision makers farmers, bureaucrats, outside experts, or others. Some scenarios are well known, e.g., the tragedy of the commons

1

narrative. Other are less known, but found across wide stretches of Africa's drylands, e.g., the eight-kilometer (five-mile) rule for spacing livestock water points apart from each other. Easily the most famous development narrative is about Africa itself, namely, the scenario concerning the continent of Except-Africa, as in "Everything works . . . except in Africa." In all cases, development narratives are used to fix and steady (that is, stabilize) decision making in situations treated as very uncertain in the absence of those scenarios. The task of policymakers, development specialists, and policy scholars is to come up with counternarratives that are just as effective, if not more so, in stabilizing decision making under uncertainty but which are far less noxious and pernicious than the development narratives currently guiding a great deal of that decision making.

One of the abiding ironies of rural development practice—and not just in Africa—is that narrative and complexity are deeply reciprocal. The more complex things are and the more things there are to be complex, the more widespread complexity becomes at the macro-level and the greater the demand for standardized approaches with wide application to deal with that complexity. The more each local case should be judged on its own merits because of its complexity, the more governments respond by insisting that one-size-fits-all programs are required for that now-widening complexity.

In this view, it is not that development narratives are too simplistic, given the world is more complex. Rather, it is because the world is complex that you have the development narratives, simplistic or otherwise. One may criticize the tragedy-of-the-commons argument as too simple-minded based on what actually happens in practice, while in the same breadth understanding that such criticism carries little force until a counternarrative to the tragedy of the commons is provided which does a better job of guiding decision making. The same holds for the other reigning development narratives of the day.

Accordingly, development narratives—hegemonic or otherwise—will dominant practice, as long as that development continues to be complex, i.e., as long as development issues increase in number, variety, and interdependence. Since development narratives are here to stay for the foreseeable future, the challenge is to come up with counternarratives to replace those development narratives that do such a disservice in stabilizing practice. *Except-Africa* shows, through the widest range of case studies yet assembled, how this can be done for rural Africa generally and for Africa's rangelands specifically. The best way to get rid of an objectionable development narrative is to go beyond criticism—does the world really need another critique of structural adjustment?—and come up with a more effective counternarrative. *Except-Africa* demonstrates that counternarratives are not only possible, but many. This introduction concludes with an illustration of the book's overall approach by developing counternarratives that work against that most famous of development narratives, Except-Africa itself.

The Book's Organization

Chapter 1 formalizes the book's argument. Development narratives are defined, a framework is provided which explains why and how these narratives are used, and specific examples of development narratives are discussed to illustrate what we can do to change them. Ten different development narratives are discussed, including those of the tragedy of the commons, land registration programs, systems thinking in rural development, rangeland carrying capacity, and government budgeting in Africa.

The remaining chapters are devoted to generating counternarratives to some of the more dominant development narratives in sub-Saharan rural development. Chapter 2 sketches four counternarratives to the tragedy-of-the-commons argument, while chapter 3 provides the most innovative counternarrative of the last several decades to conventional ways of thinking about sub-Saharan pastoralism. Chapter 4 develops a counternarrative to the dominant views about expatriate advising in Africa. Chapter 5, in turn, sketches a counternarrative to those all-too-common views about government budgeting in countries such as Nigeria, Kenya, and Ghana. Finally, chapter 6 presents a case study and counternarrative from Zimbabwe of a complex local government reform for "decentralization" there.

The six chapters are dedicated to showing how counternarratives can remake rural development in sub-Saharan Africa. In the process, they raise serious questions about conventional understandings of "power" and "power relations" in that development. The book's conclusion addresses these questions directly by asking the reader to rethink entirely the current wisdom about power in African rural development. Much of contemporary African Studies is obsessed with power narratives, be they colonial, neocolonial, or postcolonial. Yet in African rural development, power interests are by no means clear, as development issues are frequently contingent and provisional. Surviving the tangled fusion of narrative and complexity in rural development requires a politics of complexity and the conclusion sketches just such a politics for the reader's consideration.

As both an example of this book's approach and the linchpin for its subsequent analysis, let us now turn to that most pernicious of development narratives, Except-Africa.

The Except-Africa Narrative

A 1985 *New York Times* science section article ran the headline, "Spread of Deserts Seen as a Catastrophe Underlying Famine." Almost nine years later to the day, the science section appeared with the headline, "Threat of Encroaching Deserts May Be More Myth Than Fact." The former begins: "The famine now coursing through Africa poses an immediate crisis of vast proportions. But underlying today's tragedy is a more deep-seated problem that threatens the future of arid lands throughout the world. It is 'desertification,' the insidious, spreading process that is turning many of the world's marginal fields and pastures into barren wastelands . . . " The more recent article begins: "Common wisdom has it that the deserts of the world are on the march, steadily expanding, permanent converting pastures and croplands to sand dunes, and that human mistreatment of the drylands that flank the deserts is responsible. But scientists using the most up-to-date investigative techniques have found no evidence that this is true."[1]

What, one hazards to ask, will the next decade's article say? The temptation, of course, is a fallback to moderation, as in "Now this isn't to say desertification is not going on in some areas . . . " But moderation is no longer the point. Many such crisis scenarios have been, as recent work[2] underscores, destructive as well as self-destructing. The scenarios have for a time stabilized policymaking in the face of a highly complex and uncertain rural development, but in ways that have ignored or ultimately increased that complexity and uncertainty, thus giving rise to even more crisis scenarios. As Hoben (1995), Rocheleau et al (1995) and others argue, crisis scenarios have actually caused crises to take place in some cases, where uncertainty and complexity intensified as the result of failed scenarios and in the absence of effective (alternative) counterscenarios.

Two crisis narratives about Africa cry out for challenging. First, there is the crisis narrative about Except-Africa. A major financial weekly tells us investment to developing countries continues to increase, "except in Africa." A report of an overseas think-tank concludes "Africa is the exception" when it comes to development. A well-known historian notes that by the end of the twentieth century the world is likely to experience a decline in poverty *"except Africa, where things will only get worse"* (his italics).[3]

The second crisis narrative is the Doomsday Scenario for any country in Except-Africa: the birth rate of [fill in name of country] is rising; human and other animal populations increase daily; overutilization of the country's scarce resources accelerates; the government tries to create jobs but is less and less able to do so; rural people pour into the cities and the government's rural development policies are helpless in stemming the flow; political unrest becomes explosive, while politicians and civil servants grow ever more venal; and unless something is done to reverse this process, before you know it the fill-in-name-of-country is another basket case of Except-Africa.

The two crisis scenarios have stabilized policymaking for donors, agencies, and others; neither has any enduring policy relevance. In part, their problem is empirical. Except-Africa?—the average annual growth rate in gross domestic product (GDP) and GDP per capita has been worse for Eastern Europe and the former Soviet Union than for Africa, according to some figures.[4] The Doomsday Scenario for every African country?—but African governments budget and perform very differently, and such differences must matter if you believe that governments can and do have an impact (chapter 5). Africa, the basket case?—better to say, Africa the twenty-first century's reservoir of new democracies.[5]

Still, the real reason why the two crisis narratives have little policy relevance is that they do such a poor job in stabilizing the assumptions for decision making in the face of manifest African heterogeneity. Sometimes the absence of policy relevance is patent. Have you ever noticed how Except-Africa is always overcrowded when it is not underpopulated? (What expert has ever said of *any* African community, "You know, here there are just the right number of people, livestock, and wildlife!") As for the Doomsday Scenario, its neo-Malthusianism appears compelling, but the scenario has zero—repeat, *zero*—policy relevance in the absence of its providing estimates on what human and animal populations should be in place so that Africans can have markets, participate in their economic growth, and sustain their own resources . These estimates are simply not known (more in chapter 1). What is needed, and what the multinational donors *and* their critics have so far not provided, are the counternarratives that stabilize policymaking so that these estimates or their alternatives can be supplied at the level(s) where they are the most meaningful, realistic, and helpful.

The recent literature goes a considerable way in criticizing the many pernicious development narratives dominating rural development in Africa today (one thinks again of those myriad critiques of structural adjustment). Rather than critiquing the empirical merits of these and other crisis scenarios, we—you, me, everyone—will have to focus more on the equally policy relevant meta-question, What is going on when experts put forward these crisis narratives? What is the *role* of these expert narratives in decision making based on them?

The answer can be put succinctly: crisis narratives are the primary means whereby development experts, and the institutions for which they work, claim rights to stewardship over land and resources they do not own. By generating and appealing to crisis narratives, technical experts and managers assert rights as "stakeholders" in the land and resources they say are under crisis. Working on the principle that those who sustain resources are the best stewards of those resources, the crisis scenarios serve to make a twofold claim, namely, not only are insiders, specifically local residents, not stewarding their resources, but those who really know how to sustain those resources are outsiders, specifically technical assistance personnel and professionally trained, in-country resource managers. Accordingly, so this argument goes, local people must be guided by the stewardship of techno-managerial elites, be they experts in host-country governments, international donor agencies, or transnational nongovernmental organizations (NGOs).[6]

We come then to a central insight (whose complications are elaborated in chapter 4): the more crisis narratives generated by an expert elite, the more the elite appears to have established a claim to the resources it says are under crisis. What looks first to be a conflicting array of crisis scenarios and counterscenarios—first the experts said the crisis was desertification, now they don't—is not bewildering after all. Whether right or wrong, the claims and changing claims of experts serve principally to reinforce and widen the belief that what they, the experts, have to say really matters and matters solely by virtue of their expertise.

The more scenarios experts have tendered, the more topics over which they have claimed a policy-making role. The seriatim crises that Kenya, for example, has purportedly undergone over the last hundred years—epidemics, soil erosion, underdevelopment, deforestation, soil erosion again, declining biodiversity, AIDS, and all-the-time famines— serve to underscore no point better than that rural Kenyans are more and more in "need" of an ever-widening range of expert help if they are ever to overcome their all-too-many problems (see Rocheleau et al. 1995). The more the experts disagree among themselves or change their views, the more we all can be "certain" that things must be fundamentally wrong and increasingly desperate in Kenya—or why else would the experts be warning about so many different things?

What is really "fundamentally wrong," if anything, depends—fundamentally—on how Africans themselves see their rural development. That their perceptions are increasingly colored by experts is undeniable. That their perceptions differ in important respects from the experts is also undeniable (e.g., Fortmann 1995). One thing is clear, though, about these perceptions: they have evolved and continue to do so. What we know about the careers of civil servants (chapter 4) and the life histories of rural people tells us over and over again that rural development must *inevitably* be evolutionary: persons coming new to rural development start with the expectation that what is out there is waiting to be identified, realize once in the field that there are problems in determining what is actually there, later acknowledge that such problems arise in part because what is out there depends crucially on how what "it" is they are looking for is defined in the first place, and then end up in better understanding that what works best in any particular situation is tailoring practice to meet specific objectives agreed upon case by case.

Where specifically is this evolutionary rural development taking place? It is best to start by indicating where it is likely not to be found. Government, donor, and NGO institutions that persist in seeing Africa, or most of it, through the telescope of one hundred years of crises from turn-of-the century rinderpest to turn-of-the-century AIDS are unlikely to have learned much that matters. Techno-managerial elites whose very *raison d'être* is predicated on addressing one crisis after another are unlikely to have learned much that matters. A media that habitually describes Africa as a place where a reporter's one visit is enough to see the writing on the wall—where learning is never trial and error but always hit or miss, where one statistic "says it all" (an eroded hill is the sign of government indifference to desertification, a half-completed classroom means declining national self-reliance, beggars in the city foretell the Coming Anarchy), where virtually *every* news report points to collapse under such headlines as "Africa's Development Crisis," "Africa's Food Crisis," "Africa's Financial Crisis," and "Africa's Next Crisis"—is unlikely to have learned much that matters.

An important part of what has been learned is this: Except-Africa is very much a creation of outsiders. Had the experts started with nationalism and religion as the major contemporary policy issues of this and the next century, rather than population and investment, they would have ended up with Except-Yugoslavia and Except-Middle East, two places much closer to the experts' homes! Had the experts spent less time bemoaning Except-Africa's lack of roads and infrastructure, more of them would have seen the trade possibilities opened up by better roads in Kenya and Zimbabwe compared to their neighbors (more in a moment). Had they spent less time writing about crises in Except-Africa, they would have seen there is a real crisis in their one-note preoccupation with Except-Africa. Unfortunately, many experts are much more comfortable in addressing population and investment rather than nationalism and religion, and in *recommending* development rather than *doing* development.

What to do? The book's recurring theme states this author's preferred option: come up with counternarratives. Developing them will mean, quite literally, reversing old patterns of thinking. If counterscenarios are to be generated, what are conventionally treated as the causes of program failure will now have to be taken as the preconditions for successful new programs.

If the dominant development narrative asserts that (a—> b—> c), then the counternarrative is either (not-a—> not-b—> c) or (a—> b—> not-c). Thus, undertaking thought experiments where what are commonly taken to be causes of project failure are the preconditions of project success becomes one powerful way to think counternarratively. The virtues of imagining reversed causality are threefold: (1) doing so focuses on precisely the variables of observed interest (i.e., a, b, and c) and, in the process, provides the most robust test of their linkage; (2) even if a plausible counternarrative cannot be envisioned, trying to imagine one can suggest alternative explanations of the observed phenomenon; and (3) even when the analysis concludes that indeed a—> c via b, if the analyst has made a plausible case for the counternarrative, s/he has identified an alternative worth pursing, should it be found that the observed outcome of a—> b—> c is unacceptable.

Point (3) is important: to think counternarratively is to conceive of a rival hypothesis or set of hypotheses that could plausibly reverse what appears to be the case, where the reversal in question, even if it proved factually not to be the case, nonetheless provides a possible policy option for future attention because of its very plausibility. The term "counternarrative," as used in *Except-Africa*, covers the range from the pure version of a reverse causality scenario to all those other scenarios identified as alternatives to the objectionable narrative in the process of thinking counternarratively about the latter.

An example of one such counterscenario from Zimbabwe is illustrative.[7] It is commonly supposed that communal area development cannot really happen in Zimbabwe until these areas are more closely integrated with the commercial farming and related urban sectors. Substitute "subsistence" and "cash" for "communal" and "commercial," and you have a conventional development narrative for many parts of Africa.

Reverse that thinking. Imagine communal areas having closer trade and economic links with surrounding Zambia, Botswana, Mozambique, and South Africa than with the commercial farming areas or Zimbabwe's capital, Harare. Imagine also communal areas more integrated with key arid and semiarid urban centers in Zimbabwe, such as Bulawayo or Masvingo, than with that country's commercial areas. This counternarrative is actually going on in some of Zimbabwe's communal lands. As others have long noted, these communal areas have more in common with conditions in neighboring countries than they do with agriculture in Zimbabwe's commercial farming areas. The key reversal here is to recognize that Bulawayo and other centers in Zimbabwe's dry areas are much better connected by road to parts of Zambia, Mozambique, and Botswana than are Lusaka, Maputo, and

Gaborone. It is Zimbabwe's comparative advantage in communal infrastructure—notwithstanding the poor and few roads always complained about in the popular development narrative—that should, can, and must be exploited for policy purposes in such a counterscenario.

Counterscenarios will, of course, vary case-by-case. The broader point, however, still holds: reversals in thinking are required.[8] Experts will have to drastically reassess their "business-as-usual" scenarios. If African herders insist that it is not overstocking, but lack of rainfall, that is causing rangeland changes (a survey finding from across Africa), then the expert should show how this view of the herders could be true and what they can do about it. If African farmers keep growing crops in areas that the experts insist on classifying as "suitable only for extensive grazing and wildlife," then the experts must revise their agroecological classifications. If some of the so-called low potential lands of semiarid Africa have produced more cash value at the margin than the so-called high potential areas (chapter 1), then this invidious language of "low potential wastelands" should be dropped once and for all. If rural and urban Africans insist—as many do—that poor education, not rapid population growth, is their real development problem, then the expert should show how this could be true and what they can do about it. Far too many of the "business-as-usual" scenarios for the future—so popular today in sustainable development workshops and conferences—depend on ubiquitous crisis narratives that are more asserted than demonstrated. One of the abiding ironies of development practice today is that we cannot expect to "scenario" the future until we first "counterscenario" the present.

In addition to generating new counterscenarios, there are other tactics to displace or replace the offending development narrative, and they are discussed in the next chapter. One tactic is to denarrativize the offending narrative by insisting "there is no story to tell until the facts are in" (which surely should be our counter to the desertification scenario that started this introduction).[9] Existing narratives that run counter to a dominant development narrative can also be engaged. Right alongside the tragedy-of-the-commons narrative of homogeneous herders and grazing land is the narrative of heterogeneous African landscapes, households, and livelihoods. The latter becomes a counterscenario to the former when you insist that herders and their grazing land must first be differentiated (and in multiple ways) before judging the extent to which, if at all, a tragedy of the commons is taking place (more in chapter 2). Indeed, if you are able to differentiate herders and their rangeland from the start, you will never find a tragedy of the commons taking place—and that is a promise.

It is important to emphasize that potential counterscenarios are sometimes to be found within the existing repertoire of development narratives. Again, a Zimbabwe example is illustrative. The U.S. Supreme Court's *Lucas* decision on "takings" holds that government agencies must, in some circumstances, compensate those whose properties have been rendered valueless because of government regulation or other interventions undertaken after the purchase of those properties.[10] Under the earlier Convention on International Trade in Endangered Species (CITES) ivory ban (of which the United States was a leading signatory), the value of the preexisting stock of ivory in government of Zimbabwe storehouses—which ran into the millions of U.S. dollars—was reduced effectively to zero. Not surprisingly, some Zimbabweans sought to use the *Lucas* decision in seeking partial compensation—in this case from the United States—for what is a takings of their ivory. Indeed, now that some U.S.-based NGOs have "earned" what are essentially sovereignty rights as a result of the Rio Summit (that is, they are "stakeholders" able to sit down at the table and negotiate alongside developing countries over natural resource policies), they too should be expected to compensate developing countries for any takings their NGO policies entail. The broader point here is that the current repertoire of development narratives includes narratives that can be made to run counter to each other, at least under some circumstances.

"But what about the bloodshed in Rwanda?," some readers will have asked by this point. "Surely you can't counterscenario or denarrativize that away!" "What about the horrors in Liberia, Congo, Ethiopia . . . .?," you insist. Well, what about them? It should be clear by now that those who persist in starting discussions about Africa with, "What do we do about the-latest-crisis-there?," are asking a systematically misleading question. Such questions push and pull us in very much the wrong directions. First, they push us away from looking at what is actually going on elsewhere in Africa and from constructing policy-relevant (counter)scenarios in light of these observations. Second, they pull us toward techno-managerial elites whose very existence depends on getting you to keep asking "What-do-we-do-about-crisis" questions. In short, the questions pull us to an Except-Africa where nothing would get done if these elites didn't have the answers, or so they say.

The challenge before us in *Except-Africa* is to formulate many more counterscenarios that would guide rural development practice more effectively than the current crisis narratives that dominate attention today. As a first step in meeting the challenge, let us turn to a detailed discussion and illustration of what is meant by development narratives and what we can do about them.

Notes

1. Boffey (1985), pp. 17, 20; Stevens (1994), pp. B5, B8.
2. See *World Development* (1995) special section on "Development Narratives."
3. The cites are, respectively, *The Economist* (1993), p. 5; Lewis (1986), p. 30; and Kennedy (1993), p. 212.
4. *The Economist* (1994), p. 114.
5. I'm indebted to the late Aaron Wildavsky for this point. Once when we were driving into work, I complained to him about how positive points regarding Africa were almost always countered in discussions with questions like, "But what about the latest horror story there?" Aaron piped up, "Now, where do these critics think the next century's democracies are going to come from?!"
6. A more general discussion of the techno-managerial elite can be found in Roe (1988b). I am indebted to Paul Piccone, editor of *Telos*, for much of my understanding of them.
7. This counterscenario is discussed in greater depth in Roe (1992a). See also chapter 6.
8. Reversals in thinking about rural development have been called for, most notably, by Chambers (1993).
9. For more on denarrativization, see Roe (1993). A shorter version under the same title appears in Roe (1994b).
10. The *Lucas* decision distinguishes between land and property. For the details, see Sax (1993).

1

Development Narratives and Six Ways to Change Them

Introduction

What are development narratives? The short answer is that they are stories (scenarios and arguments) that underwrite and stabilize the assumptions for decision making in situations of high complexity and uncertainty. Each narrative discussed below has a beginning, middle, and end (or premises and conclusions, if cast as an argument) and revolves around a sequence of events or positions in which something is said to happen or from which something is said to follow.[1]

Rural development is a genuinely complex activity, and one of the principal ways practitioners, bureaucrats, policymakers, and other decision makers (including citizens) articulate and make sense of this uncertainty is to tell scenarios and formulate arguments that simplify or complexify that reality. (We will see why policymakers might want to make their narratives complex.) Indeed, the pressure to generate narratives about development is directly related to the ambiguity decision makers experience over that development. As noted in the introduction, the more uncertain things seem everywhere at the micro-level, the greater the perceived scale of uncertainty at the macro-level and the greater the perceived need for explanatory narratives that can be operationalized into standard approaches with widespread application. Thus, the failure of projects and programs based on development narratives often serves only to reinforce, not lessen, the appeal of some sort of narrative that explains and addresses the persisting, now increasing, uncertainty.

Such considerations raise the question, Can rural development be improved by directly addressing those narratives that underwrite and stabilize that development? The answer is Yes, and to see how this is done, six different options for changing development narratives are discussed, with examples given for each.

But first some explanation about the terminology used in what follows. It is my hope that readers will be uncomfortable with terms such as "defamiliarize," "denarrativize," "metanarrativize," and "counternarrativize." I write "hope" because the main aim of *Except-Africa* is to recast the familiar and taken-for-granted in rural development in a fresh and altogether more useful light. The objective here is, in the words of W.H. Auden, to disenchant and disintoxicate the many development narratives that dominate our understandings of African rural development. Nor do I mean only those odious narratives about "Except-Africa" and its "doomsday scenario" discussed in the introduction. There are those other development narratives taken as given and simply assumed to be the case by development practitioners and scholars alike that must be challenged, e.g., "politics in Africa is about power" or "behind the official rhetoric and policies [read: development narratives] are the power interests that determine them." Only when we have defamiliarized the familiar will we have a chance to develop new narratives that are more plausible as a platform for positive action in the future.

Briefly put then, one way to change a development narrative is to denarrativize it, an option first mentioned in the introduction. Alternatively, one could create a counternarrative (as in the following tragedy-of-the-commons example); or use the development initiatives generated by the narrative to alter that narrative (as in the case of land registration); or fill in the "details" of the narrative in order to make it less misleading (as in the systems approach example below). Another option is to identify a more tractable metanarrative that shifts attention away from the development narrative one finds objectionable. There are many instances, however, where little leeway exists to be creative. The best a person can do is to engage another preexisting narrative, which, once engaged, conflicts with the more objectionable one.

The bulk of this book is given to discussing and exemplifying the counternarrative option. For that reason, this chapter devotes considerable attention to the other five options.

Six Options

1. *Denarrativize!*

You denarrativize a development narrative by insisting that "getting the facts and figures right has to come before knowing what is the real story in question." Something like this happens, for instance, every time negative academics (Robert Chambers's term) rely on critique alone: they have simply shown that the official position has little or no empirical merits without, however, providing an effective alternative argument to the one they have so thoroughly discredited. Every reader knows of those wonderful tracts that painstakingly demolish a government or donor orthodoxy but which fall apart the minute they get to the section—if they get there at all—variously called "policy implications." There, the painstaking gives way to the painfully clear, in that no matter how effective the critique has been as a demolition job, it falls woefully short of developing a more feasible and implementable alternative to that which has been demolished. Still, criticism matters, if only in establishing just how objectionable the development narrative is.

The more general point is that because rural development is truly an uncertain enterprise and has been for a very long time, it is always (*always*) a fairly easy matter to denarrativize development scenarios simply by pointing out their factual shortcomings. To appreciate just how easy, I have purposively chosen three development narratives that have been considered by and large true within their own contexts.[2]

Narrative 1: The colonialists deserve little or none of the credit. The British are often said to have invested virtually nothing in the Bechuanaland Protectorate for much of the period prior to Independence in 1966. According to a former permanent secretary of Botswana's Ministry of Finance and Planning, "it is quite clear that nothing occurred between 1885 and 1955 which contributed significantly to Botswana's economic and financial development . . . It was a passive period, devoted to the avoidance of involvement, to the maintenance of a *status quo*." This, and like narratives, have had great currency.

The data do not warrant the conclusion. The period after 1955 was one of substantially greater development financed by Britain, but the pre-1955 period was far from static, at least in that sector—livestock—

which proved to be the country's growth engine for much of its history.

While the numbers are fragmentary, several trends were observed during the "status quo" period prior to the mid-1950s. Between the census period of 1921 and 1956, cattle numbers rose from about half a million to slightly under 1.24 million—an estimated 150 percent increase—compared to a 100 percent increase of the human population during roughly the same time (from some 153,000 to just short of 310,000). In addition, between those years for which we have comparable time series data, 1924 and 1954, cattle exports expanded from around 25,000 head to some 74,600 (an increase of some 200 percent). Income from recorded livestock sales and related products rose by more than a factor of ten between these years from £120,385 to £1,695,000, while the cattle-export price index increased less than 75 percent during the same time (from 69 to 119, with 1910 set to 100). What a status quo!

Narrative 2: Poor, female-headed households are major rural beer brewers and depend on the sale of that beer for much of their income.[3] After Independence, the majority of rural households in Botswana continued to brew traditional beer, and many of these households sold beer at one time or another, though far fewer actually sold on a regular basis. A number of researchers commented on the importance of traditional beer sales to rural poor, female-headed households, and some argued that such households were major producers of that beer (for example, see Dahl, 1978 and Egner and Klausen 1980).

The data available at the time simply did not warrant that conclusion. Most traditional beer appears to have been produced by those who can afford to produce, namely, wealthier rural households. Kjaer-Olsen found that, on the basis of her 1980 survey of thirty-eight cash brewers in three villages, the majority of beer brewers "belonged to the wealthier classes . . . In our sample, those who brewed for sale came predominately from households that were active in agriculture. 88% of those households that brewed for sale ploughed their own arable lands and of these, two-thirds did so with their own draught power." In her 1979 survey, Vierich found that, while households holding twenty-two and more cattle accounted for some 29 percent of all households sampled, they accounted for nearly 70 percent of all households selling traditional beer. Similarly another study found that while 34 percent of the sampled households held sixteen or more head of cattle, they accounted for some 44 percent of all traditional beer sellers in that sample. A different study concluded that "only relatively well-off households tend to brew [traditional beer], the capital outlay on equipment and ingredients being so high." Other studies undertaken at roughly the same time found similar findings.

Narrative 3: Marginal lands are marginal.[4] Well after Independence, some dry zones of sub-Saharan countries had faster rates of growth in per capita income, wage employment, and informal sector growth than did some of the agroecologically high potential areas. Although the percentage of the population in wage employment in Kenya's arid and semiarid lands (ASALs) was less than half that in non-ASAL areas, its annual growth rate was almost 50 percent higher. A similar trend was found in wage earnings per capita in that country. Nor was agriculture left behind in some ASAL areas: seven of the top ten Kenyan districts—in terms of average annual growth rates in total and per capita crop and livestock sales between 1980 and 1985—were classified as "ASAL districts." Similarly, project implementation rates for ASAL areas in Kenya were frequently no worse than they were for non-ASAL areas for projects like cattle dips and small-scale water supplies, at least in the early 1980s. In short, these ASAL areas were less "low potential" and "marginal lands" than simply "low density" in terms of human population.

Such examples—and their number is legion—underscore the problem with denarrativization: it increases uncertainty by undermining an existing development narrative without at the same time providing an alternative to take its place. In each example, some information has been found to construct a counternarrative—the colonialists did do something, wealthier households did produce traditional beer, marginal lands were not marginal—but we would need much more to fill in the storyline of the counterscenarios than has been provided to this date.

2. Counternarrativize!

Narrative 4: The tragedy of the commons is found through sub-Saharan Africa. The profound limitations of denarrativization in the absence of generating an alternative development narrative to replace the one denarrativized are best shown in the use and abuse of the tragedy-of-the-commons scenario.

The most obvious feature of the tragedy of the commons is its status as narrative. Garrett Hardin goes out of his way to portray it as a story having all the classic properties of a beginning, middle, and end. "The tragedy of the commons develops in this way. Picture a pasture open to all . . . ," begins Hardin in what must be the most-quoted passage in all of the common property literature. Soon we are in the midst of the story—"the rational herdsman concludes that the only sensible course for him to pursue is to add another animal to his herd. And another . . . .But this is the conclusion reached by each and every rational herdsman sharing a commons"—and the end comes rapidly and palpably into sight: "Ruin is the destination toward which all men rush, each pursuing his own best interest in a society that believes in the freedom of the commons."[5]

The data simply do not warrant this conclusion. When the tragedy-of-the-commons argument is probed empirically—for example, just what evidence is there for desertification caused by overgrazing?—the evidence turns out to be much more ambiguous, or downright contradictory.[6] Even where people agree with Hardin that range degradation is taking place and that many commons today are open-access free-for-alls, they often part company over causes. For these critics, long-term climatological changes coupled with expanding and competing land uses have led to degradation more than has the commons. A commons which, the critics hasten to add *contra* Hardin, was frequently managed in a restricted-access, not open-access, fashion until these outside pressures of climate and competing land uses undermined local management efforts.[7]

Hardin merits closer reading than some of his critics give him. "It must not be supposed that all commons are bad in all situations," he tells us; "when there were only a few million people in the world, it was all right to run the hunting grounds as a commons, though even then an area was no doubt often managed as tribal property."[8] Hardin is not saying the commons cannot be managed. Rather, "the commons, if it is justifiable at all, is justifiable only under conditions of low-population density."[9] The crux of his argument is that herders find it to their individual advantage not to cooperate in limiting herd numbers or ensuring range quality *even when* herders recognize that the overall stocking rate on the commons exceeds its putative carrying capacity and that range deterioration and live-weight loss seem on the rise.[10] In such a situation, corrective measures are largely outside the initiative of the individual herder. Either the commons has to be legislated as private property or other coercive devices, such as taxes and user regulations, have to be instituted from the outside.[11]

If we subscribe to Hardin's full argument, we should then expect to find at least two states of affairs when a rangeland tragedy of the commons is said to exist. First, even where herders agree that the range is in poor or already heavily-stocked condition, they still act in a noncooperative, competitive fashion. They should evince few, if any, collective practices for managing that commons, which, in turn, encourages its further overutilization. Second, a tragedy of the commons supposes that a privatized rangeland will be better managed (e.g., have a measurably better range condition) than if it were a commons, other factors being equal.

The most thoroughgoing test of Hardin's full-bodied version of the tragedy of the commons is found in a series of publications based on data collected during the 1979/80 Botswana Water Points Survey.[12] These data allow us to address how applicable each element of Hardin's argument is to rural eastern Botswana, an area of the country that has repeatedly been described as undergoing a rangeland tragedy of the commons.

First, do rural Batswana themselves perceive overgrazing to be taking place? The evidence was mixed. While the range condition was found to be at low levels in much of the heavily stocked eastern communal areas when assessed by standard range ecology measures, a number of Survey households indicated that lack of rainfall, rather than increase in livestock numbers, was the major culprit in perceived overstocking and overgrazing.[13] Yet there are sufficient grounds—in the form of acknowledged findings of low cattle-carcass weight and other interview information—to suppose that a significant proportion of Batswana, albeit not a majority, did in fact believe that increasing numbers of livestock were leading to overutilization of the range in the 1970s and early 1980s. It was at that time, for example, that the government of Botswana enshrined the tragedy of the commons argument as the reason for its national grazing-land policy (more on the policy in chapter 4).

If overgrazing was commonly thought to be taking place, did rural Batswana cooperate in the management of their communal resources and have management practices to do so? An in-depth survey by Louise Fortmann of communal dams constructed in eastern Botswana between 1974 and 1980 found that this was indeed the case. Of the twenty-four dams surveyed, twenty-one had some sort of collective management, be it in the form of maintenance, regulation, and/or revenue collection. All twenty-one dam groups had users who jointly regulated the use of these dams; restrictions on numbers of users, types of use, the manner of use, and/or the time of use were found as well.

Did communal management have a positive effect on the surrounding range condition, and if so, how did this compare to privatized resource management? An analysis of measurable grazing conditions around a sample of forty-six water points found that those water points owned or managed by government or groups had *better* dry season range conditions than privately owned water points.[14] No one-to-one correlation was found between private ownership, private management, and the actual restriction of livestock watering access, as one might suppose to be the case from the tragedy-of-the-commons argument.

Indeed, the finding that private rights and better range condition do not go hand-in-hand has been confirmed on a number of occasions in Botswana. Just three years after the first leasehold fenced ranches were occupied there under the World Bank's First Livestock Development Project, two-thirds of them were already overstocked.[15] Conditions did not improve under the Bank's Second Livestock Development Project. Bekure and Dyson-Hudson found that range management and condition on these leasehold ranches was often no better than in the communal areas.[16] Also, roughly fifteen years of government grazing trials undertaken periodically from the 1950s through the 1970s could show no significant difference in range conditions between those found under various fenced rotational systems and that observed under a continuous "single paddock" grazing regime approximating the communal system.[17] Finally, communal management of the dams studied in the Water Points Survey was found not only to be *ecologically* efficient relative to the next best private alternative, but cost figures indicated that this management was *economically* efficient as well.[18] In sum, the evidence has been far from conclusive that privatization of the Botswana commons increases the likelihood of improving range conditions there.

These and other negative findings have been around for a very long time, and it is tempting to dismiss the tragedy of the commons as some kind of denarrativized fable. To do so would be misguided and misses the point altogether. As a development narrative, the tragedy of the commons has continued to have considerable staying power because these negative findings and critiques—in short, denarrativization—in no way dispel the chief virtue of that narrative. Like development narratives discussed throughout *Except-Africa*, this one helps to underwrite and stabilize the assumptions for decision making. Policymakers resort to the tragedy-of-the-commons scenario in order to understand what is going on and what must be done in lieu of more elaborate and demanding analysis, particularly when such analysis leads to even more doubts and uncertainties about just what the story is behind rural resource utilization. Critiques of the tragedy of the commons are doubly troublesome for the decision maker, since they generate, rather than reduce, uncertainty when they undermine the assumptions of decision making, while at the same time leave that decision maker without the means to make the transition from the discredited narrative to whatever development narrative is needed to replace it.

In fact, the more the tragedy of the commons is critiqued and found substantively wanting, the more uncertain policymakers become—Why indeed did Batswana manage their water points collectively?—and the more pressure they feel to hold onto what scenarios they have, no matter how worn around the edges they now are. Critique, like that based on the Botswana data, never tells its own story—its point-by-point rebuttal does not have its own argument, its own beginning, middle, and end—and serves only to raise doubts that the critique itself cannot answer. What displaces a development narrative, like the tragedy-of-the-commons argument, is not a negative finding, as denarrativization of an argument does not mean you have taken away the decision maker's need to act. Rather, displacing a discredited narrative requires an equally straightforward narrative that tells a better story. The next chapter takes up the challenge of developing such counternarratives by sketching four alternatives to the tragedy-of-the-commons argument.

3. *Use Policy Generated by the Development Narrative to Change That Narrative!*

Narrative 5: Land registration increases agricultural productivity. For nearly half a century, one of the most potent development narratives in Kenya and elsewhere has been that land registration leads to increased agricultural productivity. Once land is adjudicated and registered, so the argument goes, the landowner will be in a position to use the title deed as collateral for securing credit with which to invest in improving and intensifying agricultural production on the land concerned. Dating from (if not before) the blueprint laid out in the government's 1954 Swynnerton Plan, the argument has remained popular among Kenya politicians, senior civil servants, and social scientists.[19]

The data simply do not warrant this conclusion. Empirical studies have repeatedly failed to find a positive causal link connecting the government's land registration program to expanded credit opportunities and thereby to increased agricultural productivity. Over the years, the effects of land registration in one district (Embu) have been studied in detail by different researchers, while others have undertaken point-in-time research on the same topic—much of it in the form of household surveys at the farm level—for localities in at least thirteen other districts (Meru, Nyeri, Kiambu, Kwale, Kisii, Murang'a, Taita-Taveta, Kisumu, South Nyanza, Nakuru, Kericho, Machakos, and Kakamega) covering much of the country's most agriculturally productive cropland. *All* these studies failed to confirm or raised serious doubts about the scenario linking land registration to agricultural production.[20] This robust finding is made even more striking by the equally demonstrated interregional ethnic and socioeconomic diversity of the country's rural households.

Succinctly put, it is a fairly easy matter to denarrativize the scenario tying land registration and increased agricultural production. In contrast to the development narrative, the cumulative picture left by research suggests that once landowners were registered, many did not bother to obtain their title deeds (they would never risk losing them on anything as uncertain as loan defaults); of those landowners who did obtain titles, not all of them did so to obtain credit (they may have had to sell their land or parts of it to meet school fees and other household expenses); of those who wanted to use their titles to obtain loans, not all actually received credit (farmers may not have known where to go for credit or met other requirements of the lending institution, which in turn might not have had the funds to lend); of those landowners who actually succeeded in using their titles for securing credit, a number of them used the loans for nonagricultural investments (e.g., their

off-farm businesses); of those new landholders who took over after the
registered owners die, few reregistered; and those who did not reregis-
ter or who could not have legally registered in the first place—mostly
women—were ineligible in terms of the law for title-secured loans.

Nor has the problem only been one of a low conditional probability
that, once registered, credit will be obtained and agriculture intensified. In some cases, land registration and increasing agricultural production may be negatively related. When registered, some landowners
felt (1) they could leave the land idle without fear of someone else
invoking a use-it-or-lose-it principle; (2) they now had the "freedom"
to sell land without real consent from those dependent on it and whose
labor makes it as productive as it is; and (3) they could enter land
transactions for speculation purposes only. As a result of these and
other factors, several experts concluded that Kenya's land registration
program actually increased insecurity of tenure in parts of the country.[21]

Yet the recurrent finding that registration did not increase production via the credit mechanism has not dispelled the belief of many
respected Kenyans that registration has had a positive and widespread
effect on agriculture. What then is the policymaker to do if s/he feels
compelled to pursue the topic of land registration's supposedly positive impact on agricultural productivity? One could, of course, continue to analyze the subject of agricultural credit on the hope that land
registration will indeed intensify agriculture if only credit is made
more timely, convenient, and adequate to more small-holders. Unfortunately, pushing credit has afforded about as much leverage in Kenya's
agricultural sector as pushing string.[22] Another option is to explore
other links between registration and agriculture that appear to have
potential in offering up a counternarrative relevant for policy and program development. Land registration, for example, seems to have influenced shifts in crop mixes, land concentration and fragmentation,
and the utilization of both non-farm income and credit for nonagricultural purposes. Nevertheless, if past research is any guide, this
counternarrative option will also yield mixed signals for the
policymaker. Land concentration boosts agricultural productivity in
one study, while another finds otherwise; some researchers describe
fragmentation as an ecologically valid, risk-averse response of farmers, while other researchers focus on what they see as increasingly
subeconomic holdings.[23] The policymaker who chooses this research
option will have to balance the findings of increasing complexity at

the micro-level with the widening scale of Kenya's land problems that seem to demand standard approaches to their management.

A very different option suggests itself, if the operating assumption is that both the popular narrative linking registration to production and its policy, the government's land registration program, will persist for the foreseeable future in the absence of any viable counternarrative and regardless of empirical findings that erode their credibility. The question then becomes one of focusing the policymaker's attention on those few areas where land registration offers up some promise of actually expanding agricultural production.

One prospect stands out for many of those familiar with Kenya, namely, estimating the extent to which the implementation of a land tax could intensify agricultural production by discouraging land specu-lation, absentee management, uneconomic fragmentation, and nonpro-ductive large-holdings. The argument runs something like this. Exist-ing records of the land registration program as to who is registered or holds the title deed will greatly facilitate the operation of such a tax, where it is introduced. Moreover, it is difficult to conceive of a more efficient way to update these records for the unregistered subdivisions mentioned earlier, i.e., the levy would serve as an incentive for the reregistration of land currently registered in the names of other own-ers, since the tax would presumably be assessed on those whose names show up in the records. Even though land taxation has been controver-sial in Kenya, a focus on the promising positive links between regis-tration and agriculture has the considerable merit of being consistent with the development narrative that has hitherto resisted all manner of empirical assaults on it. Indeed, the narrative's policy becomes one way of altering rather than displacing the narrative itself. The exist-ence of a huge government bureaucracy, staff and budget all commit-ted to ensuring that land registration is blueprinted across the country, inevitably increases pressure to find ways to justify their purported programmatic effect on intensifying agriculture, even if the specific mechanism for linking registration and production is no longer princi-pally that of title-secured credit.[24]

4. Fill in the "Missing Details" of the Narrative!

Narrative 6: Livestock watering points should be spaced eight kilo-meters (five miles) apart from each other.[25] For years, it had been thought that land allocation authorities in rural Botswana were following the rule of thumb that livestock watering points (each watering on average 400 head of cattle) should be spaced eight kilometers or five miles from each other in order to reduce overgrazing around those points. A study in the early 1980s, however, found the application of the rule in practice was ad hoc, varying substantially from land authority to land authority. That said, the survey found few, if any, instances where the post-Independence land authority justified a spacing closer than eight kilometers on the grounds that government policy did not officially require such a spacing.

A number of technical reasons explain why the land authorities were, in practice, unable to require such a spacing. In many localities of eastern Botswana, it was simply no longer possible to find a site for a new livestock watering point eight kilometers away from others. A more important reason was institutional. Studies of chieftainship in the Bechuanaland Protectorate prior to Independence found that chiefs and headmen often settled disputes "on their own merits," without binding themselves to a concise body of customary precedent. In the same way, the post-Independence land authorities sought to claim the right to judge each case of spacing on its own merits. Indeed, the "missing details" in the development narrative about why land authorities claimed a rule they did not follow is that such behavior was structurally similar to what often occurred under pre-Independence chieftainship resource allocation and dispute settlement. So too the post-Independence land authorities tried to establish the same claim to legitimacy that chiefs had before the advent of Independence. Thus, the development narrative that contemporary land authorities were (not) following their own rules is "filled in" with additional information: they were actually following an equally long-standing rule of case-by-case assessments.

Narrative 7: Everything is connected to everything else. Systems thinking pervades many approaches to rural development. Livestock rangeland development provides an especially good illustration of this development narrative. Few specialists, for example, would quibble with the following:

> Pastoral production is normally and correctly part of wider production systems; changes in any element have ramifications in all others.[26]

> Livestock production is a very complex system which has many interrelated com-

ponents such as climate, soil, plants, and obviously animals operating with a high degree of interaction within a certain economic and social environment.[27]

The fact that pastoralism needs to be seen in a regional perspective rather than an isolated production system for an understanding of the changes in living conditions of pastoralists has been pointed out.[28]

Why stop at "region"? The system entails, after a point, supraregional levels in a long chain of behavioral links which

starts with land managers and their direct relations with the land (. . . stocking densities . . . and so on). Then the next link concerns their relations with each other, other land users, and groups in the wider society who affect them in any way, which in turn determines land management. The state and the world economy constitute the last links in the chain.[29]

Once something has evolved into this narrative of a long-linked "system," description frequently becomes prescription. "A local systems approach holds the best hope of success in development for pastoralists," advise two social scientists.[30] "The Panel recommends a *systems approach* to all phases of project planning and execution," counsels a USAID task force on rangeland/livestock projects.[31] For Sidahmed and Koong the moral of their systems approach is clear, i.e., "any attempts towards [livestock] development should be preceded by the construction of a mathematical model which should contain all the essential elements of the current production system."[32]

As this last statement indicates, undertaking a systems narrative can be easier than living with its implications. A syllogism in the development narrative seems inescapable: integrated system, integrated intervention, right? Yet as readers well know, integrated rural development programs (particularly in the agricultural sector) have all too often been "disintegrating agricultural development."[33] Ministerial portfolios, based on apparent sectoral divisions in the political economy, do not as a rule reflect the need for intersectoral coordination and integration. Moreover, once one accepts the validity of a narrative that posits a long chain of putative causality between the international economy and the local herder, the probability of finding something wrong along the way increases exponentially. Critics continually find projects that are local successes but system failures, in a world where localized interventions, such as projects, provide little leverage in correcting what are taken to be systemic dysfunctions. Nothing works right as a system because the conditional probability of doing so approaches the vanishing point. Development syllogism thus becomes development tautology.

Yet practitioners who object to the systems narrative in rural development run the risk of having to eat their words. After all, what rural development practitioner is foolish enough to operate as if cause and effect had been repealed?

One salutary development in systems analysis has been to introduce the distinction between tightly and loosely coupled systems. Many early integrated rural development projects were designed as tightly coupled systems, i.e., everything had to occur in a sequence of steps, there was only one way to achieve the desired objective, little or no slack existed to do otherwise, and any delays or missteps rippled throughout the rest of the project cycle. What was not been sufficiently understood, however, is the loosely coupled nature of many rural development systems that set the context in which project cycles have to operate, i.e., environments in which delays have to be accommodated, the order of sequence often changes, and where slack is especially evident.[34] Moris and Thom argue, for instance, that irrigation scheme managers in many parts of Africa have to contend with what is best characterized as a loosely coupled system where a myriad of agencies, levels of authority, and formal as well as informal networks of communication are relevant to the manager's activities but not coordinated for the purposes of management.[35]

In reality, many rural development processes are best understood as a mix of tightly coupled and loosely coupled systems. Another livestock rangeland example from Botswana illustrates how this can be so.[36] Research found three tightly coupled levels of water use and management governing any given rural water point there: the site immediately surrounding the water point, the locality in which the water point is found, and the compound locality in which the water point is located (that is, the set of different localities over which the users of that water point typically reside and work during the year).

When rural Batswana are physically at the water point, they are keenly aware of the physical condition of adjacent land as well as the physical type of water source in question (e.g., boreholes, because they are mechanized, are operated differently than open wells). At the locality level, how a water point is managed and used is in turn affected by, to list several factors, the availability of labor for fetching water, which varies by locality (some household members move to the cropping fields for planting, while others, such as children who would otherwise fetch water, remain in village schools); by the locality's topography and hydrogeology; and by the locality's prevailing land uses (e.g., in Botswana, villages and grazing areas are typically dominated by borehole development, while mixed cropping and grazing areas frequently have had a greater variety of sources). Equally important, the operation of a specific water point has to be seen within the context of the availability and accessibility of alternative water sources in the locality.

Because members of rural households in Botswana have often shifted their household compounds over the course of the year—in the cropping season, they have gone to the "lands" where their field homes are and, after harvest, they have returned to their village homes for the rest of the year—one finds that the demand and supply of water have shifted as well over the course of the year across the localities concerned. It is at compound locality level that the specific water point operates as part of a sequence of water points over time and space, with households falling back from many, often surface, water sources at their lands in the wet season to fewer groundwater sources in the home village during the dry (post-harvest) season.

These three levels are tightly coupled when compared to those larger regional, national, and international domains pertinent to rural water use and management. The specific water point is at a site, in a locality, and within a compound locality at the same moment. Indeed, these three levels are able to be identified precisely because they share the same unit of analysis at the same time. This is not true for other levels. No one can doubt national considerations affect rural water use, e.g., Botswana has relied on boreholes much more heavily than, say, has Kenya in many of its arid and semiarid lands. Similarly, international considerations clearly affect water use conditions in a given county, e.g., European Economic Community (EEC) price subsidies on beef exports—which Botswana had taken advantage of, but which Kenya had not because of its relatively weaker veterinary control efforts—helped make livestock investment in Botswana a much more profitable enterprise than it has been in comparable areas of Kenya. Yet, when moving to these higher levels, it becomes very difficult to keep the unit of analysis, the specific water point, fixed in view as with the three more local levels. Just how Botswana's being a borehole culture and the beneficiary of international price subsidies affect, say, one of the thousands of open wells in eastern Botswana is certainly not clear to its average user, let alone the outside observer. These other levels are, to put it another way, connected to rural water use and management, but in a loosely coupled fashion when compared to the tightly coupled processes governing the operation of any specific water point.

What such discriminations allow one to do is to adhere to the narrative of rural development as a long-linked system stretching from the local to the international, but to "fill in the missing details" by recognizing that some systems are so loosely coupled that practitioners can treat them *as if* they were not coupled systems at all. From the standpoint of many herders, the health sector has not been "integrated" with the agricultural sector which in turn has not been integrated with the wage sector ... no matter what the government planners and African studies academics say or believe or feel should be the case. Indeed, much of the failure of tightly coupled, integrated rural development projects becomes perfectly intelligible the moment we assume that for the typical project beneficiary, "sectors" are not integrated at all, or at least not at the local level(s) relevant to the people concerned.

This is, ironically, exactly the reason why "multisectoral" programs are so needed in parts of the developing world: not because project activities are tightly coupled and functionally integrated at the sectoral level, but because multisectoral projects are, in practice, frequently loosely coupled and thereby better adapted to the "unintegrated" (read: complex) nature of development. Multisectoral projects have at times had more flexibility at the local level in undertaking different projects over different geographical areas and better chances in exploiting new opportunities as and when they arise—both major advantages in an environment characterized by the uncertainty of multiple actors, objectives, and criteria for evaluating program performance.[37]

5. Metanarrativize!

Narrative 8: The range's carrying capacity shouldn't be exceeded.[38] In a formal sense, a metanarrative is that development narrative—and there is no guarantee there is one, or if there is, that it will be only one—which the narrator needs to know in order to understand how multiple and opposing development narratives are not only possible but consistent with each other against all likelihood but with perfect logic. This is not as counterintuitive as it seems. We already encountered a very important metanarrative in the introduction, namely, the one of stewardship: the international techno-managerial elite has stewardship over resources they do not own, because they alone, so the scenario goes, can determine and adjudicate which among all those opposing and conflicting crisis narratives that make up Except-Africa.

Metanarratives come in all shapes and sizes, and the one that concerns us here is that metanarrative which allows us to make sense of all those conflicting notions and estimates about an area's carrying capacity. For one of the abiding ironies of rural development practice today is that at a time when the planet's limited carrying capacity seems increasingly obvious, specific measures of rangeland carrying capacity have come under increasing skepticism. Because the metanarrative is a difficult notion and because the notion of carrying capacity seems so obvious (when in fact it is not), the following example is difficult and is elaborated further in chapter 3.

Say the carrying capacity recommendation is one livestock unit (equivalent to 450–500 kilograms) per ten hectares in a dry range area—a not-uncommon recommendation in sub-Saharan Africa. For some time, it has been a fairly easy matter to denarrativize that recommendation (see, e.g., Roe and Fortmann 1982). First, some of these dry areas have key resources—such as localized wet areas (swamps, marshes) that allow a higher stock rate—so that the 1LSU/10ha recommendation can never be a universal one, notwithstanding those ubiquitous maps of livestock carrying capacity that suggest otherwise. Second, the negative relationship between carrying capacity and the number of shrubs and bushes ("bush encroachment") that undergirds range scorecards belies the fact that cattle do browse on bushes and that such browsing constitutes a substantial portion of the livestock diet in dry areas. Third, the actual cattle on the range may well not average between 450 and 500 kilograms; in fact, they may be half that size or less. Fourth, the carrying capacity concept all too often makes little short-term economic sense for many herders, particularly as it is this economics which drives so much of the herders' stocking rate. Last but not least, the recent literature on disquilibrium models and state-and-transition models of rangelands calls into question any once-and-for-all measure of carrying capacity, whether the range is stocked or unstocked (see also Scoones 1994).

Ideally such objections could be taken into account for any specific carrying capacity estimate, by accepting that carrying capacity has to be determined on a case by case basis in the field. (More formally, once the conventional notions of carrying capacity have been denarrativized, replace them with a counternarrative to the effect that each estimate of rangeland carrying capacity has to be done on a case-by-case basis.) Once you know the average size of the grazing and browsing animals, and once you know the biomass production of the area, the pattern of livestock movements and watering, and so on, you can—so this argument goes—produce a site-specific carrying capacity estimate for the area under consideration. Indeed, this is often what is done in practice.

The case-by-case estimation of carrying capacity seems all the more sensible in light of the apparent obviousness of the carrying capacity concept itself. Surely there has to be a finite limit to the number of livestock, or people of any given area, indeed the planet as a whole, holding constant other factors such as technological change. Surely, you cannot pack livestock into a given area, without at some point deteriorating that area demonstrably. Surely, biomass production is going down on many African rangelands precisely because carrying capacity is and has been exceeded so long, even taking into factors such as drought and climate change.

Such appeals simply will not do, at least under conditions of high environmental uncertainty as found in most of the dry rangelands of the world. To see how, we have to introduce the notion of a "Hahn equilibrium." For the economist Frank Hahn, "an economy is in equilibrium when it generates messages which do not cause agents to change the theories which they hold or the policies which they pursue" (Hahn 1984). Accordingly, agents could be in equilibrium even when markets have not cleared, or wages are rigid, or perfect competition is not always forthcoming, as long as the theories and policies that are held allow for these disparities. What is for our purposes the most interesting feature of a Hahn equilibrium are those conditions that lead to stability in the agents' theories and policies. For Hahn "equilibrium states [are] those in which agents learn nothing new" (Hahn 1984: 9). Another way of putting this is that conditions may be so uncertain that agents are unable to reliably learn anything new.

As a first pass then, the carrying capacity of any given area could be conceived as those Hahn-like theories and policies (read: development narratives) that allow agents to stabilize the assumptions for decision making in the face of what seems to them to be continuing and intractable uncertainty, such as you find in the highly variable arid and semiarid lands of Africa. Decisions have to be made, even when learning is not possible, and local carrying capacity estimates reflect those site-specific theories and policies that allow the agents in question to decide, at least for a time.

But, and here's the nub, theories and policies do change. Does these mean the carrying capacity estimates change with them? Not necessarily, and herein lies the metanarrative we are calling carrying capacity. Another economist, Brian Loabsy, suggests that we should

> add another level to Hahn's system, a level in which agents have theories about the generation of theories, and policies for the formulation of policies. Such meta-theories and meta-policies cannot be precisely specified, because it is logically impossible for the content of new knowledge to be predicted in advance or, what comes to the same thing, to be specified as the output, determinate or probabilistic, of a well-defined process. (Loabsy 1991)

Such a formulation has intuitive appeal for it implies that even when local theories and policies are changing, the system in question still may be in equilibrium in the wider sense that the changes in question are guided by broader theories and policies governing innovation in the knowledge base upon which the more local changes in theories and policies are founded.

To be specific, if the notion of rangeland carrying capacity is to make any sense under conditions of high environmental uncertainty, it has to be at this meta-equilibrium level, where "carrying capacity" would be a meta-theory about how the capacity of a rangeland to carrying a population changes over time, without however being able to predict what that carrying capacity will be in any specific instance or at any specific time. If this is so, *then carrying capacity is really a theory of knowledge generation and change over a rangeland population and area.* It is as much about technological innovation as it is about biomass increases or decline in that area and population. Like all meta-theories that cannot predict the unknown in advance, it is more at home and on sounder ground in identifying what makes for change (e.g., more livestock, changes in technology) than it is in forecasting what is ahead for that area and that population. As a theory of knowledge change and to paraphrase Loabsy, carrying capacity has no business in specifying "outputs" such as all those estimates of a specific range's specific "carrying capacity," *even when those estimates are done on a case-by-case basis.* Such site-specific estimates are only warranted on the basis of long experience and familiarity with the site concerned—which is simply another way of saying the estimator has a theory about what drives carrying capacity there and it is that theory which should be the object of question. Again, these points are developed more fully in chapter 3.

6. *Engage an Already Existing, but Conflicting, Development Narrative!*

Narrative 9: African governments can't budget. As detailed in chapter 5, disarray in government budgeting is international. Neither the developing world nor the developed countries have coped budgetarily. "How we Americans used to deride the 'banana republics' of the world for their 'repetitive budgeting' under which the budget was reallocated many times during the year, until it became hardly recognizable . . . Yet resolutions that continue last year's funding for agencies, for want of ability to agree on this year's, are becoming a way of life in the United States," as Aaron Wildavsky, a well-known expert on budgeting, put the problem years ago.[39] Continuously remaking the national budget "has now become standard practice in relatively rich nations," as well as poorer ones.[40]

It is in the developing world, however, where repetitive budgeting has received the greatest attention. Under this kind of budgeting, according to Caiden and Wildavsky's *Planning and Budgeting in Poor Countries*, the government

> budget is not made once and for all when estimates are submitted and approved; rather, as the process of budgeting is repeated, it is made and remade over the course of the year . . .

The entire budget is treated as if each item were supplemental, subject to renegotiation at the last minute . . . Repetitive budgeting . . . is found in most poor countries. Its most extreme manifestation is as cash flow budgeting where changes may be made from day to day or even from one hour to the next. (1974: 71–72)

In practice, repetitive budgeting is best measured by the gaps that perforate the national budgetary process. Substantial differences have, for example, existed between what was printed in the five-year National Development Plan of the government of Kenya (GoK) and what the GoK eventually budgeted in its three-year forward budget, between that printed forward budget and what was eventually budgeted annually in the published estimates, between what the ministries formally requested to have budgeted in the annual estimates and what was allocated them by way of official Treasury warrants, between that allocation and the documented funds made available to be spent, and between what was available and what audit reports subsequently show was in fact spent. Repetitive budgeting seems to be everywhere, as is the gap between what was initially budgeted and what is ultimately implemented (more in chapter 5). Accordingly, a very large gap can exist between what was originally planned and what is eventually implemented, and it is this gap which motivates many of the more critical accounts about the failure of large-scale government projects in both the developing and developed worlds. In this way, repetitive budgeting has itself become a development narrative explaining all matter of "failures" from top to bottom in a country's government.

Facts, again, do not always accord with this narrative linking repetitive budgeting at the national level to poor project implementation at the local level. It simply is not the case, for example, that sub-Saharan governments all budget or implement alike, notwithstanding blanket phrases like the Financial Crisis in Africa. The government of Botswana appears to have budgeted differently than Kenya, whose repetitive budgeting in government has not been as severe or disabling as it has been in, say, Nigeria (more in chapter 5). Similarly, as difficult as budgeting has been in Kenya or Nigeria, they have been able to produce yearly budgets in contrast to some more politically troubled governments like Angola, which for years did not produce a national budget. Such discriminations should be terribly important for those who believe that rural development depends in some significant measure on governmental budgetary behavior.

More empirical work on these intercountry differences is needed and would, I believe, go some way in undermining the grim narrative's depiction of national budgeting and a failed south of the Sahara. Are there other ways to weaken the narrative, other than denarrativization? Several options have already been suggested. In theory, one could try to create a counternarrative (as in the tragedy-of-the-commons example); use the policies generated by the narrative to alter it (as in the case of land registration); or fill in the "details" of the narrative in order to make it less misleading (as in the systems approach example). There are many instances, however, where the practitioner has little leeway to be creative. The best s/he can do is to engage another already existing development narrative, which, once engaged, conflicts with the more objectionable one.

A U.S. example illustrates how this has been done.[41] The California Department of Motor Vehicles (DMV) has had a reputation for long lines and slow service. The narrative of a government department mired in red tape and paralyzed by inefficiency was and is still popular to some extent in the media and the public's mind. Senior DMV managers reacted by engaging two other preexisting narratives that are also accepted in the United States and elsewhere, namely, the widespread scenarios about how "computerization improves bureaucratic efficiency" and how "personalized service is what really makes bureaucracies effective." In this case, the managers had DMV field operations computerized and initiated a program whereby service by appointment could be provided to those who before had to wait in line. The issue here is not whether these other narratives are accurate—in this example computerization and service by appointment did lead for a time to some improvement—but that their storylines ran against the dominant narrative of a government bureaucracy sunken in its own indifference to the needs of the people it is meant to serve. The temptation is to think of the actions of DMV senior managers as "public relations," but to do so would deny the highly circumscribed nature of the public arena in which they had to make decisions.

Parallel developments can be observed in government budgeting overseas. Computerization of the government of Kenya's budget was introduced when budgetary and financial management there were widely considered to be at a low point. Pinckney, Cohen, and Leonard recount how the introduction of microcomputers into the Ministries of Agriculture and Livestock Development improved the efficiency and effectiveness of scarce, skilled managers in their budgetary process.[42] They add that "the presence of the microcomputer visibly changed the technology of financial decision making . . . [It] legitimized a role in financial decision making for those who could use it, therefore making it easier for new, reform-minded individuals to participate actively".[43] Further legitimation came from the World Bank in the form of one of its elect "box" case studies for the 1988 *World Development Report*: "Overall the Ministry of Agriculture developed better management tools and information systems, aided by the introduction of microcomputers. The overall quality of agricultural programs improved markedly during this period."[44] This technology subsequently became an important part of the budget preparation exercise of the GoK Treasury and the government estimates for 1985/86 were the first to be produced by microcomputer.[45] Once again, the impression, certainly among members of the donor community, was that this extension in the use of microcomputers had also increased the budgetary and financial management capacity of Treasury officials and advisors.[46] While GoK's budgeting continued to have problems, reforms such as the introduction of microcomputers certainly helped alter its image of a repetitive budgetary process that cannot be improved.

Narrative 10. Cost-benefit analysis should be used in project appraisal.[47] Although the World Bank calculated the original internal rate of return for its large Kenya Integrated Agricultural Development Project to be around 35 percent, a Bank team needed little calculation some eight years later at the Project's completion to conclude its actual rate of return was close to zero. Many other similar instances exist where (ex-ante) cost-benefit appraisals of agricultural project proposals have provided very poor predictions of actual (ex-post) project evaluation.

The problems with cost-benefit analysis have long been noted. Shadow prices are next to impossible to compute, streams of benefits and costs are difficult to calculate, the discount rate assumes what is in the future is less valuable than what it is today, yet declining incomes in African locales mean that a monetary unit today might be worth much more a year from now, and the capital-budget bias of cost-benefit analysis has treated recurrent costs as something to be worried about in the future, precisely at a time when many African countries are in a recurrent cost crisis.

Another already existing appraisal scenario could, however, be engaged instead of cost-benefit analysis. Venture capitalism has been developed to deal more effectively with high-technology, high-risk, and high-cost investments. These are precisely characteristics of many agricultural and water projects in sub-Saharan Africa. Admittedly, the latter projects might be routine in Western countries, but a borehole project in Kenya or a farm improvement package in Zimbabwe is often more risky, costly, and technical in nature than other types of rural development there. Similarly, many of these "cutting edge" projects are designed, *pace* the venture capitalist, to foster rapid economic returns.

Existing venture capitalist appraisal differs in fundamental respects from ex-ante cost-benefit analysis. The first thing a venture capitalist looks for in a high cost, high risk, and high technology project is its proposed management framework. Project management is the *sine qua non*, precisely because the project is innovative and growth-oriented. Contrast this to a cost-benefit analysis that treats recurrent costs—that is, project operation and management—as less important than the upfront capital construction of the project.

Secondly, venture capitalists are much more willing to accept that it is not always possible to use discount rates or determine rates of return with any real assurance. In these instances, risk cannot be quantified by recourse to those probability estimates so common in cost-benefit analysis. Instead, one way a venture capitalist might seek to reduce the risk of subsequent poor project performance is to let site characteristics do the work that would otherwise have to be built into the project design itself. For example, if a proposed water project assumes a local management input, then search for areas where water remains the first limiting factor on production, where there is already a fair amount of local water management, and where those local management personnel—often women—have shown themselves to be receptive to new development innovations. In brief, the venture capitalist narrative stresses entrepreneurship in meeting development needs when all other things are not constant in contrast to the cost-benefit narrative which stresses the priority of taking action on those projects whose benefits most exceed costs, holding all other factors constant.

Final Note

The six options to change objectionable development narratives could be extended, but the point would remain the same: there are many more ways than academics commonly suppose to change a hard-to-dislodge development narrative, though the option most think is the right way—proving the narrative wrong (a.k.a. denarrativization)—has very real problems. The retort is that development narratives are hard to dislodge but only because there are power interests behind them that keep them in place. Obviously this is true . . . though far less than commonly supposed. This book is not about such development narratives. We instead are concerned with those scenarios and arguments that arise and persist as a way of underwriting and stabilizing the assumptions for decision making in the face of what everyone involved admits is high complexity and uncertainty. As we will see in the book's conclusion, the pervasive power narrative, where there is power behind every throne, is hard to sustain, when one takes complexity seriously from the outset.

Notes

1. This definition of narrative and story is the standard one (see the respective entries in Gerald Prince, *A Dictionary of Narratology*, University of Nebraska Press, Lincoln [1987]).
2. The three examples come from Roe (1987b).
3. From Emery Roe, "Who Brews Traditional Beer in Rural Botswana?: A Review of the Literature and Policy Analysis," in *Botswana Notes and Records*, vol. 13 (1981).
4. From Emery Roe, "Six Myths about Livestock Rangeland Development South of the Sahara," in *Rangelands*, vol. 11, no. 5 (1989).
5. Garrett Hardin, "The Tragedy of the Commons," in Garrett Hardin and John Baden (eds.), *Managing the Commons*, W.H. Freeman and Company, San Francisco, p. 20 ([1968] 1977).
6. Sandford, chapter 1 (1983). See also the introduction.
7. See Panel on Common Property Resource Management, *Proceedings of the Conference on Common Property Resource Management*, National Academy Press on behalf of the Board on Science and Technology for International Development, Office of International Affairs, National Research Council, Washington, DC (1986); and Bonnie McCay and James Acheson (eds.), *The Question of the Commons: The Culture and Ecology of Communal Resources*, University of Arizona Press, Tucson (1987).
8. Garrett Hardin, "Denial and Disguise" and "An Operational Analysis of 'Responsibility'," in Garrett Hardin and John Baden (eds.), *Managing the Commons*, W.H. Freeman and Company, San Francisco, pp. 47–48 (1977).
9. Hardin, p. 28 ([1968]1977).
10. Hardin, p. 72 (1977).
11. Hardin, p. 22 ([1968]1977).
12. The Survey was funded by the government of Botswana's Ministry of Agriculture and USAID through the Center for International Studies, Cornell University.
13. Louise Fortmann and Emery Roe, *The Water Points Survey*, Ministry of Agriculture, Gaborone, Botswana and Center for International Studies, Cornell University, Ithaca (1981); and Charles Bailey, *Cattle Husbandry in the Communal Areas of Eastern Botswana*, Ph.D. dissertation, Cornell University, Ithaca, NY (1982).
14. Emery Roe, "Range Conditions around Water Sources in Botswana and Kenya," in *Rangelands*, vol. 6, no. 6 (1984).
15. Malcolm Odell and Marcia Odell, "Communal Area Livestock Development in Botswana: Lessons for the World Bank's Third Livestock Development Project," paper presented to the World Bank, Synergy International, Amesbury, MA, p. 7 (1986).
16. Solomon Bekure and Neville Dyson-Hudson, *The Operation and Viability of the Second Livestock Development Project (1497–BT): Selected Issues*, Ministry of Agriculture, Gaborone, Botswana (1982).

17. Emery Roe and Louise Fortmann, *Allocation of Water Points at the Lands*, Ministry of Local Government and Lands, Gaborone, Botswana, and the Center for International Studies, Cornell University, Ithaca, p. 71 (1981); and Animal Production Research Unit, *Beef Production and Range Management in Botswana*, Ministry of Agriculture, Gaborone, Botswana, pp. 85–86 (1980).

18. Louise Fortmann and Emery Roe, "Common Property Management of Water in Botswana," in *Proceedings of the Conference on Common Property Resource Management* (1986).

19. See, for example, *Kenya Times*, "Focus on 1989 Nakuru Show—Rift Valley: Land of Plenty," Article prepared by Mr. Yusuf Haji, the Rift Valley Provincial Commissioner, Nairobi, p. 20 (29 June 1989),; and IFAD/UNDP, "Historical Perspective, Existing ASAL Programmes and Institutional Analysis," Technical Paper No. 3 written by Dr. Gideon Cyrus Mutiso, in *Republic of Kenya—Arid and Semi-Arid Lands (ASAL) Development Programme: Summary of Technical Reports on the Strategy, Policy and ASAL Development Programme 1989–1993*, Nairobi?, p. 48 (1988). The Sywnnerton Plan's policy narrative can be found in Colony and Protectorate of Kenya, *A Plan to Intensify the Development of African Agriculture in Kenya*, compiled by R.J.M. Swynnerton, Government Printer, Nairobi, pp. 8–9 (1954).

20. M.P.K. Sorrenson, *Land Reform in the Kikuyu Country: A Study in Government Policy*, Oxford University Press, Nairobi and London (1967); William Barber, "Land Reform and Economic Change Among African Farmers in Kenya," in *Economic Development and Cultural Change*, vol. 19, no. 1 (1970); Frank Bernard, *East of Mount Kenya: Meru Agriculture in Transition*, Weltforum Verlag, Munich (1972); Nancy Gray, "Acceptance of Land Adjudication Among the Digo," Discussion Paper No. 37, Institute of African Studies, Nairobi (1972); Rodney Wilson, "The Economic Implications of Land Registration in Kenya's Smallholder Areas," Staff Working Paper No. 91, Institute of Development Studies, University of Nairobi, Nairobi (1971); Simon Coldham, "Land-Tenure Reform in Kenya: The Limits of the Law," in *The Journal of Modern African Studies*, vol. 17, no. 4 (1979); Diana Hunt, *The Impending Crisis in Kenya: The Case for Land Reform*, Gower Publishing Company, Aldershot, England (1984); E.H.N. Njeru, "Land Adjudication and its Implications for the Social Organization of the Mbere," Research Paper No. 73, Land Tenure Center, University of Wisconsin, Madison (1978); David Brokensha and E.H.N. Njeru, "Some Consequences of Land Adjudication in Mbere Division, Embu," Working Paper No. 320, Institute of Development Studies, University of Nairobi, Nairobi (1977); Angelique Haugerud, "Development and Household Economy in Two Eco-Zones of Embu District," Working Paper No. 382, Institute of Development Studies, University of Nairobi, Nairobi (1981); Angelique Haugerud, "The Consequences of Land Tenure Reform Among Smallholders in the Kenya Highlands," in *Rural Africana*, nos. 15–16 (1983); Angelique Haugerud, "Land Tenure and Agrarian Change in Kenya," *Africa*, vol. 59, no. 1 (1989); Parker Shipton, *Land, Credit and Crop Transactions in Kenya: The Luo Response to Directed Development in Nyanza Province*, PhD dissertation, University of Cambridge, Cambridge (1985); Richard Odingo, "The Dynamics of Land Tenure Reform and of Agrarian Systems in Africa: Land Tenure Study in the Nakuru, Kericho and Machakos Areas of the Kenya Highlands," Food and Agricultural Organization, Rome, cited in Green (1985); Joy Green, "Evaluating the Impact of Consolidation of Holdings, Individualization of Tenure, and Registration of Title: Lessons from Kenya," LTC Paper No. 129, Land Tenure Center, University of Wisconsin, Madison (1985); Anne Fleuret, "Some Con-

sequences of Tenure and Agrarian Reform in Taita, Kenya," in R. E. Downs and S.P. Renya (eds.), *Land and Society in Contemporary Africa*, University Press of New England, Hanover, New Hampshire (1988); see also Esther Wangari, Ph.D. dissertation on land registration in Lower Embu District, New School for Social Research, NY (forthcoming), and Willis Oluoch-Kosura, in collaboration with S.E. Migot-Adholla, A World Bank-sponsored study on the effect of land registration in four localities from two districts in Kenya, Nairobi (forthcoming). Green (1985) has a more detailed review and bibliography of the literature on Kenya's land registration program.

21. For related comments on contemporary insecurity of land tenure in Kenya, see Paul Collier and Deepak Lal, *Labour and Poverty in Kenya: 1900–1980*, Clarendon Press, Oxford, p. 131 (1988).

22. For example, World Bank, *Kenya: Agricultural Credit Policy Review*, Report No. 5619–KE, Washington, DC (1985).

23. See Shipton (1985) and Haugerud (1983).

24. That the ministry responsible for Kenya's land registration program has been under increased pressure to better justify its expenditures is indicated by a memo from the ministry's permanent secretary to his staff: "During the past six months or so, His Excellency the President has on a number of occasions impressed upon this Ministry the need to expand and intensify our work in land surveying, land adjudication, and land administration so that desired goals in land tenure, and the attendant social and economic benefits, can be realized throughout the Republic in the shortest time possible . . . .A review of the performance of this Ministry over the last few years indicates clearly that our performance and output have been below expectation and that drastic changes are needed in our operational strategies, priorities and personal attitudes if we are to fulfil the mammoth responsibilities entrusted to us by the Government . . . .While it is acknowledged that external factors such as scarcity of funds, personnel and equipment may retard the implementation of the [ministry's work] programme in certain cases, it must also be recognised that the Government does not have a limitless source of funds and, therefore, it is incumbent upon us all to optimise the utilization of the scarce resources at our disposal." (Ministry of Lands and Settlement, "Programme of Work and Performance Targets for the Year 1988," Memo numbered MLS 2/001, vol. 2(16), Nairobi [1988].)

25. From Roe and Fortmann (1982).

26. John Galaty and Dan Aronson, "Research Priorities and Pastoralist Development: What is to be Done?" in John Galaty, Dan Aronson, Philip Salzman, and Amy Chouinard (eds.), *The Future of Pastoral Peoples: Proceedings of a Conference Held in Nairobi, Kenya, 4–8 August, 1980*, International Development Research Center, Ottawa, p. 21 (1981).

27. Ahmed Sidahmed and L. Koong, "Application of Systems Analysis to Nomadic Livestock Production in the Sudan," in James Simpson and Phylo Evangelou (eds.), *Livestock Development in Subsaharan Africa: Constraints, Prospects, Policy*, Westview Press, Boulder, Colorado, p. 61 (1984).

28. Anders Hjort, "Herds, Trade, and Grain: Pastoralism in a Regional Perspective," in John Galaty, Dan Aronson, Philip Salzman, and Amy Chouinard (eds.), *The Future of Pastoral Peoples: Proceedings of a Conference Held in Nairobi, Kenya, 4–8 August, 1980*, International Development Research Center, Ottawa, p. 135 (1981).

29. Piers Blaikie and Harold Brookfield, *Land Degradation and Society*, Methuen, London, p. 27 (1987).

30. Galaty and Aronson, p. 20 (1981).
31. USAID, "Suggestions for the Improvement of Rangeland Livestock Projects in Africa: A Panel Report," Washington, DC, p. 7 (1985).
32. Sidahmed and Koong, p. 74 (1984).
33. David Leonard, "Disintegrating Agricultural Development," *Food Research Institute Studies*, vol. 19, no. 2 (1984).
34. The sociologist, Charles Perrow, provides an excellent description of these general properties of tightly and loosely coupled systems (Perrow 1984). For a more detailed discussion, see the conclusion.
35. Jon Moris and Derrick Thom, *African Irrigation Overview: Main Report*, Water Management Synthesis Report 37, Utah State University, Logan, pp. 430–431 (1987).
36. More details on this illustration can be found in Emery Roe and Louise Fortmann, *Season and Strategy: The Changing Organization of the Rural Water Sector in Botswana*, Special Series in Rural Development, Rural Development Committee, Cornell University, Ithaca, chapter 6 (1982).
37. Emery Roe, "Project Appraisal: A Venture Capitalist Approach," *Development Policy Review*, vol. 3, no. 2 (1985). See also John Cohen, *Integrated Rural Development: The Ethiopian Experience and the Debate*, Scandinavian Institute of African Studies, Uppsala, chapter 7 (1987).
38. From Emery Roe, "On Rangeland Carrying Capacity," *Journal of Range Management*, vol. 50, no. 5, pp. 467–472 (1997).
39. Aaron Wildavsky, *The Politics of the Budgetary Process*, Fourth Edition, Little, Brown and Company, Boston, p. 252 (1984).
40. Aaron Wildavsky, *The New Politics of the Budgetary Process*, Scott, Foresman and Company, Boston, p. 399 (1988).
41. The example comes Timothy Sullivan, "Knowledge and Method in the Study of Public Management," paper prepared at the Graduate School of Public Policy, University of California, Berkeley (1987).
42. Thomas Pinckney, John Cohen, and David Leonard, "Microcomputers and Financial Management in Development Ministries: Experience from Kenya," in *Agricultural Administration*, vol. 14, no. 3, pp. 151 and 167 (1983).
43. Pinckney, Cohen, and Leonard, p. 166 (1983).
44. World Bank, *World Development Report 1988*, Oxford University Press, NY, p. 129 (1988).
45. Stephen Peterson, "Microcomputers and Institutional Development: Emerging Lessons from Kenya," paper prepared for the Harvard Institute of International Development Conference on Economic Reform, Marrakech, Morocco, Nairobi (1988).
46. Clay Wescott, "Microcomputers for Improved Budgeting by the Kenya Government," Development Discussion Paper no. 227, Harvard Institute for International Development, Cambridge, MA (1986).
47. From Emery Roe, "Project Appraisal: A Venture Capitalist Approach," *Development Policy Review*, vol. 3 (1985).

2

The Tragedy of the Commons

Like Garrett Hardin, this chapter's counternarratives keep to grazing and herders, but with wider applicability. The chapter concludes with a discussion of what is triangulated on by the four counterscenarios, namely, the rather surprising, but robust, finding that if we differentiate herders, herds, and their rangelands from the outset, we will *never* find a tragedy of the commons taking place.

The counternarratives are based on competing theories of resource management in the face of a highly complex, uncertain environment, as found in the arid and semiarid rangelands of sub-Saharan Africa. Triangulation of theories requires that: (1) each approach should take complexity seriously, i.e., each represents at some fundamental level a theory of uncertainty induced through complex processes; (2) the approaches in question should be orthogonal on the dimension of comparison, which, in our case, means each differs fundamentally on the core tragedy of the commons issue of resource management; and (3) each approach defamiliarizes the problem of resource management in fresh ways, i.e., more conventional analytical frameworks, such as microeconomic analysis, are often part of the problem being analyzed, which is certainly the case in the tragedy-of-the-commons debate.[1]

The approaches are orthogonal (though not perfectly so) in the following way. Both the local justice and management-under-stress frameworks equate resource management with local level, while cultural theory argues that this management represents only one or two of the handful of basic cultures possible for local resource management. Girardians will have none of that, insisting that none of these cultures—local or otherwise—are in any sense permanent, doomed as they are to disappear in crises of undifferentiation. Thus, if these divergent approaches do indeed converge (i.e., triangulate), we can be fairly confident that we are on to something that should be followed up, as in "No matter from what direction you look at this issue, you're still led to the same [conclusion, starting point, problem definition, or other desideratum]." Of course, convergence and confidence do not mean we have miraculously found "common ground" between approaches that differ so radically from each other. Rather, what we have done, when triangulation is successful, is recast a complex issue in ways that we feel confident to pursue further.

Each section below starts with extensive quotation from the relevant theorist and ends with a brief, initial application of that theory to field experience. This format of an extensive quote followed by a short application and preliminary policy implications is, I believe, the least prejudicial way for readers to appreciate the surprising number of counternarratives possible to the tragedy-of-the-commons argument.

René Girard's Stereotypes-of-Persecution Framework

First, René Girard's theory in his own words:

No matter what circumstances trigger great collective persecutions, the experience of those who live through them is the same. The strongest impression is without question an extreme loss of social order evidenced by the disappearance of the rules and "differences" that define cultural divisions . . . .We can then speak of a stereotype of crisis which is to be recognized, logically and chronologically, as the first stereotype of persecution. Culture is somehow eclipsed as it becomes less differentiated.

[The second stereotype] Men feel powerless when confronted with the eclipse of culture; they are disconcerted by the immensity of the disaster but never look into the natural causes . . . But, rather than blame themselves, people inevitably blame either society as a whole, which costs them nothing, or other people who seem particularly harmful for easily identifiable reasons. The suspects are accused of a particular category of crimes . . . .In order to blame victims for the loss of distinctions resulting from the crisis, they are accused of crimes that eliminate distinctions.

I turn now to the third stereotype. The crowd's choice of victims may be totally random; but it is not necessarily so. It is even possible that the crimes of which they are accused are real, but that sometimes the persecutors choose their victims because they belong to a class that is particularly susceptible to persecution rather than because of the crimes they have committed . . . .There are very few societies that do not subject their minorities, all the poorly integrated or merely distinct groups, to certain forms of discrimination and even persecution . . . .[I]n actuality they are identified as victims for persecution because they bear the signs of victims.

Each time an oral or written testament mentions an act of violence that is directly or indirectly collective we question whether it includes the description of a social and cultural crisis, that is, a generalized loss of differences (the first stereotype), crimes that "eliminate differences" (the second stereotype), and whether the identified authors of these crimes possess the marks that suggest a victim . . . (the third stereotype). The fourth stereotype is violence itself . . . .The juxtaposition of more than one stereotype within a single document indicates persecution. Not all stereotypes must be present: three are enough and often even two. Their existence convinces us that (1) the acts of violence are real; (2) the crisis is real; (3) the victims are chosen not for the crimes they are accused of but for the victim's signs that they bear, for everything that suggests their guilty relationship with the crisis; and (4) the import of the operation is to lay the responsibility for the crisis on the victims or at least by banishing them from the community they "pollute."[2]

From the Girardian perspective, the tragedy of the commons is a crisis and the crisis is real; the accused are herders and their adherence to communal land tenure; and their crime is to permit an overgrazing that leaves what was a once a varied range now everywhere undifferentiated and denuded. Moreover, herders for their part are poorly integrated into society and communal land tenure is considered premodern by their persecutors.

Their persecutors? Why, that's us, the experts. Our persecution—we, of course, call it the solution—is to banish them all from the "real" community: banish their tenure, banish their livestock, better yet banish the herder-as-herder. Not only that, we tell the accused that they have it within their own power to save themselves, if only they would privatize the commons, commercialize their production, and be, well, more like us.

Let's not mince words. When an international range expert (who shall go nameless) insists that private stock living off communal land and water "inevitably" means

> *no* responsibility for resource management and therefore *no* possible private investment of *any* sort . . . Until this sociopolitical situation is cleared there does not seem to exist *any* hope for *any* improvement of the Sahel grassland in the foreseeable future . . . (my italics)

this comes perilously close to sounding like persecution.[3] One solution to the tragedy of the commons is to stop this hounding of herders. That will not solve the perceived range deterioration, but it would recognize the fact that the experts have absolutely no standing in the herders' crisis. No standing? As insisted throughout *Except-Africa*, we outsiders have no standing to the extent that our statements, e.g., "overgrazing is caused by overstocking," are not accompanied in the same breadth with reliable estimates as to what levels of livestock and systems of production should be in place so that herders there can have sustainable markets, development, and resources. Outsiders simply do not know enough to provide those estimates with any degree of certainty—nor will we ever.

Jon Elster's Local Justice Framework

> *"On commons where no farmers claims appear*
> *Nor tyrant justice rides to interfere."*
> —*John Clare*[4]

First, Jon Elster's framework in his own words:

Local justice can be contrasted with global justice. Roughly speaking, globally redistributive policies are characterized by three features. First, they are designed centrally, at the level of the national government. Second, they are intended to compensate people for various sorts of bad luck, resulting from the possession of "morally arbitrary properties." Third, they typically take the form of cash transfers. Principles of local justice differ on all three counts. They are designed by relatively autonomous institutions which, although they may be constrained by guidelines laid down by the center, have some autonomy to design and implement their preferred scheme. Also, they are not compensatory, or only partially so. A scheme for allocating scarce medical resources may compensate patients for bad medical luck, but not for other kinds of bad luck (including the bad luck of being turned down for another scarce good). Finally, local justice concerns allocation in kind of goods (and burdens), not of money.[5]

From the local justice perspective, what is going on is not a tragedy of the commons as much as local justice. Herders in parts of arid and semiarid Africa exercise a fair degree of autonomy both as a community and as operators on rangelands that are often weakly controlled by central government. Moreover, the distribution of perceived range deterioration is nonmonetary in a direct and formal sense. Where livestock are typically held not for cash nor for meat but as a means of production (draft, manure, milk, or the like), the effect of the apparent deterioration is not immediately in money terms. Moreover, the de facto allocation of rangeland grazing is noncompensatory in the medium of forage and browse. Large livestock owners do not, as a rule, compensate small-holders for the shortage of grazing caused by their large herds. Nor do livestock holders compensate non-holders who cannot start or maintain herds because of insufficient grazing or water left for them to do so.

But, as Elster points out, compensation can occur to rectify some cases of "local bad luck." For instance, in the past during periods of drought, it was common for few herders, if any, to be turned away from water if they need it and if it were available. That said, local justice systems are not, in Elster's view, designed to correct for global injustice, and this is certainly true for grazing systems. Communal grazing does not compensate a herder who has had a string of bad luck, e.g., born poor, left ill-educated, allocated little land, never holding more than a few livestock and always losing those in the next drought. Elster puts the dilemma this way:

> For most people, events will turn out so that they can say to themselves, "You win some, you lose some." But by the nature of chance events, some individuals will miss every train: they are turned down for medical school, chosen by the draft lottery, laid off by the firm in a recession, and refused scarce medical resources; in addition, their spouse develops cancer, their stocks become worthless, and their neighborhood is chosen for a toxic waste dump. It is neither desirable nor possible to create a mechanism of redress to compensate all forms of cumulative bad luck. For one thing, the problems of moral hazard would be immense [i.e., if people knew they were going to be compensated for whatever happens to them, they could take more risks and thereby incur more injuries]. For another, the machinery of administering redress for bad luck would be hopelessly complex and costly.

Elster hastens to add, "These objections do not, however, exclude all forms of interinstitutional compensation." What, though, would such compensatory mechanisms look like, if they were to mitigate the global injustice of villages and rangeland communities that almost always have had highly skewed distributions of wealth, find themselves in the midst of an inhospitable arid and semiarid environment, and are vulnerable to recurrent drought? Frankly, we do not know. The injustice here is global precisely because whatever the grazing system—communal, private, leasehold, or mixed—it is not one capable of compensating for this kind of "bad luck." "There is probably not much we can achieve along these lines," Elster admits, "but thinking about the issues might have some value."

The Cultural Theory Framework

First the theory described in the words of Michael Thompson, Richard Ellis, and Aaron Wildavsky:

Our theory has a specific point of departure: the grid-group typology proposed by Mary Douglas. She argues that the variability of an individual's involvement in social life can be adequately captured by two dimensions of sociality: group and grid. *Group* refers to the extent to which an individual is incorporated into bounded units. The greater the incorporation, the more individual choice is subject to group determination. *Grid* denotes the degree to which an individual's life is circumscribed by externally imposed prescriptions. The more binding and extensive the scope of prescriptions, the less of life that is open to individual negotiation . . . .
      Strong group boundaries coupled with minimal prescriptions produce social relations that are *egalitarian*. Because such groups lack (as a consequence of their low grid position) internal role differentiation, relations between group members are ambiguous . . . .When an individual's social environment is characterized by strong group boundaries and binding prescriptions, the resulting social relations are *hierarchical*. Individuals in this social context are subject to both the control of other members in the group and the demands of socially imposed roles . . . . Individuals who are bound by neither group incorporation nor prescribed roles inhabit an *individualistic* social context. In such an environment all boundaries are provisional and subject to negotiation . . . .People who find themselves subject to binding prescriptions and are excluded from group membership exemplify the *fatalistic* way of life. Fatalists are controlled from without. [6]

From a cultural theory perspective, we must jettison the tragedy of the commons narrative that "herders" can be treated as homogeneous in their calculation and production. What is needed instead is to differentiate herders, and in ways that go well beyond the wealth categories of rich and poor. Grid/group analysis provides one powerful way to do that.

Consider the example of Botswana. In that country during the late 1970s and early 1980s, it was not unusual to find different types of "herders" and values involved in grazing the eastern communal areas. Two development narratives were said to be opposed there. On one hand, the Tswana sense of self-autonomy and individualism, it was claimed, undermined government efforts to encourage farmers to intensify their communal and group activities. On the other hand, it was claimed that the Tswana sense of tradition and community undermined government attempts to encourage individual farmers to come together as a means of promoting their own private self-interests. Dam groups and fencing groups, for instance, claimed they were hampered by having too few rules and enforcement procedures with which to ensure the contribution of individual members to help manage their fences and dams. On the other side, highly structured and legally constituted livestock ranches and water point partnerships of richer farmers ("borehole syndicates") claimed to be stymied in their efforts to modernize livestock production by members' older, traditional ties to family and tribe.

In the view of grid/group analysis, individualistic farmers, traditional society, ranches, fencing groups, borehole syndicates, and dam groups do not measure out a continuum, whose endpoints are individualism and community. Instead they can be located within a two-by-two typology measured out by "grid" and "group":

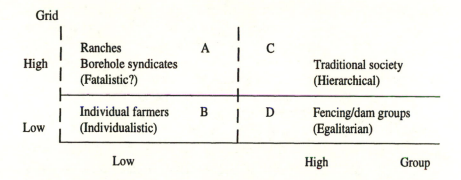

The low grid/low group cell identifies individualistic persons who are not strongly circumscribed by a sense of community cohesion or social constraint. It is here that those Motswana farmers can be located who subscribe to the Tswana "ideal" of doing as much as possible autonomously and individually.[7] The popular narrative of traditional society, on the other hand, fits the high grid/high group cell. This is essentially the image left us by anthropologist, Isaac Schapera, of a Tswana agriculture controlled through chiefly hierarchy and infused with tribal cohesion.[8]

Dam and fencing groups can be located in the low grid/high group cell, since (1) they commonly have fewer rules and regulations to abide by (at least in comparison to ranches and syndicates), and (2) they reflect interests that are more collective and group-oriented in nature (again, in comparison to ranches and syndicates controlled, as many were, by one family or person). Lastly, while ranches and syndicates do not behave fatalistically, at least in the common use of that term, their relatively individualistic members and greater number of rules and regulations puts them closest to the high grid/low group cell.

Examine the typology closely. The quadrants along one diagonal share something in common that those along the other do not—principally, a very different attitude toward risk under uncertainty. Individual farmers and traditional society along diagonal B/C are not polar opposites, as often supposed, but each embodies the same attitude toward risk aversion, though in different ways. The structure of traditional society in Botswana was, many have argued, a response to minimizing the perceived risks associated with living across a semi-arid terrain. Similarly, as others have said,[9] the individualism of Batswana is one where farmers seek to avoid reliance on friendships and alliances that prove as ephemeral under adversity as the rains are in the dry season. Depend only on yourself is the best form of risk aversion. As for the "risk-takers" in this typology, they are to be found in the borehole syndicates, dam groups, and fencing groups of cells A and D. It is along this diagonal that people have joined together to meet their requirements in relatively novel ways that fall outside or do not readily conform to the more conventional individualist or traditionally communal practices prevailing along diagonal B/C. Syndicates and groups, for example, were considered to be very much innovations and the exception in their heyday.

From a cultural theory perspective, the tragedy-of-the-commons narrative of homogeneous herders is far too simplistic. First, herders vary by locality: agro-pastoralists in Botswana do not behave like Kenya pastoralists. Second, herders in the same locality vary by risk preference: some are risk takers; others appear not to be. Third, herders vary within their risk preference. Once risk aversion is understood to embrace both individualistic *and* communalistic values (diagonal B/C), we can better understand that risk aversion itself must be variable in practice. For example, production yields under the "traditional" farming in countries like Botswana have overlapped with those under new and "improved" (read, "risk-taking") farming systems so favored by donors and governments.[10] That said, the whole notion of herder risk aversion and risk-taking can itself be counternarrativized, and we will do so in the following chapter.

The Management-under-Stress Framework

First the framework as I first formulated it:

A CPR (Common Property Resource) Management Model. We will stay with the water supply example for the moment. Comparative statistics guide the approach here to modeling local water management. There are two stages, before any outside intervention and afterwards, where the outside intervention in question is the introduction of the government livestock watering point into a locality whose residents are all herders. The following analysis would apply for any outside intervention as long as the water provided was of a larger magnitude than what locality insiders could have individually or collectively provided themselves on their own account.

The Pre-Intervention Stage

The Locality's Seasonal Response Curve. The basic seasonal relationship between a locality's water supplies and the water point management herders there undertake jointly and individually is set out in figure 1 . . .

As the wet season advances and more ephemeral water sources become available in the locality, herders respond by spending less time managing other sources: they now are able to obtain water more freely from the puddles and pools that the wet season brings. But as the dry season advances and these ephemeral sources dry up, people and their stock have to fall back to the permanent, year-round sources, leading to a period of more intensive water management on their part. In order to get the same amount of water that they do in the wet season, herders in the dry season have to expend more local management effort, both in the form of joint management at communal water points and individual management at private ones. In other words, the basic relationship is an inverse one over the entire locality . . . (the shape of the curve is less important than its negative slope).

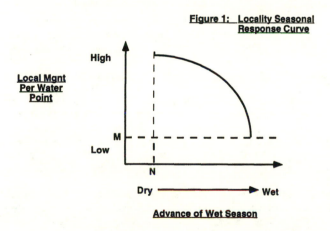

Figure 1: Locality Seasonal Response Curve

Local Mgnt Per Water Point

High

M

Low

N

Dry ———————▶ Wet

Advance of Wet Season

Points M and N in figure 1 reflect limits on local water management set by the locality's agricultural production system over the short term. Local water management will rarely, if ever, go below a certain minimum (M), even in the best of all wet seasons, since livestock always require some degree of individual or collective water management. Similarly there is a point (N) beyond which even the most intensive water point management . . . cannot compensate for the worst of all dry seasons when the lack of rains provide livestock or crops with no water whatsoever. Another way to put this is that a locality's seasonal response curve is bounded by the "worst" dry season and by its "best" wet season (worst and best defined in terms of the production system), such that in a "normal" year the locality will move along only a portion of its curve in an effort to maintain a constant water supply for meeting its production needs.

In sum, local water management occurs when that resource is under some stress relative to demand for it, that is, management occurs when water is neither too abundant or too scarce . . . .

The Post-Intervention Stage: The Outside Introduction of a New Water Point

The Short-Run and Longer-Term Effect on the Individual Herder. The near-immediate effect of the substantial increase in the locality's water supply, due to the introduction of the government water point, is to reduce the price of water for herders who respond by consuming more water. More water, in turn, means less need for their own management effort. In short, the government water point allows herders to substitute government water for their own management.

In the longer term, cheaper water alters the production-possibilities frontier for the locality, making it possible now to have more livestock for the same amount of local water management work expended before the introduction of the government water supply. Unless new limiting factors come into force [see chapter 3 for a discussion of such limits], livestock numbers will increase in the locality over the longer-term. In other words, this longer-term effect of increasing demand for livestock water may offset the short-term response of lower prices and lower levels of local water management . . . .

The Aggregate Effect over Time on Local Management. Localities fall along a continuum of outside-induced improvements in local water supplies. Figure 2 sets out the long-run locality response curve to such improvements. Line OJ shows what the government takes to be the relationship between new water point development and local . . . water point management in the locality: These are thought to be positively related, since, so the conventional wisdom has it, if water is scarce in an area, local households should be willing to provide more local management ("self-help") in order to ensure a greater water supply as and when it becomes available to them. While dividing up such a continuum is always arbitrary, three types of localities are identified. A Type I locality is one where the new water point leads to an increase in local water point management in locality as a whole, but in some cases at less a rate of increase than government thought would be the case.

Type II localities are where increased water point development by outsiders is associated with declines in water management locally. Here the effect of new water supplies is to encourage herders to worry less about managing their other water supplies. It is Type II localities where government's expectations of increased local management not only fall short of reality, but are often orthogonal to what actually does happen.

Type III localities, such as the more urbanized villages and rural towns, are where improvements in an already sophisticated government water supply system make local management of the system—at least of the pre-intervention variety conceived both by government and the locality—more and more remote. [11]

**Figure 2:   Long-Run Locality Response to Outside
Induced Water Improvements**

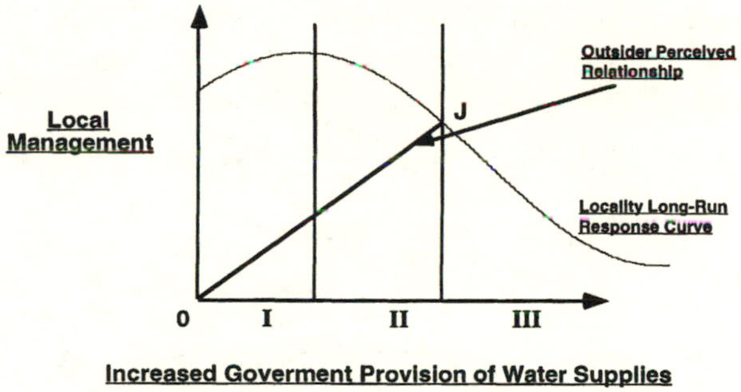

Local
Management

Outsider Perceived
Relationship

J

Locality Long-Run
Response Curve

0   I   II   III

Increased Goverment Provision of Water Supplies

From the management-under-stress perspective, the more water provided a locality by outsiders (such as government, donors or nongovernmental organizations), the more likely over time for herds to expand, range utilization to increase, and local-level water management
to decrease, holding other factors constant.[12] This, of course, is much
the opposite of what outside-sponsored livestock rangeland projects
have wanted to achieve. The idea that herders greet the livestock rangeland project by reducing their "self-help component" is particularly
troublesome. The conventional design expectation is just the reverse:
herders should be so overjoyed by having the project that they would
work extra hard to make it a success. Lurking in these worries is the
real fear of the project designer and policymaker, the silent suspicion,
more and more bordering on conviction, that if there was not a tragedy
of the commons to justify the project or policy in the first place, it is a
tragedy of the commons that is left behind.

What the above CPR model warns against are those livestock rangeland projects whose implementation rapidly transforms a Type I locality into a Type III one, as they are especially counterproductive in
terms of meeting their conventional design aims. If the policy or project
expects the target population to increase its local resource management, pay a fee for using the project's facilities, and at the same time

expand its production possibilities without increased resource utilization in the process—all as a result of the intervention—then designers and implementors must realize that the numbers of such Type I communities are probably fewer than supposed. Indeed, thirty years after independence has left rural development in parts of Africa with many Type II and III localities, whose chief limiting factors on expanding further production now vary from locality to locality (i.e., they are never guaranteed with certainty) and can no longer be presumed to be water, grazing, or labor alone.

Conclusion

It would be a fairly simple matter to end the chapter with the last paragraph. But notice the connection that cuts across the four counternarratives—namely, the need to differentiate herders and the herder context, if the aim is policy relevance.

The empirical finding that herders are frequently differentiated is, of course, not new.[13] What is new is the methodological imperative that insists the analyst first differentiate herders, their herds and rangelands—and differentiate them in multiple and crosscutting ways—before assessing whether or not the tragedy of the commons applies to the case at hand. To put it more forcefully: if you differentiate herders, their herds and rangelands from the outset (whatever the metric of differentiation), you will never find a tragedy of the commons taking place. A rather stunning finding, it is the best indicator of the counternarrative status of the four approaches sketched above. Moreover, what you do find in practice will be much more useful—namely, rangeland use should be analyzed on a case-by-case basis given multiple, if not unique, differences are always at work in the field. In short, Hardin got it wrong from the start: you can't "picture a pasture open to all" that does not exist, period.

That there are at least four plausible alternatives to the tragedy of the commons argument is of course due to the fact that what is being explained—behavior across the sub-Saharan drylands—is sufficiently complex as to accommodate such differences. If rangelands were everywhere and always just one way causally, then ultimately those of us who insisted that this causality was some other way would come to our senses and see the rangelands as they really are. That this does not happen—that people go on and on being surprised by how many different ways you can account for rangeland behavior—tells us that the rangelands and their use may never be just one way causally, i.e., they are constantly changing. And if they are constantly changing in causally complex ways, then with this constant change comes even more uncertainty and pressure for ever more counternarratives to make sense and better triangulate on what is going on. Narrative and counternarrative are thus at the heart of livestock rangeland development. More generally, the implications for our understanding of "power relations" in such an environment are profound, as we shall see.

Since counternarratives are part and parcel of the development of the sub-Saharan rangelands, let us now turn to a very different way in which to differentiate herders, one that in the process sets out this book's most robust and innovative counternarrative to that long-standing development narrative about the herder's risk-averse adaptation to ecological stress under arid and semiarid conditions.

Notes

1. For more on triangulation, see Roe (1998).
2. René Girard, *The Scapegoat* (translated by Yvonne Freccero), Johns Hopkins University Press, Baltimore ([1986]1989). The page references to the quotes are: 12, 14; 14, 21; 17, 18, 21; and 24.
3. Others have noted the persecutory nature of what passes for expert range advice, i.e., Sandford (1983: 17): "A further consequence of the Mainstream view [of, e.g., range management experts] is an astonishing inhumanity towards the destitute of pastoral societies."
4. John Clare verse from his *Shepherd's Calendar* is quoted in Raymond Williams, *The Country and the City*, Hogarth Press, London, p. 136 ([1973]1985).
5. Jon Elster, *Local Justice: How Institutions Allocate Scarce Goods and Necessary Burdens*, Russell Sage Foundation, New York (1992). The quotes are from pages: 4; 133; and 134.
6. Michael Thompson, Richard Ellis, and Aaron Wildavsky, *Cultural Theory*, Westview Press, Boulder, CO (1990). The quotes are taken from pages: 5, 6 and 7. The notion of risk as a form of cultural bias is explored specifically in Mary Douglas and Aaron Wildavsky, *Risk and Culture*, University of California Press, Berkeley (1982). A longer version of this section is found in Emery Roe, "Individualism versus Community in Africa? The Case of Botswana," *Journal of Modern African Studies*, vol. 26, no. 2 (1988d).
7. See Hoyt Alverson, *Mind in the Heart of Darkness: Value and Self-Identity Among the Tswana of Southern Africa*, Yale University Press, New Haven, CT, p. 133 (1978). Also see A.B.J. Willett, *Agricultural Group Development in Botswana*, vol. 1, pp. 36–41 (1981).
8. Isaac Schapera, *Native Land Tenure in the Bechuanaland Protectorate*, Lovedale Press, Alice, South Africa (1943).
9. Alverson, pp. 133–134.

10. Clive Lightfoot, "Agricultural Research for Development of Small Farmers: A Closer Look at Traditional Technology," *Botswana Notes and Records*, vol. 14 (1982).
11. Material for this section is drawn from Chapter 5 of Emery M. Roe, "Uncommon Grounds for Commons Management: Making Sense of Livestock Rangeland Projects South of the Sahara," unpublished Ph.D. dissertation, University of California, Berkeley (1988). The quotes are from pages: 216–218, 225, and 227–229. Some of these ideas were introduced in Emery Roe, "Last Chance at the African Kraal: Reviving Livestock Projects in Africa," *Proceedings of the 1987 International Rangeland Development Symposium*, Winrock International, Morrilton, AR (1987a). For a short review of evidence on common property resource management, see Emery Roe, "Six Myths About Livestock Rangeland Development South of the Sahara," *Rangelands* , vol. 11, no. 5 (1989).
12. Chapter 3 introduces the complications with this ceteris paribus condition.
13. See, for example, Pauline Peters, "Embedded Systems and Rooted Models: The Grazing Lands of Botswana and the 'Commons' Debate" in McCay and Acheson (1987); and Jean Ensminger, *Making a Market*, Cambridge University Press, Cambridge (1992).

3

Old (Risk-Averse) Pastoralism versus New (High Reliability) Pastoralism

with Lynn Huntsinger and Keith Labnow

Introduction

Except-Africa demonstrates that counternarratives to objectionable development narratives in African rural development are not only possible but plentiful. That said, little attention is given to fleshing out these counternarratives in the kind of detail needed to guide policy or projects on the ground. This chapter is the exception. Considerable time is spent developing the most innovative counternarrative proposed in *Except-Africa* and drawing out its implications for real-time policymakers and researchers who are concerned with African pastoralist development. We believe this counternarrative radically changes the understanding of African pastoralism and how to approach it.

Summary

The study of pastoralism—and not just in Africa—continues to center on the implications of *unpredictability* in rangeland ecosystems for pastoral societies and land use patterns (Sandford 1983a, is the starting point of any such study). The development narrative that conceives of this unpredictability as risk, and pastoralists as risk averters, makes sense where rangeland unpredictability is in fact the core exogenous driver of pastoralist decision making. We argue instead that the central concern of pastoralists is to manage a predictably unpredictable environment better, so as to establish a "reliable" flow of lifesustaining goods and services from rangeland ecosystems that are in fact an endogenous part of their production systems. Our counternarrative is of pastoralists as a high-reliability institution in the face of unpredictability and stands in contrast to the development narrative of pastoralists whose risk aversion is purportedly an ecological adaptation to that unpredictability. In short, the discussion of risk aversion in chapter 2 was the start, rather than the end, of analysis.

For our purposes, think of the risk-averting pastoralist as engaged in an attempt to avoid or escape the high hazards of ecological unpredictability, given that the pastoralist has no control over the probability of those hazards occurring. The pastoralist in search of reliability is, in contrast, actively engaged in ongoing efforts to reduce the probability of those hazards s/he cannot avoid by managing temporal and spatial diversity in grazing opportunities and diversity in livestock capabilities and response. Rather than being risk averse in trying to avoid hazards altogether, pastoralists accept and even take risks in order to respond to high-consequence hazards they cannot avoid.

This counternarrative follows directly from what has been called the New Range Ecology, which tells us that range management must shift its orientation from the expectation of herders eventually achieving some kind of a stable relationship with the environment to an "opportunism" that allows herder management in the face an absolute certainty of unpredictability. The high reliability counternarrative shifts the focus of analysis from "risk aversion" to reconceptualizing pastoralist activities as driven by the opportunities for management afforded through the use of a complex technology—particularly, the livestock—whose hazards stem directly from a reliance on the unpredictable, unstable forage production characteristic of arid and semiarid rangelands. In that other high reliability organization—nuclear power plants—you find computers, cooling systems, alarm systems, and other complex structures constructed so as to harness the unstable power of the atom. Pastoralism is harnessing the unstable power of the range. In both cases, the attempt is less to avoid hazards than to accept and manage them better.

The distinction between risk aversion and reliability seeking is subtle, but has important implications for policy approaches to pastoral development. It also has ramifications for understanding the ecological aspects of the interactions of pastoralists and the environment. To appreciate those aspects better we must turn to what has been called the "new range ecology."

The New Range Ecology

The New Range Ecology seeks to accommodate range management to the complexity and inherent unpredictability of rangeland ecosystems. Clementian models of plant succession have long provided a simple, hitherto compelling framework (read: development narrative) that permits evaluation of the ecological status of rangeland ecosystems and prediction of response to management, including development of recommended carrying capacities and stocking rates (Behnke et al 1993). Increasingly, the shift in rangeland ecology is away from simple assumptions and models to a greater appreciation of the complexity of vegetation dynamics as they interact with herbivory and random events or "disturbance" on rangelands. In between alarmingly simplified succession models that assume an orderly and predictable progression to a "climax" equilibrium state, and equally alarmingly complex diagrams that appear frequently today in symposia papers purporting to illustrate rangeland ecosystem dynamics, the need has grown for models or frameworks that maintain the virtues of simplicity but capture more of the complexity (and thus the unpredictability) observed on many rangelands around the world. The New Range Ecology, which focuses on the disequilibrium conditions of rangelands, offers state and transition models as one such option (Westoby et al. 1989).

State and transition models do not assume a linear progression for vegetation development on a given site. Instead they offer a variety of end and transition states, with a number of possible pathways or transitions between them. In the disequilibrium environments characteristic of rangelands, state and transition models make it clear that operating scale and management objectives take on different roles than those conceptualized in more traditional models of rangeland vegetation dynamics. In many rangeland environments, transitions are more strongly driven by random, unpredictable events and contingencies than by stocking rates or patterns of herbivory. Managing for particular vegetation states becomes unrealistic in these cases, where instead the process of maintaining reliable production over different operating scales despite unexpected shifts takes priority. For ecologists, this means both rethinking approaches to the evaluation of ecological change and the development of goals and standards of management and focusing on the interrelationships of ecosystems, management, and disturbance.

What does this mean for our understanding the ways pastoral people interact with rangeland ecosystems? The answer: it is now much easier to see pastoralism as more akin to what has been termed *a high reliability organization*. The details follow, but simply put, the New Range Ecology tells us that achieving a "steady state" or equilibrium between stocking rate and forage production is not possible on many, if not all, arid and semiarid rangelands (Behnke et al. 1993). Instead, the interaction of pastoralists and their surrounding conditions has created an institution of reliably maintaining high (i.e., peak) levels of livestock in order to exploit the expected but unpredictable production of low-quality vegetation. In this view, livestock are best thought of as part of the complex technology adapted by pastoralists to utilize and "smooth" a highly volatile, unpredictable and inherently "dangerous" forage resource key to their production system. Livestock are mobile, have the sophisticated digestive capacity to process fibrous vegetation, and are ideally suited to a diverse landscape where production varies over time and from place to place and where grasses and shrubs are the forage supply. In effect, the rangeland-livestock production system is technology adopted and adapted by pastoralists to provide a steady flow of human sustenance from the herbivory of animals in an environment whose only certainty is its high spatial and temporal diversity. In the high reliability counternarrative, while herd and herder mobility is an important management tool, ability to cope with diversity and change in any given place is fundamental.

The New Pastoralism and High Reliability Theory

Unfortunately, the New Range Ecology has been patched onto the Old Pastoralism, or more properly, the outdated—and we argue erroneous—development narratives about pastoralism and its policy implications. The Old Pastoralism views pastoralism as a risk averse adaptation of herders and herds to environmental and ecological stress, particularly variability in rainfall and grass cover. In this development narrative, anything that ensures or assists herd mobility is to be encouraged and anything that hinders it is to be discouraged. The Old Pastoralism's implications are that the range as common property or otherwise communal resource is a good thing, while borders, agricultural encroachment (particularly on dry season grazing land), privatization of the range, and fenced ranches are a bad thing, because they inhibit or otherwise retard herder and herd mobility. According to the Old Pastoralism, pastoralism is fast becoming impossible—a conclusion that ignores the options our high reliability counternarrative affords.

The development narrative that pastoralism is a risk averse adaptation to a highly variable environment has been virtually unchallenged over the last fifty years. It dominates analysis about, as well as development projects for, pastoralists (e.g., see Swallow 1994; Dahl and Hjort 1976; Galaty and Johnson 1990).[1] It is now time to challenge the assumption, both because of the New Range Ecology and because the performance of most development projects has been so disappointing (e.g., de Haan 1994; UNDP 1994: 1).

The starting point in rethinking pastoralism must be questioning the centrality given to herder risk aversion. A moment's reflection makes clear some problems with the risk aversion narrative—if it were simply a matter of pastoralists being risk averse, then why ever do they stay and live in such hazardous environments? Why haven't they all long ago flooded into the towns or agriculture or into something less risky?

The answer is that herders, instead of seeking to avoid risk altogether, have in all the important senses accepted it. To see why, we must be clear about what is meant by risk aversion and high reliability, at least as development narratives. Formally, risk is defined as the magnitude of a hazard multiplied by the probability of that hazard occurring. In risk-averse pastoralism, both the hazard and the probability are large, with the paradigmatic case being the inevitable droughts in an arid and semiarid environment. From the risk averse perspective, the way herders respond is (1) by accepting that the probabilities of these hazards occurring are largely outside the pastoralist control, and then (2) by trying to avoid the hazards altogether (e.g., they move the herd to where they think the grass and water are better) or by trying to reduce the magnitude of the hazard directly (e.g., "spreading the risk" through separating the herd across a large geographical space). In both cases, the attempt is to ensure a minimum survival level of the herd, thereby ensuring the survival of the herders (e.g., Ellis 1993: 89).

The New Pastoralism counternarrative based in high reliability theory interprets pastoralist behavior quite differently. Both the hazard and its probability are large in high reliability pastoralism, although unlike risk-averse pastoralism, it is much more focused on probability than hazard. Accepting full well what the hazards are of living and working in an arid and semiarid environment, pastoralists act in ways that enable them to maintain their large herds and ways of life in as highly reliable a fashion as they can. In formal terms, pastoralists seek to ensure their capacity to maintain very high, peak levels of livestock in the face of the hazards that cannot be otherwise avoided. They do this by avoiding management mistakes and other failures in a manner that allows them to reliably reduce the probabilities associated with otherwise highly probable hazards of living in their dryland environment. In high reliability pastoralism, the hazards cannot be avoided and the probabilities must be managed instead, in large part because what the risk averse narrative treats as exogenous to pastoralism, the high reliability counternarrative treats as endogenous to pastoralist production, namely, the highly variable environment of rainfall and grass cover.

This is not to say that all hazards are avoidable (in the risk-averse development narrative) or that all probabilities of hazards are reducible (in the high reliability counternarrative). Consider the hazard of low and erratic rainfall. No pastoralist behavior, whatever its nature, can change the hazard arising because a semiarid and arid rangeland has, by definition, twenty inches (500 milimeters) of rainfall or less per annum nor can pastoralist behavior change the hazard arising because even this little rainfall is erratically distributed over any given area there. On the other hand, how the hazard of a severe drought having a 0.5 or greater probability of killing half or more of the herds in one out of every ten years is understood and treated by pastoralists varies by whether one is talking about risk-averse or high reliability pastoralism. From a risk-averse perspective, pastoralists will be searching for better grazing and water as a way of escaping the worse effects of the drought and as a way of increasing the chances of being left with a minimum survival herd after that drought. From a high reliability perspective, pastoralists will be managing the spatial and temporal diversity of their rangeland as a whole by using different areas in different ways so as to increase the chances of producing and maintaining peak herd sizes even through the drought. The implications of these differences are considerable.

At the most general level then, risk-averse and high reliability pastoralisms overlap in the sense that high reliability pastoralists are very "risk averse" when it comes to one special class of risks—those where the consequences of management error are catastrophic. That said, at all other levels that matter, the difference between, on the one hand, averting failure by avoiding hazards whose probabilities cannot be controlled so as to maintain a minimum survival level of the herd and, on the other hand, seeking reliability by managing high-hazard, high-probability events into lower probability ones so as to avoid failures and maintain peak herd levels cannot be overstressed. The difference entails other formal distinctions between risk-averse and high reliability pastoralism important for our understanding of pastoralism and its wider implications. The contrasts between the two development narratives of pastoralism are summarized in table 3.1. We take up these distinctions in the following sections.

High reliability theory is a relatively recent development of organization theorists, many located at or around the University of California at Berkeley, who have been interested in how complex organizations and institutions maintain their activities in situations where failure, error and accidents are highly probable. The question is (e.g., Demchak 1996: 97), How do some institutions, with complex technologies and in predictably unstable environments, still manage to perform in a reliable, safe fashion, even when their first mistakes might well be their last? High reliability organizations studied in the West have included air traffic control systems, nuclear power plants, electricity companies, hospital intensive care units, and naval air carriers, among others. We nominate pastoralism to the list of high reliability organizations, by arguing that pastoralism shares most—maybe even all—of the same attributes as these other organizations.

According to two high reliability theorists, Todd La Porte and Paula Consolini (1991: 21), the operating challenges of high reliability organizations "are twofold: (1) to manage complex, demanding technologies, making sure to avoid major failures that could cripple, perhaps destroy, the organization; at the same time (2) to maintain the capacity for meeting periods of very high peak demand and production whenever these occur." Notice the goal is twofold: maintain safety and *at the same time* meet peak production requirements (see also La Porte

Table 3.1
The Old and New Pastoralisms

Risk Aversion	High Reliability
Primarily avoids risks	Primarily accepts and takes risks
Averts failures by avoiding hazards whose probabilities cannot be controlled so as to maintain a minimum survival level of the herd	Seeks reliability by controlling the probabilities of hazards so as to avoid failures and maintain peak herd levels
Complex environment with simpler and more flexible technologies	Complex environment integrated with complex technologies
Drought response crucial to evaluating risk aversion	Drought response largely irrelevant in evaluating high reliability
Because cattle have multiple functions, they enable herders to be risk averse	Because herders can maintain cattle in a highly reliable fashion, cattle take on multiple functions
Learning through trial-and-error testing	Learning in ways that avoid testing the limits of error
Herd mobility over a large common property range is crucial	Herder experience with a wide range of scale-dependent resources, whether public, private, or common property, is crucial
Redundancy of livestock reduces chances of losing all the herd	Redundancy of livestock increases chances of producing a peak herd
Carrying capacity of the rangeland sets limits on how many livestock the rangeland can support	Carrying capacity of pastoralism is the limits set by pastoralist experience with different operating scales and critical phases of rangeland production

1996). Maintaining peak livestock loads is precisely the core problem pastoralists face when confronting erratic rains and other potential disruptions.[2]

The pastoralists' biggest challenge, like the challenge confronting all high reliability institutions, is to reduce the number and magnitude of their errors, given that the hazards associated with making highly consequential mistakes are so high. In the words of another high reliability theorist, Gene Rochlin (1993: 16): "A highly reliable organization is often defined as one that has already been judged on empirical or observational grounds to provide a desirable activity, product, or service at a desired or demanded level of performance while maintaining a low rate of error or accident." High reliability institutions are all the more notable, according to Rochlin (1993: 15), because "these organizations have not just failed to fail; they have actively managed to avoid failures in an environment rich with the potential for error." That ability to actively and reliably manage to reduce the chances of hazardous mistakes occurring, rather than to avoid the hazards, has been the distinguishing hallmark of much of pastoralism.[3] For us, it is not risk aversion only or even primarily, but rather high reliability, that explains the pastoralist's "uncanny ability to survive and sometimes prosper under considerable adversity" (World Bank 1987: 29).

Moreover, complex technologies and the wider, uncertain task environment ensure there can be no "equilibria" to which high reliability institutions are driving or from which they are departing. Here the link to the New Range Ecology could not be more explicit: "In the research conducted by the Berkeley group, virtually every manager interviewed appeared to believe that there is not a steady-state or a stable 'resting point' for the high performance system under their management," according to high reliability theorist, Paul Schulman (1993: 35). In order to identify the links better, the following section sketches nine of the twelve features that have been identified for high reliability institutions, and illustrates how these attributes are to be found in the pastoralist literature, a fraction of which has been reviewed here. Reconceiving pastoralism in this way we summarize as the New Pastoralism counternarrative.

The New Pastoralism of High Reliability

Clearly reliability matters to pastoralists, and examples abound. According to Reckers (1994: 49), "The diversity of herd stocks [among Kenya pastoralists] allows a more efficient use of the rangelands and facilitates a more reliable supply of food." Reliability is at a premium for pastoralists, because they are found in areas "where the natural resources that population is technologically capable of exploiting are unreliable" (Spooner 1973: 4). What does "reliability" mean precisely? Rochlin (1993) has summarized the principal features of high reliability institutions in his "Defining 'High Reliability' Organizations in Practice: A Taxonomic Prologue." The work of other high reliability theorists, particularly Todd La Porte, is used to supplement and extend this list of primary features. In articulating our counternarrative, we have collapsed the features identified by Rochlin, La Porte and their colleagues into a dozen interrelated characteristics of high reliability institutions, of which nine principal ones are summarized here. No pretense is made that all theorists describe the features in the same way or that the features they describe apply to all pastoralists. What is important for our purposes is that each feature comes from the work of high reliability theorists and is found in the very same literature that has been used to justify the currently dominant development narrative of risk-averse pastoralism.

High Technical Competence

High reliability institutions "manage technologies that are increasingly complex, requiring specialized knowledge, specialized management, and a variety of esoteric skills at the operational level" (Rochlin 1993: 14). "High technical competence" is how La Porte (1993: 1) summarizes this characteristic.

It has long been noted that pastoralists have had and continue to have very detailed knowledge—sometimes called indigenous technical knowledge (e.g., UNDP 1994)—of the range, key resources, cattle and other livestock they manage as part of their production systems (e.g., Dyson-Hudson 1988, p. 702 on the Turkana; Hobbs 1989, p. 111 on Egyptian Bedouins; and Oba 1985, pp. 37, 39 on other Kenya pastoralists). Several important corollaries follow from the high technical competence requirement of high reliability institutions.

The first is what the requirement entails, namely, "continuous training" (Roberts 1988, figure 3). As La Porte (1996: 63) puts it: "Continuously attaining this [technical competence] entails attention to recruiting, training, and staff incentives. It puts a premium on recruiting members with extraordinary skills and/or an organizational capacity to develop them *in situ* via continuous training." "The East Pokot possess an immense plant knowledge," according to Reckers (1994: 51), where "Every child is able to learn and identify plants and knows their value in terms of human and animal consumption." As Spooner (1973: 17) notes that the pastoralist's "intimate and detailed knowledge of his territory . . . must be continually rehearsed and revised. This knowledge is the foundation of the technology of successful nomadism, and represents a huge and continuous investment in time and energy."

A second corollary of maintaining high technical competence is, La Porte (1993: 3) argues, the need for an "Extensive data base characterizing technical processes [and] the state of the system in operations, including performance data" (see also La Porte 1996: 63). Charles Perrow (1994: 218), another organization theorist who has engaged high reliability theory, calls this the need for "Experience with operating scale—did [the institution in question] grow slowly, accumulating experience, or rapidly with no experience with the new configurations or volumes?" The more extensive the database and experience with differing operating scales, the greater the chances the organization can act in a reliable fashion, other things being equal.

The detailed experience with and knowledge of different operating scales in livestock herding and holdings combine to be one of the preeminent features of pastoralism. Some of pastoralism's scale dependence is captured in statements such as "the pastoralists' flexible responses to the spatially and temporally distributed pasture and water have enabled them to exploit an environment which would have been impossible to exploit under other forms of land use systems" (Oba 1985: 52). Or, "Such periods of stress [e.g., droughts] are met by migrating to other areas, i.e., expanding the spatial scale of exploitation" (Manger 1994: 14). Or, "In the arid context, it is precisely the two factors of space and time, rather than number of animals, that determine sustainable carrying capacity and have been used efficiently by traditional pastoral managers of extensive rangelands" (UNDP 1994: 21). Or, as Behnke, Scoones, and Kerven (1993: 73), summarize:

> Cattle forage at different spatial scales. At the widest scale, animals move between different savanna types . . . .[S]patial heterogeneity thus has an impact on the interactions between population and resources, at different levels in a hierarchy of scales. The persistence of cattle populations can be interpreted in terms of the exploitation of environmental heterogeneity at different spatial scales.

As will be seen, the experience of herders with different operating scales and the fact that different resources are scale-dependent have profound implications for reconsidering the importance of land tenure—especially common property regimes—in pastoralism.

Just as experience with operating scales is important to high reliability institutions, so too is their experience with critical phases of operation. "Experience with critical phases," Perrow (1994: 218) tells us, is imperative in this regard: "if starting and stopping are the risky phases, does this happen frequently (take-offs or landings) or infrequently (nuclear plant outages)?" Here too the cognate is well-known in pastoralism in the form of pastoralist cycles of moving between wet and dry season grazing and other resources over time (e.g., Reckers 1994: 51).[4]

High Performance and Oversight

High technical competence in a high reliability institution must be matched by continual high performance. "The public consequences of technical error in operations have the potential for sufficient harm such that continued success (and possibly even continued organizational survival) depends on maintaining a high level of performance reliability and safety through intervention and management (i.e., it cannot be made to inhere in the technology)" (Rochlin 1993: 14). Accordingly, "Public perception of these consequences imposes on the organizations a degree of formal or informal oversight that might well be characterized as intrusive, if not actually comprehensive" (Rochlin 1993: 14). "The organization will be judged to have 'failed'—either operationally or socially—if it does not perform at high levels. Whether service or safety is degraded, the degradation will be noted and criticized almost immediately" (Rochlin 1993: 16). La Porte (1993: 7) adds that: "Aggressive and knowledgeable formal and informal watchers [are] IMPORTANT. Without which the rest [i.e., high reliability] is difficult to achieve."

Precisely this need for constant oversight (surveillance and monitoring), both formal and informal, in order to maintain pastoralist survival, safety and reliability is nicely captured in several references. Spooner (1973, p. 17) quotes a researcher who found that the Tibetan nomad "remains alert to the faintest whisper that riders have left their own encampments or have been seen at large." Lancaster and Lancaster (1986: 42) write of the herder:

> He needs an enormous amount of information. The most likely place to acquire such information is from other people, so he needs to be able to assess the reliability of informants. To do this he must know who they are. Usually the most reliable informants are those to whom he is related, for their interests are in common, the reliability diminishing the further away genealogically that the informant is.

As the quote implies, the success of surveillance and monitoring depends crucially on the number of reliable informants and participants. Perrow (1994: 218) describes this feature as follows: "Organizational density of the system's environment (vendors, subcontractors, owners/operators . . . etc.)—if rich, there will be persistent investigations and less likelihood of blaming God or the operators and more attempts to increase safety features." Some of this drive to a denser form of management in pastoralism is glimpsed in statements such as Spooner's (1973: 9): "Where a nomadic group relies on a number of different species, herding requirements . . . require a higher degree of cooperation between families than would be necessary if they could specialize in one species." We return to the importance of families from a high reliability perspective in a moment.

Constant Search for Improvement

A feature related to high technical competence and continual monitoring in these high reliability institutions is the constant drive to improve operations. "While [high reliability organizations] perform at very high levels, their personnel are never content, but search continually to improve their operations" (Rochlin 1993: 14). They seek "continually to *search for improvement* via systematic gleaning of feedback" (La Porte 1996: 64).

For Ekvall (quoted in Spooner 1973: 16), the pastoralist is not "satisfied with generalities: he has a well-developed question and elicitation technique that seeks specific and essential items of information," adding that "At the same time he is continually on the alert for other resources to exploit" (Spooner 1973: 23). "Every morning the herd owner decides upon a new route for the daily livestock migration," Reckers (1994: 50) found among Kenya pastoralists.

The constant search for improvements is aided by what La Porte (1993: 7) calls "Systematic, consistent individual and group rewards for discovering error, performing acute analysis, and proposing potential solutions." Indeed, such search is often in the form of "Formalized processes of discovery and review" (La Porte 1993: 7). Roberts (1988: 37) adds, "personnel are trained that when they see a problem they own it either until they solve it or until someone who can solve it takes responsibility for it." Some of this formalized search and discovery in assuring high reliability is captured in the following quotes (the first from Spooner 1973: 16; the second more recent in Agrawal 1992: 23):

> Herders leave their campfire to waylay passers-by for news, and men ride out from the encampments to intercept approaching or passing caravans for news of places and events both near and far . . . .The price for completely reliable information is high, but information for which a price has been paid rates well as evidence and has a standard market value . . .
>
> The *nambardar* [chosen leader] in the *dang* [social unit of migratory pastoralists] often undertakes reconnaissance missions to gather information regarding rainfall and grazing availability. They travel five to twenty miles ahead of the *dang* and gather information on the state of vegetation over the proposed route. They look at the state of water-points and find out if the farmers with whom they are acquainted are present in their villages. Since *dangs* move almost every day, such reconnaissance missions are invaluable for getting advance information which will help the movement of the *dang*.

The constant search for and discovery of new information and improvements leads to permanent innovations in some pastoralist behavior and technology. Hobbs (1989: 113) concludes of the Egyptian nomads he studied: "The Khushmaan apparently have had to innovate in order to protect their resource base because their ideal of common access to resources could not guarantee sustainable resource use during times of prolonged drought. . . . In view of the nomads' abilities to adapt themselves to some of the world's most marginal conditions, this innovation is not surprising."

Highly Complex Activities

"The activity or service [of a high reliability organization] is inherently complex, in that tasks are numerous, differentiated, and interdependent" (Rochlin 1993: 15). This too is found throughout pastoralism (in addition to preceding quotes, see the literature review by Dyson-Hudson and Dyson-Hudson 1980). "All nomadic movements involve complex decisions," in Spooner's (1973: 21) summation.

One conceptual advance of the New Range Ecology has been to clarify better the inseparability of herder environment and technology in the arid and semiarid areas of the world. The great failing of the risk-averse pastoralist narrative has been to draw too rigid a line between the two, arguing that the herder's environment is unpredictable and complex, while herder technology is simpler and more flexible (see Spooner 1973: 4; Abercrombie 1974: 13). In fact, the herder's production technology is very complex. It includes the spatial and temporal variation and interrelated dynamics of water, vegetation, and other key resources—all too often lumped misleadingly together as "the external environment"—as well as the links between this variation and dynamics and the livestock behavioral and physical characteristics. Coping with this complexity necessitates specialization across communities and within the herder household and the herds themselves (Bonte 1981). Different household members or communities specialize in different aspects of livestock and environmental management, for example. At the same time, the composition of the herds are often specialized at the household level.

For high reliability organizations, "It is impossible to separate physical-technical, social-organizational, and social-external aspects; the technology, the organization, and the social setting are woven together inseparably" (Rochlin 1993:16). But not *totally* inseparable: " . . . it must also be shown that the reasons for failure did not arise from exogenous factors outside the organization's possible range of control (e.g., through an 'act of God' or a technical failure in an area of design or implementation not within its power to identify or correct)" (Rochlin 1993: 22).

The notion that high reliability depends on what we can manage or fail to manage, rather than on what we cannot manage or is outside our control, has implications for the reconsideration of the role of drought and drought response in pastoralist behavior. A considerable amount of the literature on pastoralism, particularly the more recent variety, has been devoted to gauging the effect of drought on pastoralist peoples. Much of this literature has been preoccupied with pastoralist drought responses (e.g., Dahl and Hjort 1979; de Haan 1994).

High reliability theory suggests that it is crucially important to distinguish—if not practically then at least conceptually—those droughts that are "an act of God" in the Rochlin sense from those that are the product of human—including pastoralist—error and mistake (which some droughts are). From a high reliability perspective, pastoralism does not "fail" when a drought unexpectedly occurs nor should pastoralism be evaluated in terms of how effectively pastoralists respond to such an "act of God." To reiterate, the successes and failures of pastoralism, like other highly reliable institutions, must be evaluated in terms of and equated with that which people can and actually do manage, such as peak herd size, movements, and distribution.[5] To insist that a widened range of drought response and management (e.g., food distribution programs, food-for-work projects) must become part and parcel of pastoralist behavior risks repeating the very same mistake made with fenced ranching schemes of the 1960s and later— namely, the misguided insistence both that pastoralists should be reliable in a ways they are currently not and that they should be evaluated on how well they meet these new standards of reliable performance.

High Pressures, Incentives and Shared Expectations for Reliability

"The activity or service [of a high reliability organization] meets certain social demands that require performance at the highest level of service obtainable within present safety requirements, with both a desire for an even higher level of activity and a penalty (explicit or implicit) if service slackens" (Rochlin 1993: 15). The social demands on pastoralists to cooperate in order to maintain peak reliability (in this case the safety and high production of the herds) has been much commented upon. As was seen a moment ago, where nomadic groups rely on different livestock species, herding requirements often require a higher degree of cooperation between families than would be necessary if the groups were specializing in one species (Spooner 1973: 9). For Lancaster and Lancaster (1986: 45), "the Rwala see themselves as managing an environment in cooperation with the other users of it for the benefit of all. This moral duty is not only to their symbiotic partners, but to generations on both sides of the nomad/settled equation as yet unborn."

Neville Dyson-Hudson notes that a Karamojong pastoralist manages his herd and family in "mutual association" (in Spooner 1973: 13). "Families recognize a household head (usually male) who has most of the apparent responsibility for herd management decisions. All family members engage in herding activities. Children are especially important for the day-to-day maintenance of animals" (Kuznar 1991: 99). "There are also traditions for mobilizing work parties or age-groups according to the age grades of young women with a female leader or young men with a male leader" (Shanmugaratnam et al. 1992: 56). For Lancaster and Lancaster (1986: 44), "Owing to the general unpredictability of the environment no one could ever be sure where he would be the next year, the following year or the subsequent one. So a man needed a variety of *khuwa* [brotherhood] relationships with a variety of settlements." Similar passages can be found elsewhere in the pastoralist literature (e.g., Dahl and Hjort 1976: 133–134). One virtue of organizing high reliability around kith, kin, and neighbors is they provide greater chances of, in La Porte's words (1993: 7), "Relatively assured resources for/to carry our failure-preventing/quality enhancing activities" as well as, in Perrow's words (1994: 218), "Close proximity of elites to the operating system—they fly on airplanes but don't ship on rusty vessels or live only a few blocks from chemical plants."

Hazard-Driven Flexibility to Ensure Safety

"The activity or service contains inherent technological hazards in case of error or failure that are manifold, varied, highly consequential, and relatively time-urgent, requiring constant, flexible, technology-intrusive management to provide an acceptable level of safety [i.e., reliability] to operators, other personnel, and/or the public" (Rochlin 1993: 15). This accent on flexibility in securing safety is a preeminent feature of pastoralism. For example,

> Nomadic pastoralism, as practiced in East Africa, presupposes much organizational and spatial flexibility. Not only do households constantly redistribute themselves over the terrain, in response to climatic fluctuations and the needs of herd management, but membership of pastoral households, too, is continually changing as labour is allocated and reallocated between management units. (Dahl and Hjort 1979:29)

For Spooner (1973: 22) "the seasonal variability . . . requires a certain amount of fluidity in social organization". "The [pastoralist] strategies are in harmony with the yearly cycle of rainy and dry seasons and are modified when needed: e.g., by expansion or shifting. In this way menacing situations are controlled" (Reckers 1994: 51). According to El Wakeel and Abu Sabah (1993: 37), "transhumants roam large areas to look for better and safe grazing areas." Also, "the ungrazed belts between areas effectively used by wildlife and those used by livestock noticed during aerial surveys in Maasailand are not evidence of the abundance of pasture, but are 'safety belts' deliberately created by the pastoralists to protect their herds from infection by wildlife" (UNDP 1994: 71).[6]

One primary way in which organizations aspiring to high reliability develop the required flexibility is to ensure redundancy is built into their operating systems. By redundancy, organization theorists mean high levels of duplication (where two units perform the same activity separately), overlap (where two units have the same activity together), or both. The argument is that the more redundant (back-up) modes of problem-solving there are, the more reliable performance can be, if any one mode of problem-solving fails (Roberts 1988; Rochlin 1993; Sagan 1993). Fallback or back-up water points and grazing lands, as well as overlapping grazing areas, have long been a property of some pastoralist systems (see, e.g., Fortmann and Roe 1981; Sandford 1983b; UNDP 1994). Redundancy extends to other pastoralist resources: "In sum, the Khushmaan have three redundant and reinforcing rules that protect their trees: no tree anywhere should be cut; groups of trees within particular areas should not be cut; and specified individual trees should not be cut," writes Hobbs of Egyptian Bedouins (1989: 106). Clearly, though, the most important redundancy built into the pastoralist system to ensure its high reliability is its many livestock. What outsiders perceive to be too many cattle are in reality cattle kept because they are duplicates of each other. When one dies, others are there to take its place. Such, indeed, is the meaning for pastoralists of the much-vaunted "safety in numbers."

But it is "safety in numbers" with a twist. According to risk-averse pastoralism, pastoralists keep as many animals as possible in order to increase the chances of being left with a minimum or better herd size after the next drought or other catastrophe (e.g., Hobbs 1989: 103). In this view, safety in numbers means the greater the number of livestock, the better the chances some will survive, worse comes to worst. High reliability pastoralism offers a very different interpretation of large herds. From its perspective, pastoralists keep as many animals as possible in order to increase the chances of producing a peak herd size as safely and for as long as they can before and during the next drought or other catastrophe. What looks to be a minimum herd size left behind after the drought ends is, from a high reliability perspective, the peak herd size pastoralists have managed to maintain through the end of the drought. By actively assembling and maintaining large herds, pastoralists create a production system that pressures them to manage these herds in a safe and reliable fashion, such that they, their herds, and the societies they represent have even more to lose if they fail. La Porte (1996: 61) puts the point this way: "As societies come to depend on systems designed and deployed in ways that risk putting their operators, consumers, and citizens in harm's way, demands for [high reliability] performance are insistent." In this view, safety in numbers means the greater the number of livestock, the better the chances that they will be managed safely and reliably, before and while the worst happens.

Culture of Reliability

High reliability institutions "face the challenge of being highly reliable, both as producers (many under all manner of demanding conditions) and as safety providers (under conditions of high production demands). This suggests an organizational culture integrating the familiar norms of mission accomplishment and production with those of the so-called 'safety culture'" (La Porte 1996: 64). For Roberts (1988, figure 3), this organizational culture is a "culture of reliability."

Some of this culture of reliability and safety can be glimpsed in descriptions of pastoralists generated from the Old Pastoralism's risk-aversion framework. According to Dahl and Hjort (1979: 18),"safety first" is the motto of subsistence operations like those of pastoralists, adding: "Insurance and security are central themes in the East African pastoral societies and expressed both in the social structure and on the level of individual action." "To distribute one's cattle resources is," in Spooner's view (1973:13), "a form of insurance against natural hazard and enemy depredation." Western (1979: 94) found that, among the important selection criteria for Maasai settlements is a "location . . . that will minimize the hazards, production losses, and general discomfort of the occupants, and provide the essential settlement materials." The problem with such descriptions is that they get only half the picture: the safety is there, but so are the peak production requirements, where what is minimized is less the hazard of operations than the probability of their occurrence.

Reliability is not Fungible

"Because of the consequentiality of error or failure, the organization cannot easily make marginal trade-offs between capacity and safety. In a deep sense, safety is not fungible" (Rochlin 1993: 16). What this means is that there is a point at which high reliability institutions are simply not able to trade-off reliability for other desired attributes, such as money.[7] Money and the like are not interchangeable with reliability; they cannot substitute for it: in short, high reliability is simply not fungible.

When this principle is applied to pastoralism, it leads to an unexpected finding. Namely, the conventional argument that pastoralists keep cattle (or other livestock) because cattle have different functions—e.g., provision of draft, milk, dung, brideswealth, etc.—gets it backwards. From a high reliability perspective, it is because cattle are not fungible that cattle have multiple functions. Indeed, a signal feature of pastoralism is the pastoralist's inability to trade off livestock for other ways to achieve "reliability" in herd numbers, like bank accounts or fenced ranches. Accordingly, it is not surprising that cattle or other such livestock have taken on multiple functions as little, if anything, else can substitute for them in terms of securing the pastoralist priority of high reliability. Just as there is no substitute for the high number of safely traveled airplane passenger miles in ensuring that passengers can use airplanes for a variety of different reasons, so too there is no substitute for the high numbers of livestock in ensuring that pastoralists can rely on those livestock for a variety of different purposes. From a high reliability perspective, because cattle are maintained in a highly reliable fashion, they can have multiple functions. We return to the issue of nonsubstitutability below.

Limitations on Trial and Error Learning

It is commonly said that pastoralism is a product of long trial and learning, e.g., "grazing systems developed through trial and error by pastoralists have been handed down from generation to generation" (De Boer, Yazman, and Raun 1994: 24). Yet the high reliability organization, according to Rochlin (1993: 16), "is reluctant to allow primary-task related learning to proceed by the usual modalities of trial and error for fear that the first error will be the last trial." While high reliability institutions do have search and discovery processes, and often elaborate ones as we saw, they will not undertake learning and experimentation that expose them to even greater hazards than they already face. They undertake learning only within the bounds that they control. As Rochlin (1993: 16) puts it, "Because of the complexity of both technology and task environment, the organization must actively manage its activities and technologies in real time, while maintaining capacity and flexibility to respond to events or circumstances that can at most be generally bounded." High reliability organizations "set goals beyond the boundaries of present performance, while seeking actively to avoid testing the boundaries of error" (Rochlin 1993: 14). Trial-and-error learning occurs, but in ways that avoid testing the boundary between system continuance and collapse or how to act when that boundary is breached.

Such is why the experiments with fenced ranches for pastoralists have so frequently failed. They failed not because pastoralists were "traditional"—herders who constantly search for improvements and adopt them scarcely qualify as traditional in any conventional sense. Nor did the projects fail because they were too "modern"—pastoralists know a great deal about complex technologies and decision making, as we have seen. Rather, fenced ranches failed because they posed a kind of trial-and-error learning whose "errors" threatened the very reliability of pastoralism—namely, ranches were unacceptable precisely because they insisted fewer than peak-load livestock be maintained. Over and over again and quite literally, when pastoralists tried to become ranchers, this first error as pastoralists proved to be their last trial as ranchers.

A Proposed Test of the New Pastoralism Counternarrative

While our review has been based on secondary data sources, clearly a remarkable congruency exists between what has been described in the pastoralist literature and the major features of high reliability institutions. Nonetheless, this chapter's review has not been comprehensive. Obviously, some secondary sources are out-of-date, pastoralist societies are constantly changing (indeed that is the point of the high reliability theory), while our source material originated in very different conceptual frameworks and models (particularly that of risk aversion). A much more difficult problem is that there is no clean way to distinguish risk-averse and high reliability pastoralism in terms of overt pastoralist behavior only, e.g., in both cases, herds and herders move and their responses vary over time and space. Only detailed research of pastoralists will uncover the kinds of distinctions identified above.

That said, these limitations do suggest a way to test the applicability of high reliability theory to pastoralist behavior. We did not find quotes or references for three additional characteristics of high reliability institutions identified by organization theorists:

"Their search for performance and suspicion of quiet periods continually regenerates operational challenges even during times when they [i.e., high reliability organizations] seem to be working well" (Rochlin 1993: 14). In particular, "Groups compet[e] to discover error, 'located,' or attached to different levels of hierarchy [or] different reporting issues" (La Porte 1993: 7). In terms of the pastoralist literature, we would be looking for references to the effect that pastoralists rarely if ever rest in their often search for relevant information or are always on the lookout for such information.

"Common access to data bases [is found in high reliability organizations]. All operating . . . groups [have] access to same data, so can view, review situations before and after fact. Provides roots of realistic alternative views" (La Porte 1993: 3). In particular, "Information on errors—is this shared within and between the organizations? . . . Can it be obtained, as in air transport, or does it go to the bottom with the ship?" (Perrow 1994: 218). In terms of the pastoralist literature, we would be looking for references to the effect that pastoralists regularly come together to share the same information, e.g., during the evenings, around their fires, or in assemblies.

High reliability organizations "structur[e] themselves to quickly move from completely centralized decision making and hierarchy during periods of relative calm to completely decentralized and flat decision structures during 'hot times'" (Mannarelli, Roberts, and Bea 1996: 84). In particular, these organizations have a "flexible delegation of authority and structure under stress (particularly in crises and emergency situations)" (Rochlin 1996: 56), where "other, more *collegial*, patterns of authority relationships emerge as the tempo of operations increases" (La Porte 1996: 64). In terms of the pastoralist literature, we would be looking for references to the effect that, in times of emergency, pastoralist elders and leaders would be delegating decision-making powers to those who were dealing with the crisis first-hand.

As a test of the applicability of the New Pastoralism counternarrative, we predict that primary research as well as a more thorough review of the secondary literature would find these features (as well those already described) to be central to pastoralist livestock production.

Policy Implications of High Reliability Pastoralism

We have already discussed implications of high reliability theory for reconceiving features attributed to the risk averse narrative of pastoralism. There are many wider policy implications of high reliability pastoralism, and we conclude by drawing them out for pastoralist development; for the key issues of pastoralist mobility, land tenure, herder risk aversion, and "overgrazing"; and for the future of pastoralism generally.

Development Implications

High reliability theorists warn against trying to use the theory to design reliable institutions (e.g., Rochlin 1993: 13). Certainly, there is no cookbook here. Equally important, there are very real costs—economic, organizational, personal—to maintaining a high reliability organization; one simply cannot assume that all such organizations have net positive value (Rochlin, personal communication). For example, whatever one's position on overgrazing, keeping livestock as a form of "redundancy" entails costs (if simply herd management costs) in addition to the benefits already mentioned. Boundary avoidance in trial-and-error learning is also not without its own costs. Other costs will become clear momentarily.

That said, development implications do follow from the New Pastoralism, and they are different from those of the currently hegemonic Old Pastoralism. Commonplaces such as the following four—chosen at random—must be rethought and challenged, when the high reliability elements of pastoralism are foregrounded:

1. The future of pastoralism depends on the ecological restoration and sustainable utilization of the available rangelands, on the improvement of livestock productivity, and the resolution of resource conflicts in ways that facilitate the integration of pastoralism, agriculture, and silviculture in areas suitable for their coexistence. (Shanmugaratnam et al. 1992: 2).

Wrong. The future of pastoralists may have nothing whatsoever to do with the ecological restoration of rangelands, or livestock productivity, or the resolution of conflicts, or even the integration of pastoralist communities into the wider society (on the latter, see chapter 6).

2. Policies to sedenterize herders have hindered them from practising the most effective strategy for managing risks in areas of great environmental uncertainty: the option to move to areas of higher natural productivity in any given season or year. (UNDP 1994:39)

Wrong. If by managing risk what is meant is ensuring high reliability, then there is nothing that says sedentary pastoralists are not or cannot be highly reliable in their sedentary behavior (see Gefu and Gilles on sedentary pastoralists). While in no way justifying policies of forced sedentarization (see Johnson 1993), the crux here is not mobility itself but developing strategies that provide forage as reliably as possible over time.

3. If accepted that rangelands are generally robust and resilient, future rangeland management policies should be more concerned about resolution of resource use conflicts/equity/civil security/drought-preparedness and economic efficiency . . . . (Vedeld 1994: 20)

Wrong. If the New Range Ecology and high reliability pastoralism are the case, then pastoralist-to-pastoralist links are the priority, and these may have little, if anything, to do with current resource conflicts, equity and security issues, let alone drought response (more in a moment).

4. Rangeland resources must be co-managed by local communities and government authorities. (Behnke et al. 1993).

Wrong. Co-management makes sense only when both the communities and government agencies concerned approximate high reliability institutions. Anything otherwise is a recipe for mismanagement (more also below).

A high reliability critique of the commonplaces that dominate thinking about pastoral development and management could easily be extended. But the aim of *Except-Africa* is to move from critique to counternarrative, and high reliability theory is significant precisely because it has positive implications for the directions pastoral development and management should take. Only three development implications are identified below, and none of the recommendations are new. What is innovative is that the recommendations *must be the core of pastoral development strategies*, where the pastoralism of interest is high reliability rather than risk-averse pastoralism:

1. First and foremost, the central driver of any major pastoral development (e.g., encouraged by the donors and major lenders) should be those activities that *promote pastoralist-to-pastoralist links*. Such links, of course, are already underway, though at the periphery rather than in the center. Currently, contacts between pastoralists as individuals and in groups are promoted primarily by NGOs and through small government projects rather than by the major donors and lenders; moreover, they are never treated as the central engine of pastoralist development. That has to change when dealing with high reliability pastoralism.

The core priority of promoting pastoralist-to-pastoralist links follows directly from the major role that search, improvement, and learning play in a pastoralism bounded by the avoidance of error. Pastoralist-to-pastoralist links that facilitate such bounded search, improvement, and learning can be encouraged in three ways:

- first, through intrapastoralist innovators and innovations (e.g., diffusion of innovations developed within a given pastoralist group or community);
- second, through interpastoralist links focused on the so-called traditional pastoralist learning and innovation areas of livestock disease control, breeding, and feed supplementation, where innovators in one pastoralist community work with pastoralists from other communities, be they within or outside the region or country of concern; and
- third, through interpastoralist links that focus specifically on major challenges analogous to that Boeing faced when it moved from propeller engines to producing jet engines. Namely, how can pastoralists maintain a culture of high reliability when they move from "producing" livestock to undertaking other "livestock" activities, such as ostrich (or wildlife) farming, ecotourism, or other income-generating innovations in livestock production and utilization.[8]

Note that the links we have in mind are much more varied than the popular wisdom that pastoralists should get to know how other pastoralists run their common property institutions. How one actually designs specific pastoralist-to-pastoralist links will vary from case to case (again, there are no recipes here; in one case the focus may be on veterinary care, in another, wildlife management). Clearly, pastoralist associations, which are the focus of more and more pastoralist development efforts (e.g., de Haan 1994), could facilitate some of the links we recommend. Nevertheless, a high reliability perspective suggests having a specific pastoralist agency (ministry, government initiative, national commission) whose goal is to ensure that *all* key pastoralist development projects focus *primarily if not exclusively* on promoting pastoralist-to-pastoralist contacts.[9]

2. Another important development implication follows from the fact that pastoralists are not the only high reliability institutions in arid and semiarid environments. Each of the nine features for high reliability could well have been found in the government of Botswana's Veterinary Department and the Botswana Meat Commission in the 1970s and early 1980s. Agropastoralism in Botswana and these gov-

ernment of Botswana operations were very similar at that time, notwithstanding the conventional view that the former was "traditional,"
the latter "modern."

Why is this important? Because there is nothing "exotic" about
pastoralism (see also Gefu and Gilles 1990). What is of note is the
high reliability, given their complex technologies and uncertain task
environments. That is, what really links activities like pastoralism,
veterinary departments, and abattoirs is their commitment to highly
reliable peak-load production, not that they all have something to do
with livestock or are lumped together in something called "the livestock sector."

Why is that important? Because without that commitment to high
reliability there can be no real "livestock sector"—which explains why
Botswana had one in a way that was manifestly not the case in Kenya
during the same period, when the Kenya Meat Commission was in a
shambles and the government of Kenya had veterinary control problems in pastoralist areas of the country. There are times when the best
thing one can do to improve the reliability of pastoralism is to stop
trying to get pastoralists to be "more modern" and instead improve the
reliability of linked institutions such as vet departments and meat com-
missions. If these latter institutions cannot be made reliable in their
own peak-load throughputs and if the objective is to keep pastoralism
as a highly reliable institution in those areas in which it operates (an
objective *Except-Africa* commends), then it is best to get rid of the
latter institutions altogether in the areas concerned.

3. The third development implication of a high reliability perspective runs counter to the popular recommendation that pastoralists require common property tenure regimes, because such tenure arrangements facilitate herd mobility and movement. In high reliability terms,
the relevant issue is not that, but rather the fact that the more experience high reliability institutions have with different operating scales,
the more reliably these institutions can perform. There is an access
issue here, but it is one of ensuring access to scale-dependent resources. From a high reliability perspective, what is threatening about
loss of grazing area due, e.g., to agricultural encroachment, is not that
it restricts herd mobility as such, but that it reduces the experience of
herders with managing herds at different scales of operation.[10] Reduce
our experience with operating scales and you threaten our ability to
perform in a highly reliable fashion.

One herder response to a reduction in operating scale has been to compensate for that loss by accessing other scale-dependent resources hitherto un(der)-accessed. For example, the herders' response may be a shift to confined feeding of stock at selective times of the year, using improved grasses grown in plots near the herder's compound or gardens. Whatever the case, the land tenure issue cannot be one simply of ensuring land remains common property, as the prevailing Old Pastoralism would have it. Grazing land may better remain common property if it is not encroached; but one cannot argue in the same breadth that the plot of improved grasses should as well remain common property. The better argument is that such plots should be private property. The issue is really one of access to scale-dependent resources, not that all scale-dependent resources should be common property, or for that matter, private property. From the New Pastoralism perspective, different scale-dependent resources will have different access requirements, and therefore require different tenure regimes.

Little in the three recommendations should be surprising, but taken together they constitute a new flashpoint not only in the way development practitioners think about pastoralism, but also in the way they undertake that development. In this time when many larger donors have turned away from anything to do with livestock and pastoralists, especially in Africa, it is important they know they have turned away far too early and with much yet that can be done, albeit what needs to be done is not what they have been trained to do.

Implications for the Key Pastoralist Issues of Mobility, Land Tenure, Herder Risk Aversion, and "Overgrazing"

Four themes that dominate the Old Pastoralism are challenged by the New Pastoralism counternarrative: the need for herder mobility, the need for stable and secure common property tenure regimes supporting that mobility, the herder risk aversion said to be driving those needs, and the "overgrazing" that arises when trying to meet those needs.

Mobility. From the perspective of a high reliability institution, herd and herder mobility is important, but only because it is a scale- and phase-specific routine comparable to the standard operating procedures for bringing in airplanes, providing hospital intensive care, or supplying electricity over a power grid. Mobility is not just movement; it is also defining and staking out the operating scales at which high reliability is to be achieved over the critical phases of pastoralist production. To reiterate, risk-averse pastoralism holds that, when pastoralists move from one part of the range to another over the course of the year, they are escaping dry conditions and need a large area to provide such a retreat in order to minimize the effects of or otherwise avoid altogether the hazards they cannot afford to risk. High reliability pastoralism holds that in making such movements, pastoralists are managing the spatial and temporal diversity of their operating scales and enhancing the reliability of high levels of production by using different resources over these scales at different times in response to hazards that must be risked. Mobility is not just about herds moving where; it is also about managing the where so that herds can move.

For example, a risk averse perspective would focus on how the Batswana shift their livestock watering over the course of a year from ephemeral, surface water sources during the rainy season to more permanent wells and boreholes late in the dry season. From this viewpoint, herders are retreating from surface water sources as they dry up and falling back to the fewer, year-round water points. In contrast, the high reliability perspective focuses on the multiple levels of water use and management governing any given specific water point in that fallback system discussed in chapter 1: namely, the site immediately surrounding the water point, the locality in which the water point is found, and the compound locality in which the water point is located (that is, the set of different localities over which the users of that water point typically reside and work during the year). Indeed, it is at compound locality level that the specific water point operates as part of the fallback water point system, with herders falling back from the many surface water sources in the lands (i.e., their cropping fields) to the fewer permanent water sources in the village of residence. In this way, what is being reliably managed by the herders is not only a fallback water point system, but the production and consumption system(s) as well. The importance of such spatial and temporal diversity of multiple operating scales and phases key to ensuring the reliability of high levels of production thus becomes much more apparent and central in the high reliability counternarrative than in the risk-averse development narrative.

Land tenure. The problem with tenure is the reverse of the problem with mobility. While there has been too much fixation on movement as movement in pastoralism, the preoccupation with tenure has been to focus too much on stability and security[11] to the exclusion of negotiation and change (on the importance of negotiation in high reliability institution, see Schulman 1993: 44). Land tenure arrangements are important not because they provide stability, but because they are negotiated and changed in ways that realize highly reliable behavior over critical scales and phases needed to ensure that reliability.[12] The accent on negotiation follows from the fact that highly reliable behavior requires continual search, improvement, and informal mechanisms of oversight—three concepts at odds with a tenure that is prized simply because its rules are said to be secure, public, and purportedly "tried and tested" (UNDP, 1994, p. 42) in promoting mobility .[13]

Herder Risk Aversion. As for the preoccupation with risk aversion, it is not difficult to see why pastoralist behavior has been so uniformly described as risk averse. For many the antithesis of reliability is risk (Schulman 1993: 34), and, in practice, both risk aversion and reliability seeking may sometimes be occurring simultaneously, e.g., as when Mace (1990: 2) writes of pastoralists "having to decide how to invest their livestock wealth between slow-breeding but relatively reliable and potentially fast-breeding but risky species" (in her case, camels and smallstock respectively). Similarly, much has been made in the literature about the risk-spreading practices of pastoralists who loan their livestock out to others (e.g., Dahl and Hjort 1976, 1979; Sandford 1983a); what also is going on is that in so doing pastoralists are learning about the different operating scales and critical phases over which herds can be managed more reliably.

That said, it should be clear by this point that reliability-seeking behavior, as described through its nine principal features, is very different from the conventional view of risk-averse pastoralism. Behavior that is developed around high technical competence and highly complex activities; requires sustained high levels of performance, oversight, and flexibility; is continuously searching for improvements; maintains great pressures, incentives, and expectations for safety; and establishes a virtual culture predicated on maintaining peak (not minimum) livestock numbers in a highly reliable fashion is not what we customarily think of as "risk-averting" behavior. Again, apart from being averse to catastrophic risks, high reliability pastoralism is characterized in its most important respects by risk-accepting, if not risk-taking, behavior.[14] Similarly, as developed above and summarized in table 3.1, the contrast between risk-averse and high reliability pastoralisms, at least as development narratives, could not be starker on virtually all the key dimensions.

"Overgrazing." Last but not least, what about overgrazing and the putative land degradation caused by pastoralism? It is the singular failing of the vast literature on pastoralism that so much of it starts out by assuming "overgrazing and degradation" are the issue to be explained.[15] In writing this chapter, we put an embargo on even talking about overgrazing until after we had thought out and articulated the high reliability counternarrative of pastoralism. Our assumption was that, if we had anything new to say about overgrazing, it should follow from our approach, rather than be a prior assumption to that approach.

It turns out that we have something new to say. As noted earlier, the most commented-upon finding of the New Range Ecology is that it is difficult, if not impossible, to define the carrying capacity of a given rangeland. This does not mean, however, that there is no carrying capacity for pastoralists. There is. Chapter 1 argues that carrying capacity is really a theory (or theories) of knowledge generation and change for the given rangeland population and area. One such theory—and the one *Except-Africa* recommends to all readers—has been presented in this chapter, namely, that of high reliability theory. The upshot here is that while there is no carrying capacity of the range, there is the carrying capacity of high reliability pastoralism.[16] What sets the carrying capacity of this pastoralism are the limits on peak-load production already described for high reliability pastoralism: knowledge about the livestock production on a given rangeland is generated through pastoralist experience of working at different operating scales, through different critical phases of production, and under the pressures that limit trial-and-error learning and put a premium on ensuring reliable production through adversity. Carrying capacity is defined, in other words, as the limits on peak production derived through the long familiarity and experience pastoralists have with the range over which they operate. While the limits on what the rangeland itself can support are as important as the amount of electricity the power lines can take, the number of beds in the intensive care unit, and the level of contamination that water in the nuclear reactor can tolerate, these factors only become limits by virtue of being part and parcel of the complex production technology that drives the institution in question to be a highly reliable one. Sustainability matters, but it is sustainability of the production system that ensures the sustainability of the land in high reliability pastoralism.

For some, destocking the range is comparable to reducing the number of airplanes in the sky—both are geared to reducing perceived overutilization of a common property resource. But this is the wrong analogy. Destocking any area, particularly when what is being destocked is the breeding herd, is really comparable to removing the number of computer tracking monitors in an air traffic control room. In both cases teh problem of reliably maintaining peak performance remains the same—the planes are still in the air, the pastoralists still on the ground. Breeding herds, like the computers, are what generate the reliability now being threatened by the removals.

Thus, we are not certain if the "overgrazing issue" makes any sense whatsoever as currently formulated. We are certain, however, that any scenario about pastoralist overgrazing of rangelands has zero policy relevance in the absence of its demonstrating what activities should be in place so that pastoralists can manage whatever they manage in as reliable a fashion as they currently are managing their livestock. Moreover, such demonstrations are most likely to evolve, if at all, through the pastoralist-to-pastoralist links recommended above. Or to put it another way: if overgrazing is important as a major threat to the rangeland, then as a threat it literally has no meaning until tied directly to the carrying capacity of high reliability pastoralism being studied. As we shall see in the next and final section, there is a threat to high reliability pastoralism that strikes at the heart of its capacity to produce peak herd sizes reliably over time—and that threat is *not* "overgrazing."

Implications for the Future of Pastoralism

The past fifteen years have witnessed a major shift in prevailing views about pastoralists, initiated in great part by Stephen Sandford's path-breaking and path-setting *Management of Pastoral Development in the Third World* (1983). In the past, the mainstream view held that pastoralism had many problems and what was wrong was by and large internal to pastoralism itself. The "endogenous" perspective argued, among other things, that pastoralist systems put a premium on the short-run objective of accumulating as many livestock as possible and on using traditional communal grazing systems, both of which, in this view, led to a disregard of longer-term considerations of rangeland conservation and environmental enhancement. What happened over the last fifteen years has been a shift to a more "exogenous" perspective on pastoralism, where perceived rangeland deterioration has been explained by factors largely external to the pastoralist systems, including agricultural encroachment on wet-season grazing, ill-conceived government policies (e.g., nationalizing rangeland, enforcing pastoralist resettlement), and a highly variable climate that makes it very difficult to determine just what is rangeland "deterioration" and the role that livestock numbers may have in "it." In crude terms, the older mainstream view held that pastoralists were acting irrationally because of their preoccupation with the short-run, while the newer view holds that pastoralists are actually acting rationally in the face of factors largely outside their own control. The risk-averse narrative of pastoralism is never more inadequate than when used, as has too often been the case, to support the endogenous and exogenous perspectives both at the same time.

The counternarrative of high reliability pastoralism pulls us back to an endogenous perspective on pastoralism and thus runs counter to much of the exogenous perspective developed by the revisionist literature of the last two decades. In a nutshell, the benefits of high reliability pastoralism are precisely its dangers. La Porte (1996: 67) summarizes the problems generally:

> [High reliability organizations] are at once a source of benefit and worry. As the benefits become crucial and the potential damage from missteps becomes grave, the difficulties of maintaining public trust and confidence grow. . . . The degree of difficulty will, in large part, be a function of the following conditions. . . .
>
> - Operations are beneficial but hazardous in their design, that is, the work is intrinsically dangerous;
> - hazards are evident and likely to extend well after the benefits have been gained;
> - the benefits of the production system have already accrued to past and present generations with high costs still to be borne by future ones;
> - overall success or failure of the operations is hard to determine for several work generations;
> - there is reasonably rapid change in the technical aspects of the work, the core technologies, or information about the environment where it is deployed; and

- there is hostility to current or future operations based on learning from past . . . practices.

These conditions, along with ever present competition for resources generally, combine to reinforce the sense of public dependence on the skills and integrity of managers and operational leaders. This, in effect, intensifies the public's perceived vulnerability and their hope—perhaps against hope—that organization leaders are worthy of the public's trust and confidence.

The difficulties for high reliability institutions overall have a remarkable fit for pastoralist institutions as well. Yes, outside factors such as encroachment and government policy have made pastoralist operations even more hazardous than before (the first bullet above), but it is because pastoralism is already a very dangerous occupation that these factors come to pose even more hazards. To continue with the above bullets, the benefits of pastoralism ebb and wane, but hazards persist; past generations have clearly benefited from pastoralist practices in ways that future generations might well not; as it has been demonstrated again and again, only after a lengthy period can the success or failure of pastoralism practices be determined (e.g., with respect to assessing livestock-induced changes in range condition); and the technical core of pastoralism has been changing with the increasing adoption by pastoralists of modern veterinary care and the cash economy, among others changes. Perhaps the one threat that embodies most of these concerns is pastoralists expanding their peak herd sizes to a point where irreversible collapse of the forage, water, or other input resource is threatened (see Ludwig, Hilborn, and Waters 1993)—though this concern is precisely why high reliability pastoralism resists such boundary testing and insists on constant oversight of resource and production conditions. To repeat, there is a carrying capacity at work, albeit of high reliability pastoralism itself and not of the land *per se*.

Finally and most important for our purposes, high reliability pastoralism is profoundly preoccupied with the short run rather than the past immediately behind or the longer-term ahead. As Schulman (1996:74) puts it for high reliability institutions generally: "The organization is only as reliable as the first incident in front of it, not the many successful operations behind it." High reliability pastoralism, in the New Pastoralism's endogenous view, cannot afford *not* to be preoccupied with the short-term, as so much is riding on reliably maintaining peak herd sizes. Accordingly, irrationality is an important part of this newer endogenous view as well: it would be incredibly irrational and irresponsible of pastoralists—just as it would be for hospital intensive care units, nuclear power plants, air traffic controllers, and large utility corporations—not to be fixated on their short-run performance. Indeed, *we* would be irrational to accept anything less in a world that is populated, as this one is, by hospitals, power lines, airplanes, and the millions upon millions of pastoralist livestock all over the globe.

The good news, in sum, is that high reliability pastoralism fills a unique niche in the world's arid and semiarid lands. To adopt Demchak's description of high reliability organizations (1996: 97): "In general, their functions are non-substitutable and considered socially essential, forming a natural monopoly . . . " The bad news is that this natural monopoly for making what has been in many cases the best human use of an otherwise inhospitable landscape is itself a highly precarious niche. It is precarious because what the exogenous perspective takes to be external factors, such as highly erratic climate and rainfall, are in fact endogenous factors core to pastoralist technologies and production systems. Hazards do not "happen" to pastoralists; they are built into pastoralist production by virtue of their accumulating and keeping peak herds in such a way that high-probability hazards would pose even more catastrophic consequences for pastoralists, were they not able to reduce the probabilities by managing their livestock safely over time and space. Drought is all but inevitable, but pastoralists are the ones who make it a hazard whose consequences have to managed for better or for worse.

In this way, the great betrayal of many, if not most, government and donor-initiated policies and projects for pastoralists has been that they have been killing pastoralism from the inside. Fenced ranches, grazing schemes, resettlement projects, and other rangeland reforms, combined with the unwillingness and inability of governments to stop the whittling away of pastoralist areas due to outside incursions—agricultural, security, or otherwise—have served only to up the stakes for pastoralism and make it even more hazardous, posing new risks that pastoralists must try to manage but find all the more difficult to surmount. It is like taking workaholics who are already producing to the limit, and then knowing they will continue to try to produce that much after you have ensured that they have even more to work on than they had before. The real threat here, *pace* La Porte and other high reliability theorists, is that pastoralists themselves will lose trust in their own capacity to respond reliably to such misguided interventions.

So what is the future of pastoralism? The answer, this chapter insists, depends profoundly on just what pastoralism we are talking about. If pastoralists are only risk averse as the Old Pastoralism would have it, then the future is bleak: it depends on giving back to pastoralists the mobility and tenure arrangements that, quite frankly, will not be given back to them. If pastoralists are highly reliable as the New Pastoralism insists, then the future is less bleak, at least to the extent that they have significant things to learn from each other by way of improving their changing operations. Either way, the future of pastoralism is precarious. Understanding why this is so is today's real challenge for the environment and development of the world's arid and semiarid lands.

Notes

1. There, of course, have been criticisms of the ecological approach by some, e.g., the critique of Spooner (1973) by Dyson-Hudson and Dyson-Hudson (1980). For another critique of the ecological approach, see Bonte (1981).

2. For example: "Whether movement is regular and seasonal, contingent, or a combination of contingency and regularity, the producer's strategy within non-equilibrium systems is to move livestock sequentially across a series of environments each of which reaches peak carrying capacity in a different time period." (Behnke et al.1993: 11)

3. Obviously, high reliability organizations may attempt to control or manage the hazards directly, but more often than not their behavior is organized around trying to reduce or otherwise favorably affect the probabilities (Rochlin 1993: 19).

4. Other critical phases include breeding, weaning, and culling cycles.

5. The current view among many experts runs directly counter to this conclusion. According to one long-time observer (Gilles 1994:16): "Droughts continue to be regarded as 'acts of God' which are not part of the normal operation of semiarid ecosystems. [Such traditional] understandings of resource management prevent the development of a means for systematically addressing drought and drought management."

6. For more on the importance of flexibility (sometimes called, opportunism or opportunistic management) in pastoralism, see UNDP (1994), Scoones (1994), Gilles (1994), and Sandford (1983a).

7. As Schulman (1993: 34–35) puts it: "Reliability demands are so intense, and failures so potentially unforgiving, that only a sharply reduced amount of trial-and-error learning about causal relationships is permitted. Managers are hardly free to reduce investments and arrive at conclusions about the marginal impacts on reliability." We discuss the limitations on trial-and-error learning in the next subsection.

8. The challenge of keeping pastoralist high reliability in tact while such basic production changes are underway is akin to the well-known paradox in philosophy, i.e., "We've had this hammer in our family for so long we've lost count of all the times we've had to change its head and its handle!"

9. There, of course, are ecologists and other technicians who would insist that pastoralist-to-pastoralist diffusion of livestock and herding innovations could worsen

rangeland conditions considerably (see our next section). Nonetheless, the fact that pastoral networking is a growing focus of the major donors—e.g., World Bank, GTZ, Oxfam—is very encouraging from the high reliability perspective.

10. The argument that agricultural encroachment is limiting the effectiveness of pastoralists bears a striking, albeit uncomfortable, resemblance to the argument that pastoralists are overgrazing their rangelands. For over fifty years now, veterinary and livestock officers in Africa have been saying that herders are seriously overstocking and degrading their rangelands, all the while the herders have been managing to increase their numbers and the numbers of their livestock (see, e.g., Fortmann 1989). In parallel fashion, for over fifty years now people in Africa have been saying that pastoralists are seriously endangered by agricultural encroachment of their rangelands, all the while pastoralists have been managing to increase their numbers and the numbers of their livestock (see, e.g., Dahl and Hjort 1979; Scoones 1994). Both cases, rather than portending the imminent collapse of pastoralism, have demonstrated the high reliability resilience of pastoralists in the face of real and persisting adversities.

11. With respect to the stability argument: "Spatial demarcation with secure, defensible usufruct rights is a basic condition for the sustainable management of the rangeland . . . " (Shanmugaratnam et al. 1992: 8). The importance of common property regimes based upon "well-established" pastoralist institutions is stressed by UNDP (1994: 16).

12. On the negotiation of tenure rules, see UNDP (1994). On the existence of flexible tenure regimes, see Scoones (1994; also Vedeld 1994).

13. Needless to say, privatizing rangeland could (though not necessary would) interfere with a habitually renegotiated commons. That said, national policies and initiatives, which were to have led to privatization of rangelands, have not always in practice done so, i.e., privatization itself can be a negotiated tenure regime (see chapter 4).

14. Though high reliability behavior has nothing to do with and is in fact orthogonal to the press-on-regardless-technique of relying on luck and chance that Brian Walker (1993: 87) seems to recommend in some livestock herding situations under arid and semiarid conditions.

15. For example: "A basic parameter in the working of a pastoral system is the relation between carrying capacity for the area and demographic practices, i.e., the growth rate of man and animals. The basic issue is whether the stocking rate exceeds, is in balance with or below the theoretical carrying capacity" (Manger 1994: 5–6).

16. A commendable counterweight to static carrying-capacity estimates of one beast per n hectares has been the notion of opportunistic strategies of pastoralists for adjusting livestock numbers to variable forage conditions. The notion, however, has the problem of tying these strategies to limits on what the land can support rather than limits set by pastoralism itself.

4

Expatriate Advising

This chapter makes the transition from livestock rangeland development to the broader role of development narratives in sculpting the African countryside. The development narrative of interest here concerns expatriate advisors, and this narrative and its counternarrative are elaborated through the career of one such advisor, James Leach, known not only for his work on livestock rangeland reform but also for his achievements in other areas of rural development. The case study underscores the complexity of rural development and why that complexity necessitates development (counter)narratives for policy-making there. I begin on a personal note.

Introduction

Leach and I were walking against the wind across Norfolk's Holkham Park on a sunless day. It had been a long walk and by the time we reached the cenotaph of Thomas Coke, the English agriculturalist and innovator, my hands were pocketed and cold. I shifted from foot to foot, not really paying attention, as he read the memorial out loud. On finishing, he turned to me and said, "You asked earlier what kind of values I believed in. Well, that's very much my philosophy," nodding to the words. As he walked away I read quickly the phrases, "Public Service . . . activated by Duty . . . Independence marked his Political Career." This too is my reading of Leach, known both for his earlier work in Nigeria and Kenya and for being an architect of one of the most famous African land reform efforts, Botswana's Tribal Grazing Land Policy (TGLP).[1]

Much has been written about TGLP. Missing up to this point has been an insider's account of it. In fact, we have few accounts by expatriate advisors of their role in government decision making, though a wealth of literature is critical of their involvement. Leach is among the exceptions, as he has written about the lessons learned first in Kenya as the chief advisor to the Special Rural Development Program and then in Botswana as that country's principal advisor on rural development, involved not only in TGLP, but in other large-scale development thrusts during his six years there.[2] His record of the process leading up to TGLP points to counternarratives that are considerably more realistic (read: complex) than those development narratives which currently drive common understanding not only of TGLP specifically and but also of expatriate advising generally.

Expatriate Advisors and TGLP

The most widespread development narrative about expatriate advisors is that they subvert government by bending policy to their own ends. That "foreign experts only 'advise' is a myth. They inscrutably and unobtrusively make policies," as one critic put it for expatriate advisors in Africa (Tandon 1973: 146). Similar criticisms have been made in the case of the Tribal Grazing Land Policy, initiated by the government of Botswana (GoB) in 1975 and intended to avert what was said to be a tragedy of the commons taking place on Botswana's grazing lands (e.g., Peters 1987).

Prior to the policy and with few exceptions, tribal land in Botswana was held communally, that is, tribespeople (Batswana in the plural, Motswana in the singular) could not hold title to this land in their own names. By the early 1970s, cattle numbers and the drilling of livestock watering boreholes had increased at such a rate that widespread overgrazing and overstocking were perceived to be taking place in a number of the communal areas and threatening to take place in many others. TGLP was meant to stop that perceived overutilization. The policy made it possible for local land allocation authorities (the land boards) to alienate tribal land for specific individuals, who could thereby exclude the livestock of others from grazing and watering there. To this end, the 1975 government White Paper recommended that tribal grazing areas be zoned into three categories:

1. Land suitable for *commercial* purposes (primarily cattle ranching) that would be leased to Batswana and developed on an exclusive basis, either individually or in groups.
2. Land which would remain *communal* in nature, save for the introduction of stock limitations.
3. Land to be set aside as *reserve* areas, which would be available for future generations or for non-ranching uses, such as mining, wildlife, or arable agriculture.

It was expected that commercial ranching areas would be located primarily in the western (Kalahari "sandveld") region of Botswana, by and large thought to be open grasslands, uninhabited except for a few cattleposts (i.e., sites where Batswana or other cattleowners already had sufficient water, grazing, and labor to keep their cattle). It was also expected that the communal areas would substantially coincide with the eastern ("hardveld") area of the country where most rural Batswana and much of their livestock were located. The policy's implementation was, as Robert Hitchcock and T. Nkwe point out (1986:94–95),

> to be approached in a phased manner. Phase 1 would be the zoning of the land, based on land use, water points, soil, and range surveys. Phase 2, which would be initiated during the time the zoning was ongoing, was a large-scale consultation campaign. The public was to be informed about the policy through a massive radio campaign . . . Feedback concerning the policy was to be encouraged, and the White Paper promised that the Government would take appropriate action in order to put the people's views into effect . . . Finally, there would be a phase in which grazing land would be demarcated, allocated, and leased.

The major criticisms directed against the policy are discussed in the next section. What must be noted here is that the involvement of expatriates in the policy's development is a major narrative of that criticism. "TGLP was conceived in an expatriate written report," Mpho Molomo (1989, p. 240) tells us. "The spark that set off the search for a new policy" was a 1971 Botswana conference, which "was somewhat unusual. All but one of the active participants were expatriates," according to Louis Picard (1980, pp. 325–326). "The foundations for that [TGLP] rhetoric," Picard continues (1980: 327–328), "were provided by the expatriate advisors who wrote the various policy studies which preceded the 1975 Grazing Land Policy. Of these reports, the most important was prepared by Robert Chambers and David Feldman in February of 1973." The Chambers and Feldman report will figure prominently in Leach's account of the events leading up to the White Paper.

Responsibility for writing the TGLP document had been coordinated by the Rural Development Unit in the Ministry of Finance and
Development Planning, whose head and then chief advisor was James
Leach. The unit worked in close cooperation with planning officers in
the Ministries of Agriculture and Local Government and Lands, and
these planning officers, "almost all of whom were expatriates, were
central to the writing of the policy" (Picard 1980: 331). Picard notes
that a number of versions of the draft policy "had been prepared, all
by expatriates" and that opposition to the TGLP planning exercise was
also led by expatriates in government administration (1987: 248, 246;
Picard 1980: 346). Many of these expatriate critics worried that TGLP
was really a land grab by politicians and senior civil servants intent on
alienating communal land for their own private and economic purposes. As Jack Parson (1981: p. 249) summarizes the matter,

> Expatriate technical assistance was exceedingly important in this whole process.
> From articulating the problem of overgrazing, to generating proposals to overcome
> it, and in their involvement in land-use planning, expatriates in consultancies,
> reports, and as line personnel, were indispensable.

Did expatriates actually make policy, as the development narrative
would have it? For Picard it is "a curious fact of political life in
Botswana that while sensitive political decisions are made by
Botswana's political elites, much of the debate over proposed policy
takes place among Botswana's expatriate administrators" (1980: 331).
Leach's own view (1981: 268) is: "Undeniably, expatriates working
for the Government have contributed substantially, but Botswana officers have increasingly taken over responsibility not only at top management levels but throughout the structure, and all the critical decisions have been taken by them." Many commentators have persisted
in arguing otherwise. For them, expatriates are an integral part of the
Botswana elite that frames policy. According to P.P. Molutsi (1989:
107),

> Given [Botswana's] weak political institutions, the expatriate personnel who played
> the role of techno-bureaucrats in government invariably found themselves in key
> decision-making positions . . . It can be argued therefore that a large number of
> expatriates have become part of Botswana's ruling class in the post-colonial pe-
> riod.

To the question "Why do the civil servants develop policies like the
Tribal Grazing Land Policy?" Molutsi answers that these policy deci-

sions "have been implemented largely by expatriate dominated parts of [the GoB] bureaucracy which are interested in promoting their continued presence in the country" (1989: 112). Such sentiments are widespread within development circles in and outside Botswana.

While the views of expatriate critics of the policy have been given considerable attention, the same cannot be said for those advisors who worked to articulate and promote TGLP. Fortunately, as senior civil servants—local and expatriate—retire, more and more of them are in a position to record their government service. This account paints a more complicated counternarrative than those familiar theories which treat economic class and self interest as reliable predictors of personal motivation and bureaucratic behavior.[3] The complication is nowhere better illustrated than in Leach's account of TGLP.

The Tribal Grazing Lands Policy from an Advisor's Perspective

James Leach's fullest treatment of TGLP is in his final report for the United Nations. After summarizing the history leading up to the White Paper of 1975, he continues in a passage that bears close reading (1980: 7):

> A lengthy process of public consultation followed, culminating in a notable nationwide radio learning group programme in 1976 which reached one sixth of the adult population. Thereafter a process of comprehensive land-use planning commenced, while a number of development projects were prepared on livestock, wildlife, and land boards. A regular series of detailed reports have been submitted . . . A study of these reports reveals that the process embraces a wide spectrum of activity. It should be recognized that TGLP is a process that will gather momentum over a number of years. The period under review saw the design and commencement of that process.

The recurrent term, "process," holds a special place in Leach's development lexicon. He returns to it again and again. For Leach, development is "fractious and unpredictable" and always about processes as much as it is abut outcomes: "Rural development is a process of social and economic change and quick results should not be expected," he reminds us (1982: 300). Indeed, what distinguishes Botswana for Leach is that, while "many of us, who are engaged in the business of development, both expatriates and nationals, expect results too quickly," the Botswana "leadership believes in the importance of processes, as well as programmes and projects" (1981: 268). Thus, when Leach reiterates

(1981: 267) that TGLP "initiated a long term process of land use planning and land tenure change," he is underscoring that the Policy, like other major development thrusts, cannot be measured solely in terms of whether or not its original stated objectives were achieved. Change in policy direction should be expected, and it would be a distinct failing of the process if it could not accommodate change. More formally, "process"—not the popular development narrative about expatriate advisors as the power behind the throne—is the counternarrative that stabilized decision making under high uncertainty and complexity during Leach's time in Botswana. Two kinds of processes have bearing for Leach when evaluating the performance of TGLP, namely, those which TGLP initiated and the wider processes in which TGLP was embedded and intended to reinforce.

The Wider Processes

TGLP was an exceptionally important development thrust of the Rural Development Unit, which Leach originated. Largely a one-person operation until the arrival of a Botswana local coordinator of rural development in 1975, Leach served as coordinator of rural development and later as senior rural development advisor to the unit until his departure in 1979. The unit was decidedly opportunistic in its approach to development, with "one thing leading on to another: there are many things that might be done to accelerate development, but there are also formidable constraints of manpower and executive capacity; it is often best in such circumstances to start with those tasks which appear possible and practicable, and to seize opportunities thereafter to move forward one or two steps at a time" (1981: 268).

The observation sounds banal and would be, were it not that its implications run counter to a major criticism of expatriate advising. "Perhaps the most important achievement" initiated by the Rural Development Unit, continues Leach, "has been the organization of a system which has enabled many people, both official and non-official, to make a useful and significant contribution ... The release of talent and energy was secured by a variety of measures, the most important being the widespread dissemination of information, ideas and advice so that people got caught up in a surge of creative development" (1981: 268). More and more Batswana civil servants were drawn into rural development, as they became involved in the development thrusts sponsored by the unit, which included a nationwide accelerated rural development program of infrastructure construction, an arable lands development initiative, comprehensive district planning, and the organization of drought and disaster relief. Linkages between the operating ministries and Batswana officials multiplied as a result, leading to more Batswana decision making, not less.

TGLP Processes

Considering TGLP as an open-ended process rather than a preexisting blueprint calls for reconsidering much—though not all—of the TGLP criticism. Three charges against TGLP stand out in the literature (e.g., Parson 1984; Hitchcock and Nkwe 1986; Molomo 1989a). The Policy's designers are accused of having:

1. Assumed wrongly that the land to be alienated for commercial purposes was largely uninhabited and unutilized;
2. Assumed wrongly that TGLP's basic technical package—primarily fenced ranches having rotational grazing, stocking rates according to carrying capacity, and water development—was feasible, that the demarcation of the ranches would not take priority over reserving land for communal and other uses, and that these ranches would thereafter absorb excess cattle from already overstocked eastern communal areas; and
3. Set into motion a land grab by the rich cattle-owning elite against the poor peasantry. TGLP "resulted in a blatant process of primitive accumulation . . ." according to Mpho Molomo (1989a: 66; also Parson 1981), "through which substantial numbers of Batswana were dispossessed of their land." With TGLP, "administrative and political elites designed changes in land tenure which would ultimately benefit those same administrative and political elites" (Picard 1980: 316). "TGLP has emerged primarily as a mechanism for a variety of medium and large-scale cattle owners to advance their position through exclusive land rights which amount to a form of dispossession," Parson (1981: 249) assures us.[4]

Let us examine each charge, in addition to the earlier one that expatriate advisors were furthering their own interests in the process.

Vacant land. It is true that many of the policy's designers supposed land in western Botswana demarcated for commercial ranching purposes was basically uninhabited, unlike the more populated communal areas of eastern Botswana. "These TGLP ranches are miles from anywhere," Leach stated in an interview.[5] "We're not talking about the communal areas . . . or anywhere near the villages . . . What we're talking about is the so-called 'open areas.'" To be fair, Leach was by no means the only one in government who believed them empty. The interviews Picard held with expatriate and Batswana district-level officials in 1975 (Picard 1980: 341–348) do not raise the issue in any notable way and I distinctly remember operating at that time on the assumption—erroneous, it turned out—that the western areas of the district for which I was developing a pilot ranching project were also largely uninhabited.

Wrong technical assumptions. A number of Batswana and expatriate officials in the districts, including myself, believed the Ministry of Agriculture's argument that fenced ranching and other improved range management practices would increase the effective carrying capacity of grazing land in the western areas. Leach, at the center of the TGLP formulation process, had a different view: Fenced ranches "were experimental . . . .It wasn't conclusive that we really knew whether the ranches would work." The expectation of TGLP insiders was that, as more information was gathered on what worked or did not work in terms of ranching and land use planning, TGLP would be adapted and modified accordingly. The experimental nature not only of the technical package, but of TGLP itself, becomes clearer when the land alienation issue is examined in more detail.

Land grab. If TGLP were a land grab, then that should have been evident on the ground itself. Simply demarcating ranches on a map with no further legal follow-up does not mean land alienation has taken place in the field, particularly if the exercise has no practical effect on how herders graze in the area under question. Signing ranch leases makes a weak land grab somewhat stronger; sinking private boreholes for livestock watering purposes makes it even stronger; and fencing the ranch perimeter makes it a very strong land grab indeed.

Such qualifications surface in a World Bank report which, after a decade of TGLP, concluded that "[o]nly limited areas of grazing were demarcated into commercial ranches," that "in some cases public uncertainty over the intentions of [TGLP] and its effects delayed the demarcation process," and that "some large land owners . . . were not necessarily interested in ranch development" (World Bank 1985: 10).

Moreover, the default rates of the commercial ranches financed by World Bank credit under TGLP have been high. By 1990, of the over 480 ranches demarcated (most under TGLP), some 280 had been allocated and of these, 240 had had leases signed (Robert K. Hitchcock, personal communication).

The overall impression of TGLP implementation was of commercial areas not fully demarcated for ranches, of demarcated areas not fully developed (no water, no fencing), or where developed, often only a borehole had been sunk, and where the borehole was actually operating, frequently no fencing had been put in place to close the area off to outside graziers. "In almost all the ranches financed [through TGLP], the managerial input continues to resemble that of a traditional cattlepost situation," sums up one informed observer (Merafe c.1988: 57). According to a later GoB report, the TGLP "ranches which were established to manage cattle commercially are hardly different from the communal areas" (Government of Botswana, Ministry of Agriculture 1991: 7). In other words, while people were doubtless displaced by TGLP, it was never clear if this would not have happened anyway under so-called traditional practices. Indeed, the displacement could have been much greater in the absence of TGLP.

For it remains one of the enduring ironies of the policy that its designers saw it primarily as the mechanism to *stop a land grab*, in this case the one that had already been taking place in the form of the uncontrolled drilling of livestock boreholes giving their owners *de facto* rights to wide tracts of surrounding grazing.[6] In fact, Leach thought I was talking about this unrestrained drilling when I first raised the issue of "land grab." He went on to express dismay when the nature of the critics' charge was made clear:

> It was always conceived, the whole TGLP was conceived as an ongoing process. That's what I keep on saying, it was always conceived by we who formulated it as a process. Not as a fixed policy which had been decided once and for all. So I mean, this is why I am scathing about this accusation, because it's completely misconceived what was behind the whole process. The whole idea was to set the process in motion so that . . . if this method of ranching didn't work out, either in the communal areas or in the commercial areas, then something might be done about it . . . . TGLP was a flexible system, because nobody was sure that anything would work . . . . It seemed to me that there was absolutely no doubt that there was a genuine attempt to have a multifaceted policy for development of the ranching system . . . Of course, senior politicians and civil servants were agnostic, as we all were, to be honest, agnostic about whether any of it would work, but at least it was worth a try, because there would be order in this process.

The Policy, to repeat, was designed to slow down borehole drilling, not fuel a land grab. Nor was the policy designed to be the definitive answer to perceived overgrazing. Rather, in the process of bringing the chaotic drilling under control, "hopefully the formula for cattle would come out of the TGLP". The policy's approach to addressing the stated overgrazing problem would be "a step at a time process" in Leach's words: "The policy right from the start said it wasn't hard and fast."

TGLP's sequence of zoning, demarcating, leasing, drilling, fencing, ranching, and monitoring and evaluation, moreover, provided TGLP critics with multiple points of intervention to lessen or redirect the rate of land enclosure (e.g., rezoning land, delaying demarcation, and reducing donor support for ranch development, among others), particularly as it became clear the "formula for cattle" in Botswana would not be forthcoming from TGLP alone. The process did not turn out the way Leach and other TGLP designers thought it might—rural development is increasingly a sideshow in the rapidly urbanizing and wage-dominated Botswana—but that there was a process open to intervention rather than a blueprint which was not is precisely what distinguishes TGLP from that other famous sub-Saharan land reform, Kenya's land registration program (see chapter 1).

TGLP as process was also a matter of necessity. To an outsider, the TGLP formulation exercise may have looked like a conspiracy of rich against poor,[7] but to insiders it smacked of different people contributing to different decisions in different ways and at different times to an outcome by no means assured or foreordained. Expatriate advisors may have written the White Paper, but the presence of advisors was no guarantee that a policy would be formulated or implemented.[8] It "was such a long process of consultation and discussion," notes Leach, "both leading up to the production of the TGLP paper and then the whole consultation process." Consultation, moreover, convinced Leach and others that many Batswana outside the government, like many TGLP designers inside, "accepted the reasoning for grazing reform, they were willing to give it a try, but they were agnostic as to whether it would be good or bad." Some people, of course, were not agnostic and really believed from the outset that TGLP would work as planned. But it is precisely that widespread sense of uncertainty and high contingency to which Leach refers, both over whether there would be a TGLP at all, and if so, whether it would work, that has been sorely missing in the critical literature.

While the process was open-ended, for Leach its rationale was never in doubt. Just as the Rural Development Unit "was a vehicle for implementing part of the national development plan," so too TGLP was to provide the framework for implementing policies established or agreed upon in principle by the government beforehand: " . . . all these things were in theory there in the development plan, at least the statements of intention, if nothing else. Now they had to be converted into public activities, so what we were hoping was to formulate activities to implement a policy already decided upon . . . We were operating on the basis of the earlier 1973 government policy paper in response to the Chambers and Feldman report. That's what we were implementing, don't forget." When asked about the differences between this earlier policy paper and that of the 1975 TGLP statement, Leach responded:

Leach: I don't think they were significant. It was only a development of the ideas. I honestly don't think they were. The overall spirit of what Feldman and Chambers were after was to have some kind of development, some kind of process which would gain control of land use [i.e., the uncontrolled borehole drilling] and conserve land at the same time. That was what they were after, and that's what we were after . . . .
Interviewer: So let me get this right. What was new about TGLP?
Leach: Just implementation. Working out something, a process which would actually convert a lot of stated intentions, working out how to do it in the realities of rural Botswana.

This notion of TGLP as framing a process for implementing decisions already taken casts some of the criticisms against TGLP designers in a rather different light. For example, Picard (1980: 335) quotes a unnamed member of the Rural Development Unit addressing critics of the draft TGLP statement in May of 1975: "You should not persist in discussing a policy which has already been decided. These decisions were made two years ago . . . " Picard may be right in assuming this was an attempt to bring closure to that specific discussion; certainly there were other efforts by central government staff to present TGLP as a *fait accompli* to the districts. But the point here is that such a statement should not be surprising nor is it even unwarranted in the circumstances. Indeed, it is the only plausible one when the operating assumption is that TGLP was primarily a framework for implementing policies that had already been a matter of record for years. As Picard (1980: 327) himself notes, the main lines of TGLP were made public in a 1972 policy paper on rural development, some three years before the TGLP paper.

Conceiving TGLP as a process for implementing decisions already taken casts the TGLP role of expatriate advisors in new light as well.

The expatriate role. A fine line exists between implementation and policy-making in sub-Saharan Africa, with its often large gap between what a policy says to do and what actually gets done on the ground. Picard could therefore be correct in asserting that "much of the debate over policy takes place among Botswana's expatriate administrators," even when all that those administrators think they are debating are the difficult details of implementation. Certainly, *ex ante* decisions over implementation may turn out to be *ex post* policy-making, since the way policies are implemented can ultimately entail their substantial revision later on.

In order to evaluate the role of expatriate advisors in government decision making we must, however, have a clear idea as to what they thought they were doing in the first place. Their intentions matter as much as those consequences, intended or not, of their behavior. Why making this distinction is essential becomes readily apparent in the TGLP case. For what looks to outside critics like elite expatriates making policy appears very much different to expatriate insiders who have been given the charter by senior Batswana politicians and civil servants to work out implementation details without having to consult that elite every step of the way. This distinction is reflected in an extended interview excerpt, one which at first reading seems to support the charge that TGLP was designed specifically to advance elite interests, but which on closer inspection is really saying something quite different. The passage starts with Leach's earlier remark about the policy's implementers:

> We were operating on the basis of [the 1973 government policy paper]. That's what we were implementing, don't forget. That was our authority . . . .Now, what we then said is, "Before we go any further, if we're going to pick this up, we'll look at it first of all to say how we'll do it, or at least get an idea. Then we'll take it step by step." So that's the process. Then, when we had worked out the proposal which we felt could stand up, we went to Quett Masire [vice president, later president of Botswana] . . . . The whole principle of the thing was to work out a policy which could be used realistically by Batswana given the actual political situation of the big cattle owners, what would work given Quett Masire's own interests, personally, and others of his fellows, what he could do politically. So it

had to be designed to take all that into consideration, because *that's the only way that any effective policy could be implemented.* I well remember that the whole idea was to design something which had a little in it for everybody, so far as it could, or if you were being restrictive, was it restrictive in a way which was politically possible, that could be backed and defended? Because everything had to be something which could be defended in the public consultation process. And what was intended was certainly honestly intended . . . . Naturally, those who had an interest in developing cattle ranches were keen on TGLP, but to me, it was a legitimate interest. They would have wanted to develop ranches in the areas where nobody else would develop ranches, if they could be developed. I don't think there is anything illegitimate about that . . . It's not only in Botswana that you have a skewed income where people who have money can have the money to develop what amounts to the frontier being pushed into the Kalahari . . . .So I don't think it was wicked, is my point . . . I think it was a genuine development intention. (italics added)

It is one thing to argue, as the critics do, that large cattle owners instigated TGLP as a way of seizing the commons for their own interests. It is quite another thing to maintain, as Leach does, that TGLP was first and foremost a national development thrust (i.e., "pushing the Kalahari back") and that its successful implementation, like other thrusts at the national level, necessarily depended upon the cooperation of major segments of Tswana society, including but by no means limited to large cattle owners and senior civil servants. If this latter argument is controversial, it is not at all clear why, as similar reasoning is widespread and found unexceptional throughout the rural development and implementation literature. The critics' rebuttal, of course, is to argue that the development thrusts being implemented were themselves the product of elite and expatriate interests. But if TGLP was more complicated than the critics have portrayed, why then should we expect the formulation of preceding policies to be any less complicated?[9]

Furthermore, in contrast to the uncomplicated development narrative of a homogeneous political elite intent on furthering their cattle-owning interests, it was the need to create and maintain that elite's consensus over what was politically feasible by way of developing the country that kept a short rein on TGLP designers. Referring to the involvement in the TGLP formulation process of Sir Seretse Khama, Botswana's first president,[10] Leach notes,

Seretse went along—he wasn't enthusiastic about this thing, but he went along with it, and he listened carefully to what was said, weighed up in his mind and felt that this was a risk worth taking . . . I mean, he looked at it, all right. There's no question he didn't know what was happening: he knew what was happening. And he jolly well satisfied himself that this was something which he could live with, politically . . . .When [the chief secretary, a close aide to President Khama] was ordered to go through it absolutely word by word, he went through it absolutely word by word in a two-day session. They were very on the ball about seeing that this thing was operating in such a way it was not going to be damaging politically.

Another enduring irony of the TGLP exercise was that the views of those Batswana, like the vice president, who were involved in the exercise actually took on added importance and weight precisely because so many expatriates were involved in writing the White Paper. Speaking of the Botswana citizen, who took over as coordinator of rural development in 1975, Leach remarks: He "had a lot to do with the mounting of TGLP . . . He took very much the lead, as the head of the RDU . . . And in the consultation process, he really played a major role . . . He was the most senior Motswana; in fact, the only real Motswana who was speaking in this coterie of expatriates who were devising the detailed programme." Other Batswana civil servants played a crucial role in the process leading up to the TGLP exercise. The Motswana coordinator of rural development at the time of Leach's arrival was "a tower of strength" when permanent secretary in the Ministry of Agriculture during part of the TGLP exercise. Before that he had been the main organizer for the Chambers and Feldman visit and had been at that time "very much the ideas man, very much Quett Masire's right-hand man on rural development matters," in Leach's view.

Thus far, the role of expatriates in the TGLP exercise has been sketched in very general terms. What, though, about Leach's motives specifically? The narrative discussed earlier asserts expatriates are motivated by considerations of economic class and self-interest directed to securing donor penetration and their long-term employment prospects. Were this the case, then we presumably would see a pattern of advancing these interests over the course of the expatriate's career, even if from time to time that expatriate were influenced by other factors. To put it bluntly, even if it could be shown that an expatriate's actions during the TGLP exercise did not fit the critics' narrative of expatriate motivation, it could still be argued that we must look to his or her career up to that point, not to isolated incidents in it, in order to perceive the expatriate's real motives over time.

In order to do justice to this argument, we turn now to a brief description of Leach's career up to and through his tenure in Botswana.[11] The critics are surely right in insisting that Leach's background is important to our understanding why he did what he did in the TGLP exercise. What the critics miss is the complex interplay between background and political environment. The record of Leach's career makes it clear that the reason why he was considered such a successful advisor in Botswana by those around him is to be found in the remarkable "goodness of fit" between, on the one hand, the political and institutional setting then posed by the government of Botswana and, on the other hand, the personal and professional values and socializing experiences that Leach carried to his government position.[12] Rarely in his career had the demands of his task environment corresponded so well to his abilities to meet them as in Botswana. The same was not true for Leach in Kenya. Such careers illustrate a counternarrative about how the fortuitous and by no means assured tangency of values, socialization, and institutions considerably complicate the static notion that expatriate advisors, whether they know it or not and with few exceptions, encourage and promote predictably similar, if not the same, material interests.

Leach's career also underscores what is so misleading in believing that these advisors are a bygone era, and that rural development initiatives identified so closely with expatriates, like TGLP, have had their day. The reader will find much that is unique in his career. Few of today's rural development consultants, academics or experts share a similar chronology. But different chronologies embrace parallel learning curves. Leach's pattern of learning from experience and from risk-taking, combined with personal values that stress hard work, commitment to mission, and probity, all of which operate within a political and organizational context where goodness of fit and timing are of the essence, is precisely the amalgam of patterned behavior found among some of the more successful and respected African civil servants working today in rural development (for Kenya, see Leonard 1991). The persisting pattern of behavior means that risk-taking policy efforts, like TGLP, are to be expected, be they initiated by more Africans or by fewer expatriates in the future.[13] Far from being a vanishing breed, such administrators and their initiatives are—as they have always been—critical to the shaping and success of rural development policy.

Leach's Career and its Relationship to the TGLP Exercise

James Leach began his rural development career in 1946–47, when, along with others, he took the famous "First Devonshire" Course. Devonshire proved to be an important part of redirecting the British Colonial Service.[14] The course was "very formative . . . .from the point of view of our indoctrination, education, professional preparation— that really was my professional preparation." When asked why his published work and his involvement in major policy initiatives, such as TGLP, emphasized coordination and consultation over the much more pressing reality of interministerial rivalry, Leach mentions this training specifically:

> During the First Devonshire Course, we learnt that one of the jobs of an administrative officer was to deal with the interdepartmental battles . . . I used to say, as a Provincial Secretary to my Assistant District Officers and District Officers in Eastern Nigeria, "If you have a continual disagreement and battles with departmental officers, I will always hold you responsible no matter how responsible the other man is . . . .because it is your job to find a way to work with people, and not to quarrel with them."

Devonshire was to resonate for Leach throughout his career, and not just in the formulation of TGLP.

Nigeria, 1948–1967

After the course, Leach was posted to Eastern Nigeria, where he eventually became one of the most senior provincial secretaries, serving after Independence as rural development adviser to the Eastern Nigerian government. His Nigeria career, during which he received the MBE and OBE, involved him in what are today considered core rural development activities in sub-Saharan Africa, viz., infrastructural and social service projects, district and provincial development plans, prototype research and development programs, major institutional reforms, and the training of local administrative officers.

Leach was to draw on this wide-ranging operational experience when serving as an advisor in Kenya and Botswana. The shift from public works to development in Nigeria was very similar to what it later became when he was in Kenya; development projects Leach had constructed earlier in his career were very much like the ones he worked with later in Botswana's Rural Development Unit; and, more generally, what he had been doing in Nigeria is what he would find district commissioners and district authorities undertaking in Kenya and Botswana as well.

Leach's work with the Ibo greatly influenced what would be his continuing belief in the value of coordination, information, and persuasion to the process of rural development:

> My thinking developed partly because of my First Devonshire Course and all the indoctrination there, and secondly because of the reality of making development work in this changing, this rapidly changing political situation, so that we learned to work in an intensely democratic society (the Ibo society in Eastern Nigeria) . . . .I learned the—what you would call it—the human management side simply by dealing with Ibo villagers. There was no way you could bully Ibos . . . You had to persuade them in order to get anything done. So that was largely the result of my field experience, not the result of my bureaucratic experience.

One hears a great deal of this field experience with villagers behind Leach's repeated call for development as process: "Those of us who have lived in small rural communities anywhere in the world should remind ourselves constantly of the dynamics of village life and of the nature and time-scale of changes when they do occur. Social engineering is all very well, but it is fatally easy to forget that human societies, like human beings, are fractious and unpredictable" (1982: 300).

Well-known bureaucratic changes in the Colonial Service were also transforming the functions and responsibilities of the administrative officer in Nigeria in ways that reinforced Leach's field orientation and his career-long preference for rural development over routine administration:

> Our role . . . .was changing, as it does in every country from the original, traditional role of the colonial administrative officer to that of a field officer in a developing country . . . .You see, one of the things we campaigned for and eventually got rid of was the court work, which was tremendous in the early days . . . Once we got rid of that, we were free, and I shirked as much as I could after my first years of that work. I regarded it as just a waste of time . . . .Undoubtedly this development work, the development and local government work were our two main thrusts . . . And we went through a great deal of experimentation and trying to make these local Native Administrations, district councils and county councils, trying to help them to work. We were their advisors.

Preference for field activities was not without costs. It reinforced what for Leach "was a personal failing which I think lasted all my career: I always reckoned that the job was what mattered, and I seldom, if ever, gave any thought to the impression I might be creating."[15] "I've always just totally concentrated on the work and its own merits," though "I would only do a job where I felt I was making a useful contribution." As a result, "I think I'm poor on politics, on the political." In Leach's view this explained why he was never offered a permanent position at the center in Nigeria, which, in turn, meant that he "lacked expertise in the business of negotiating in the headquarters." "I never gained what would then be called secretariat experience." But it was precisely a secretariat position into which Leach moved when he went to Kenya, and these limitations, if that is what they are, came to haunt him with a vengeance there.

Kenya, 1968–1973

When Leach became the Coordinator of Rural Development Pilot Projects at the headquarters of the Kenya Ministry of Finance and Economic Planning, he organized one of the best known early development efforts in sub-Saharan Africa, Kenya's Special Rural Development Program (SRDP).[16] In addition to many articles, SRDP figures prominently in two books that brought Africa to the attention of a generation of development specialists, Robert Chambers's 1974 *Managing Rural Development: Ideas and Experience from East Africa* and Uma Lele's 1975 *The Design of Rural Development: Lessons from Africa.* SRDP helped pioneer the strategy of integrated rural development;[17] the Program's labor-intensive rural road-building program, village polytechnics, and rural industrial centers had spin-offs not only in Kenya but in other countries; and its influence on later government of Kenya (GoK) development efforts, such as the district planning process and the arid and semiarid lands program, can easily be traced.[18] Even SRDP "failures" have been important, as its maize credit program was one of the first efforts showing the often weak link between agricultural credit and increased crop production. Leach's own conclusions about SRDP register the same themes that were to preoccupy him later in Botswana and the TGLP exercise:

Rural development is an enormous and complex subject which defies succinct definition and cannot offer precise prescriptions . . . [I]t is unlikely that such problems will be solved in a swift and tidy way: it is more realistic to hope for marginal and spasmodic improvements through a whole series of different initiatives. In these circumstances, efforts to evolve mechanisms to mobilize initiatives and to release latent resources of talent, energy and enthusiasm probably have a considerable pay-off in the long-term of national development. It is believed that the SRDP made a good start in pioneering such a process. (1974: 364)

SRDP never lacked critics. Senior GoK officials differed over its usefulness, as did outside evaluators. As with TGLP later, one common complaint about SRDP surfaced fairly early one, namely, criticisms over the Program's heavy expatriate component. Uma Lele (1975: pp. 148–149) notes "that, had there been a greater Kenyan content to SRDP from the outset with experienced Kenyans of high rank and prestige stimulating the effort, much of the delay in planning could have been avoided . . . For although expatriates were technically qualified, they simply did not have the authority or the position to elicit the action required by the Kenyan bureaucracy." Subsequent experience, it must be said, has proved that even experienced and high-ranking Kenyan civil servants have great difficulty in moving the GoK bureaucracy (e.g., Leonard 1991).

Still, Leach was his own harshest critic when it came to his expatriate involvement in the program. "SRDP implementation suffers because I am concerned with so many horizontal linkages . . . not to mention donor negotiations. The whole operation depends far too much on me," he wrote at the time. Seventeen years later Leach was of the same mind: "Yes, the thing is that undoubtedly I was trying to do too much single-handed, and not much of it washed off." "But," he continues, "I was under the impression that I was expecting to be there another two years." His contract was not renewed, though, and that surprised him: "It never occurred to me that there would be any difficulty. I was amazed when I later received a note that they didn't propose to seek an extension." He "regarded the job as only half-finished" and because completing the job was his top priority, leaving SRDP proved particularly disturbing for him.

Leach's problem as SRDP coordinator stemmed in considerable part from his field orientation and secretariat inexperience:

I wasn't sufficiently experienced, you see, in all this headquarters' negotiation to fully understand what was going on. I was just straightforward expressing what I thought at the time without worrying too much about it. You see, my problem with Kenyan civil servants is that I treated them all like Ibos. I well remember the best incident that explains this was once, some terrible disaster—in ministry terms— some terrible disaster happened. Like a typical Ibo, I simply burst out laughing. And [a senior Ministry official] rounded on me really angrily and said, "*What* are you laughing at?" And that I realized, in a flash of inspiration, that was what the problem was, that he simply didn't understand. He thought I was being sort of hopelessly irresponsible.

"I am quite prepared to say that I didn't have rapport, that I missed out on things," concedes Leach. Yet other expatriates had good rapport with high GoK officials, at least in the early days of SRDP, and this seemed not to have helped the program either. In Leach's view, one has to look elsewhere than to expatriate involvement to explain why SRDP's continuation never had the commitment of senior civil servants (about the lack of high-level commitment, see Leach, 1974: 358). "Something went wrong" with SRDP: "But what, I can never put my finger on it." A personal shortcoming may again have been involved, but also much more:

> I had this unease, and I shouted loudly, but that didn't have any impact . . . that was maybe a personal failing of mine. I couldn't get through, and I couldn't get anybody else to get through. And it wasn't just me . . . Nobody has ever been able to understand why such an imaginative programme didn't catch the imagination of imaginative Kenyans . . . .It's a bafflement, then, to me. It really is a bafflement. If things went wrong in Botswana, I could understand why they went wrong.

The remark about Botswana is illuminating. For Leach's most succinct statement as to what "went wrong" in SRDP is also couched in a comparison between Kenya and Botswana. "Somehow we'd lost my Permanent Secretary's support . . . You see, that was the point, that somehow I'd lost the PS's ear, which I never did with Quett Masire in Botswana. I always had his ear."[19]

Botswana, 1973–1979

Advising in Botswana posed a different set of circumstances for Leach than did either Kenya or Nigeria. The "style suits the local scene," as he puts it (1981: 268). True, there were similarities and connections. Noted previously was Leach's ability to apply his Nigeria background with local governments to Botswana. Work with the Ibo also stood Leach in good stead with Batswana, whose traditions placed a very high premium on consultation and persuasion. Similarly, in Botswana as in Kenya, his official terms of reference were very wide; he was located in a central ministry of finance and planning; he acted as a secretariat for the government's chief Rural Development Council; and in the case of TGLP, he even worked with personnel who had been instrumental in SRDP.[20] TGLP and SRDP were also similar in a way that summarizes the key themes of Leach's published work: "Basically, the same process of communication and discussion, involving all the people and identifying all the people who should be involved, and talking with them in this process of advising on TGLP, and thinking up how it would be pursued. So it was the same process as the SRDP."

Botswana was, nonetheless, different and these differences mattered profoundly. "I used my previous experience and was influenced by it, but not, I believe, exclusively and certainly *not* in connection with choices of what I should or should not do, which were dictated by circumstances on the spot". When asked what was more important in his work in Botswana—securing the operations of the Rural Development Unit or putting into place processes such as TGLP—he countered: "The answer to that is neither, consciously. It was much more empirical than that . . . .It is more true to say that the previous experience may have been utilized as we were thrashing about trying to develop what we were trying to do, but it certainly wasn't in our minds as such. I was responding mostly to some outside thing, not what I said should done or what I thought should be done." The fact that each country had the force of its own circumstance placed real limitations on what even the best expatriate advisors could do, a point which TGLP illustrates for Leach:

> I mean, we recognized in the TGLP . . . that it was a pretty sophisticated thing we were trying to do, and that probably it wouldn't survive in its present form, but it was a good thing to set up, and show what could be done, show what the potential was . . . But you could never give it life, expatriates can't give a thing life. They can get it started, then depending on the internal situation, it will take root or it won't take root.

Leach's innovation was to see how being able to respond to "the internal situation" then in Botswana did not mean that the development had to be ad hoc and unfocused as a result. The key for Leach was the Rural Development Unit and its sequence of development initiatives, only one of which was TGLP: "What we were trying to do was to provide development thrusts, that's why I kept on using that expression, thrusts in rural development, so that you could make an impact on one thing after another, and thereby not be just diffused over the whole field." In practical terms, this sequential approach meant that the various initiatives sponsored by the Unit during the last half of the 1970s showed a remarkable degree of linkage, as in the case of TGLP leading to subsequent innovations in land use planning and arable lands development.

The mix of contingency, timing, and sequence in the national development process is reflected in how the Unit's specific focus on TGLP came about. During its first development thrust, the accelerated rural development program, Leach was building up the Unit and systematically reviewing the Chambers and Feldman report and the 1973 government response to it, both of which were his charter, so as

> to work out how to move, on what and in what order. I followed initially the apparent priorities of the report, but practical considerations soon stepped in to impose priorities—
>
> e.g., Dryland Farming—clearly a priority but no way ahead until dryland farming projects produced results in 3–5 years . . .
>
> Water—RDU helped wherever it could, but the Ministry of Mineral Resources and Water Affairs had this pretty well in hand.
>
> So *Cattle* and *Boreholes*—an obvious area of interest in Botswana. Indeed, I remember so well the *lack* of interest from Seretse down to a Motswana planning officer in dryland farming contrasted vividly with the immediate and intense interest of all Batswana, whether cattle owners or not, in cattle and grazing.

One cannot stress too strongly the importance for the TGLP exercise of the Batswana preoccupation with cattle, and not just among the elite. "Why was TGLP chosen?" Leach asks rhetorically: "The answer is, we repeatedly said, 'You talk about cattle and everyone's face lights up. You talk about crops and everybody's face drops.' . . . I remember this actually being discussed in the Rural Development Council." For Leach who could never interest key Kenyans in SRDP, the contrast could not have been starker.

Having the ear of Batswana, like having the ear of the vice president, who chaired the Rural Development Council, proved decisive for TGLP. Leach's being positioned in the Rural Development Unit was essential in this regard:

> We were the special unit who were, as it were, the experts on rural development, and we had a voice. Why were we accepted? Because we had the ear of the vice president, and everybody knew that. Everybody knew that we could walk in, I and then [the succeeding two coordinators of rural development], we didn't even go through the permanent secretary. We had direct access to the vice president in the small number of cases where either he wanted us, or we wanted him. Because it was both ways. And this was very important indeed.

If the vice president "wanted anything he'd ask, and if you had something you wanted to tell him or ask him, it was perfectly easy to get to him . . . I'd just go in and see his secretary, and if he was available, he would see me." Having the ear of the vice president was also an especially important consideration in Leach's preference for the Botswana citizen who subsequently became the Coordinator of Rural Development. Leach had been advised that the candidate was very much his own man and not known for his easy relations with other Batswana, let alone expatriates. Leach, however, favored him precisely because he "got on well" with the vice president; he "was constantly talking . . . with Quett Masire on the effect of TGLP . . . He was aware much more that we were of what would be the political issues. So while we were doing all the writing of the Policy paper, he was also talking with Quett." Being able to carry on a discussion with the vice president took on added importance, as Dr. Masire had a "fantastic grasp of development issues" and "this incredible ability . . . of being able to keep cool and not to have his judgement clouded by emotion."

Leach was advised at other points in his career to choose the more pliable counterpart amenable to the ends of others, but for him "that's too Machiavellian. That would have been to behave like a true [donor name deleted] advisor . . . I would never sink to that level." In fact, Leach's behavior is at odds in other respects with the charge that expatriates were intent on using TGLP to promote their continued presence in Botswana. He did not negotiate with donors over funds and he always saw himself first and foremost as a government of Botswana advisor, not the representative of any donor agency: "That was always my policy . . . It had its advantages, but the advantages were for the work, but not for me. Because once I got out on the limb, you were really out on the limb. Nobody would protect you." No one asked him to stay longer than six years in Botswana and "it never occurred to me to suggest that I should stay longer, because it was part of my philosophy to hand over, to create a Rural Development Unit which would be run by Batswana—which in fact is what happened." Indeed, it is a point of pride to Leach that he was *not* replaced. His SRDP departure had cast a long shadow: "I was conditioned by my Kenyan experience, where I had been pushed out early, so I wasn't about to try to prolong my own stay" in Botswana. "The only thing Quett said to me," at Leach's going-away party, "was 'I can't thank you enough for what you've done for us.' That's all he said. It was reward enough, after what I had in Kenya." Leach's work in Botswana proved to be of no help in securing his next posting, just as during his career all his jobs "came up fairly fortuitously."

What then really motivated Leach in the TGLP exercise? For some, a colonial career combined with phrases such as "having the ear of the Vice President" and "gaining control of land use" are proof enough to convict. For others, terms like "coordination" are jargon, while "process" is nothing better than a rationalization of actions taken for other reasons. For many, a parallelogram of higher-order forces from Culture, Politics, Economy, and Society can always be erected to ensure human intentions have no functionally independent role whatsoever in accounting for why people, like Leach, do what they do.

On the other hand, the brief review of his career from Devonshire through Botswana offers a more parsimonious and comprehensive answer to the question of motivation: Leach believed what he said and what he believed is already there for everyone to see, in his writing. It is of one piece. In addition to keywords like "process" and "coordination," phrases from his SRDP article

> an experimental programme . . . catalyst for the formulation of specific rural development policies and programmes . . . . deliberately operating within the normal framework of government . . . .intercommunication was a better watchword than decentralisation . . . .No formula is foolproof, and no absurd claims are made on behalf of this one . . . (1974: 358, 360, 361, 362)

are matched seven years later in the Botswana article by

> The role of the Rural Development Unit was largely catalytic . . . .Coordination is, in fact, better achieved through communication and information linkages, through consensus and negotiation, than by directives and orders . . . .The rule has been at all times to work 'through the system' and at no point to bypass it. There is a place for experimental or special projects . . . (1981: 267, 269)

These themes, in turn, reverberate a year later in his review article on rural development in Botswana, Kenya, Nigeria, Tanzania, and Zimbabwe:

> A central concern must be to emphasise mechanisms to achieve cooperation and consensus . . . .Dialogue and communications are more important than structures . . . . Establishing a mechanism for oiling the wheels of interdepartmental communication and cooperation is much more important . . . . Experiments are prematurely written off as failures . . . .a step by step approach, learning by experience, is

almost invariably more effective than attempting to get everything right from the beginning . . . whenever possible, the existing mechanism or institutions should be utilised . . . (1982: 298, 299, 300, 302)

More than just a commitment, this constellation of themes—in effect, this counternarrative to an all-powerful advisor—communicates Leach's very real enthusiasm for the working mechanics and uncertainties of rural development. His drive was everywhere evident in the TGLP exercise. We had been talking about the Policy, when at one point, Leach looked out the window and wondered, "maybe I shouldn't have done as much as I did." Then he paused, shook his head and smiled, adding quickly "but I was so keen on creating the linkages. . . ."

A Last Counternarrative:
Public Service as the Other Face of Development

Sometimes the best that governments can do is to ensure their public servants, be they local or expatriate, have extremely productive and effective careers in public management. Rural development specialists frequently think otherwise. Development, we are told, means results on the ground and, yes, people matter, but surely it is to confuse means and ends by claiming the people in question are civil servants and not the public.

Unfortunately, the results of rural development have always been difficult to assess. Conflicting evaluative criteria have become commonplace and multiple perspectives on development are taken as a matter of course. That's part of the complexity. Today, the very same intervention can be evaluated as a success, as a failure, or even if it were a local success, it still would be a failure at some more global level. The upshot at times is worthy of Alice in Wonderland. If TGLP had succeeded as the critics thought it would, then they would have considered it a disaster; the fact that its implementation has fallen short of the critics' predictions, however, has not made it a success for them. In the critics' view, the real "success" would have been ensuring that the government of Botswana did not undertake TGLP in the first place. Yet, if the criterion is one of having not done something, then why isn't that government praised more often for all the things it hasn't done?

When agreement over ends and outcomes is in doubt or otherwise difficult to achieve, questions of the means and processes take priority. It is unfortunate, then, that very much more attention has been given in the literature to identifying and debating the ends rather than means of rural development. Of course, the line between development process and outcome is not always clear (as when people's increased participation in rural development becomes an end in itself). Yet, as long as extensive uncertainty and complexity in evaluating sub-Saharan rural development outcomes persist, development specialists will have little recourse but to let questions over means govern the evaluation of rural development, namely, are the processes fair and honestly managed, open to scrutiny, capable of learning from mistakes and of evolving into new areas? More important, these questions take on salience, even when their answers move us not one step closer to identifying the contingent and local ends toward which the processes are taking us.

When Leach reviewed the first draft of the preceding three paragraphs, he dissented strongly:

> I for one would not want my performance in rural development evaluated in terms of success on processes simply because it is so difficult to evaluate anything else! Results still must count, even if the results are not those originally intended. So while you have chronicled some of the outcomes of TGLP, you do not comment further—so what? How did different people react, when things turned out like this—at all levels: Quett, others in Government, the civil service, cattle owners, rich and poor, etc.? Did the machinery institutions set up under TGLP continue and cope or did they atrophy? That is what I am interested in . . . The proof of the pudding is in the eating—if the processes and institutions couldn't and didn't cope with what actually happened, then they were flawed.

Here I disagree with Leach. If evaluative criteria continue to be multiple and conflicting, as I believe they will, we shall never "know enough" to decide one way or the other whether TGLP was a failure as its critics maintain. What we can do instead, though, is note here the implications of this unflinching regard to be judged on results, not just processes, a regard many Batswana and Kenyans alike esteem in their own civil servants.

For if Africans consider the measures of effectiveness of their senior government officials to be hard work, long hours, measured risk taking, political support, and a professional commitment to public policy and government mission, as Leonard (1991, chapter 12) found in Kenya, then those are the standards every civil servant is to be evaluated on, African, expatriate, or otherwise. This, in turn, leads directly back to my own argument: enhancing public service must itself be fundamental to undertaking rural development, at least in those cases where development is evolving under conditions of high complexity and where processes, rather than outcomes, are the focus of evaluation. Increasing the number of opportunities for good people to become successful public managers over the course of their government careers not only reinforces, I believe, the standards of managerial excellence, it also is core to the enterprise of making the processes of development work more effectively.

Here, too, there must be no illusions. Even if ways were found to improve the chances for highly successful careers in public management, much would still depend, as just seen, on the fit between public manager and the political environment for public management, and on the all-too-frequent fact that, even where the fit is remarkably good, the public manager's writing a policy need in no way ensure that policy will be implemented or managed as written. Nonetheless, while these careers in public service are not a sufficient condition for advancing rural development in the field, they are to my mind the underacknowledged necessary condition. Public service is the other face of development, an all-too-hidden, but very real counternarrative to results-oriented development, and it is the career or life cycle of the public servant—this link between public management generally and rural development policy specifically—that deserves much more priority and attention by development specialists everywhere. We encounter the public service counternarrative in the next two chapters as well.

Notes

1. The Policy was described by one expert in the late 1970s as "probably the most open and comprehensive land reform programme being undertaken anywhere in the world at this time." Quoted in R.K. Hitchcock and T. Nkwe, "Social and Environmental Impacts of Agrarian Reform in Rural Botswana," in J.W. Arntzen, L.D. Ngcongco, and S.D. Turner (eds.) *Land Policy and Agriculture in Eastern and Southern Africa*, The United Nations University, p. 93 (1986).
2. Leach's publications include: "The Kenya Special Rural Development Programme," in *Journal of Administration Overseas*, vol. 13, no. 2 (April 1974); "Rural Development, Botswana: Project Findings and Recommendations," United Nations, TC/BOT-72–028/1 (1980); "Managing Rural Development in Botswana," in *Public Administration and Development*, vol. 1 (1981); and "Administrative Coordination in African Rural Development," in *Agricultural Administration II* (1982).
3. As for the theory underlying this article's analysis, it is much more modest and

decidedly of the middle-range, to adopt Robert Merton's term. Indeed, it is Merton's 1972 critique of Insider and Outsider epistemology which allows us to understand how an insider, like Leach, can function as an outsider when it comes to analyzing the institutions and processes of which he was a part. The Outsider doctrine holds that knowledge about institutions and groups is only accessible to Outsiders who are supposedly unprejudiced and unbiased by membership in them (Merton 1972: 30–31). But as Merton points out (1972: 22), Insiders and Outsiders occupy crosscutting roles and social statuses. Leach was not just an "expatriate advisor": Like others outside government, he was a Christian, father, writer, and development specialist; like local civil servants elsewhere in government, he was a manager, expediter, colleague, and expert (see Roe 1988a). To put it more formally, Leach had many of the very same ascribed and achieved social statuses as did those who were not expatriate advisors. To the extent role and status matter for human behavior, Leach was an outsider in ways commonly slighted by subscribers of the Outsider doctrine. It is, however, important to recognize that Leach's view on matters is only one perspective, albeit a vital one, of what went on inside the TGLP exercise. A fuller treatment of the multiple perspectives to be taken on the Policy, as on Leach's career, remains to be written. Recording these perspectives, however, would complicate even further the received wisdom that it is primarily economics which drives the expatriate career. It is noteworthy that focusing on careers in government as a way of understanding better the interplay of politics and bureaucracy is one of the principal features of the New Institutionalism in political science (e.g., March and Olsen 1984: 744).

4. A more subtle elite analysis has been advanced by John Holm. He argues that TGLP represents a struggle between three different elites in Botswana, each with its own interests, namely, government civil servants, the political elite (primarily central government politicians), and those private cattle owners who were not politicians or civil servants:

> TGLP is for civil servants a means to regain control of public lands. It is a means to insure government power relative to private economic elites . . . TGLP is far from being an instrument of the cattle holding elite. Rather civil servants have moved it ahead to promote their institutional and personal interests . . . .The political elites—in Cabinet and Parliament particularly—are in between. (Holm1985: 167)

The desire to gain greater control over land use was certainly one of the chief factors motivating senior civil servants and expatriate administrators. Still, intra-elite interests were by no means homogeneous, as will become clear.

5. Unless otherwise stated, unreferenced quotes of James Leach are taken from the edited transcript of an interview the author held with him over the course of several days in early 1989. The interview was an outgrowth of an earlier article (Roe 1988a) calling for more research on expatriate advisors in Africa.

6. The borehole-driven land grab is described in Colclough and McCarthy (1980: 117–118).

7. The sense of conspiracy is nicely captured in a passage from Picard (1980: 330):

> While there was relatively little activity at the national level with regard to land, one development was quietly taking place in the western part of Southern District which was to lay the groundwork for land use. Throughout the year there was quiet planning toward a pilot project in the Western Ngwaketse tribal areas located in the Kalahari Desert. With large scale involvement of

USAID in the later stages of the project, the pilot program was designed as a model for the grazing policy [i.e., TGLP] as a whole. The project was kept somewhat confidential because of the elections. The file for that year notes that the Project Memorandum is "not for general distribution," and the project was not made public until March of 1975 . . .

I wrote the project memorandum. As I recollect, the attempt to keep the project low-profile was primarily because the District's traditional chief had been suspended, thereby unsettling a number of matters, including land issues. None of my files were for general distribution, a bureaucratic formality existing before my arrival. I do not recall the often contentious consensus-building process leading to the project as in any way "quiet."

8. For a Kenya example of expatriate advisors who wrote an important policy document but whose impact on the policy's subsequent implementation and direction was considerably less direct, see Leonard (1991: 207).

9. Another retort of the critics is to argue that, even if we could prove TGLP were well intended, the road to hell is paved with good intentions. But cases where bad intentions lead to good outcomes are also well known in land reform, as when the Sywnnerton Plan, implemented to blunt the Mau-Mau and forestall Kenya Independence, led nonetheless to a boom in small-holder production there. By this line of reasoning that sees in good (or bad) intentions the probability of bad (or good) consequences, why then cannot we not imagine what the critics take to be an ill-conceived TGLP leading ultimately to a resurgence of small-holder livestock production in Botswana?

10. Both presidents of Botswana are commonly referred to in the country by their first names, Seretse and Quett. Use of first names, thus, does not necessarily denote personal acquaintance.

11. I owe this paragraph's ideas to my reading of Leonard (1991).

12. This is not unique to Botswana or other parts of Africa. Doig and Hargrove (1987: 15, 12) note that the political connections of U.S. public administrators can be instrumentally critical to their managerial successes, and that over the course of their careers, major American public administrators have had a mix of successes and failures. I thank a reviewer for pointing me to this reference. The importance to U.S. public managers of finding and keeping key constituencies within government is also stressed by Wilson (1989: 202–205).

13. Moreover, it is increasingly the case that the expatriate advisor concerned is African in origin. For more on risk-taking, see chapters 2 and 3.

14. The effect of the Devonshire Committee on the British Colonial Service is described in Heussler (1963). The course was not Leach's only early experience with respect to public service. Born in 1925, Leach came from a family of public servants. His grandfather, A.F. Leach, was an author and lawyer, while his uncle, Gordon Leach, had been in the Indian Civil Service and his father, Thomas, was one of the first civilian Provincial Governors in the Sudan Civil Service. James Leach "followed in my father's footsteps." As he explains it, "in those days the professional class here in England very much followed from father to son—it goes in families. Still does to some extent . . . So in my case my family is very much a professional family of lawyers and civil servants." "The whole ethos," of Leach's later schooling "was public service" and he "really never thought of anything else." Leach went on to serve in the army during World War II and was recruited into the Colonial Service at the end of the war.

15. His preoccupation with work and the impression this made on others are nicely captured in an interview excerpt:

> My interpreter . . . refused to drive with me, I was such a devastatingly fast driver . . . I had three accidents in one tour, so much so that I was blackballed by all the insurance companies of Nigeria. They wouldn't insure my car . . . .So I went dashing about at my work, totally impervious to the impression I was creating. I remember being mortally offended by one of my colleagues. He said, "You really must get your file work done. You can't go on dashing around like this, and leaving all your files lying about." And I was mortally offended, because I thought what I was doing was more important.

16. For comments on Leach's role as SRDP's operational head responsible for its day-to-day management, see Doggett (1973, especially the section, "USAID Meets James Leach," including pp. 91 and 111).

17. See, e.g., International Labour Office (1972).

18. The effect of SRDP on district planning is mentioned briefly in Heyer and Waweru (1976: 214; see also Doggett 1973). In some cases, the influence of SRDP has been indirect. For example, one of the major problems highlighted by the Program was "the inordinate amount of time it takes field officers to receive from Nairobi authority to incur expenditure" (Nellis 1972: 6). This problem was not tackled on a national basis until the GoK's major district planning innovation of the early 1980s, District Focus for Rural Development. District Focus allowed Treasury and the operating ministries to bypass the provincial tier of government when sending the authority to incur expenditures down to the districts. The prototype for this innovation was the Machakos Integrated Development Program (MIDP), which was also the first of Kenya's Arid and Semiarid Lands (ASAL) Programs. The officer, who was instrumental in establishing MIDP and later the ASAL Program and who was permanent secretary of the Treasury at the time of District Focus, had also been an important participant in the SRDP, when serving as a planning officer in the Ministry of Finance and Economic Planning (for more details, see Leonard 1991: 190–209).

19. Leach's comments about "having the ear" of a senior civil servant in Kenya's Ministry of Finance and Economic Planning illuminates his field orientation and headquarters' problems:

> About the only people who had [the official's] ear continuously were academically oriented people, who understood his mind and way of thinking—it tortured me to have a discussion with him. I simply had to write down what he said very fast, and not respond at all, and then go away and work out what he had said: . . . such a complex mind, speaking very quietly so I could only just hear him. He was a very difficult person to work for, work with, unless you were an academic . . . but to my practically oriented mind, it was just absolute agony.

20. John Gerhart, whom Leach considered as part of the in-team for SRDP, served as an advisor in Botswana's Ministry of Agriculture in the first days of the TGLP exercise. "If anything, John was more fundamentally important than I was in the conceptual stage of TGLP . . . .I remember at a very early stage, I can definitely remember, John Gerhart coming out with the tragedy of the commons thing, because he said 'Have you heard of the tragedy of the commons?' And at that time, I hadn't." As the chapter indicates, Robert Chambers also played an important role in SRDP and in the early formulation of what eventually became TGLP.

5

Boom-and-Bust Budgeting

with Eddy Omolehinwa

Introduction and Overview

As discussed in chapter 1, the policymaker frequently does not have the option of creating a new counternarrative. The best he or she can to do is engage an already existing development narrative, which, once engaged, conflicts with the more offensive one. Below is an example of that tactic, ending with a suggestion for a new counternarrative.

An important feature of the Except-Africa scenario is the view that "African governments can't budget!" For those of us who strongly object to the development narrative of African-governments-are-hopeless, our objections have been altogether too weak. Basically, we have been left to point out that developed country governments cannot manage budgetarily either.

This chapter engages a more complex narrative, one whose difference opens counternarrative ways of looking at the very real problems governments have today in budgeting in many developing countries. This different narrative I call "boom-and-bust budgeting." Our examples are from Africa, but boom-and-bust budgeting can be found in other countries. The chapter's argument is that by understanding boom-and-bust budgeting, we will be in a better position to appreciate just how narrow and misleading is an Except-Africa narrative that focuses only on the "bust" to the exclusion of the "booms" in Africa.

Boom-and-Bust Budgeting—
The Role of Repetitive Budgetary Processes

Economic boom-and-bust cycles are familiar to countries across the globe and show no signs of disappearing any time in the near future.[1] What happens to government budgeting in these cycles? Have governments taken advantage of booms in order to enhance budget control? Have these gains been carried over so as to ameliorate or otherwise avoid the next bust?

The early work of Naomi Caiden and Aaron Wildavsky suggests that increasing a country's resources should improve the budgetary capacity of its government. These increases would, Caiden and Wildavsky felt, reduce or eliminate the repetitive budgeting they found to be so characteristic of poor countries with unpredictable resource flows. Under repetitive budgeting, to repeat a point made in chapter 1, the government

> budget is not made once and for all when estimates are submitted and approved; rather, as the process of budgeting is repeated, it is made and remade over the course of the year . . . The entire budget is treated as if each item were supplemental, subject to renegotiation at the last minute . . . Repetitive budgeting . . . is found in most poor countries.[2]

Note that the addition of resources alone need not diminish repetitive budgeting, if the supply of those resources remains unpredictable.

Wildavsky grouped countries along two dimensions: (1) how wealthy (rich or poor) they are in terms of mobilizing sufficient resources, controlling expenditures, or both *and* (2) how predictable (certain or uncertain) these flows of expenditures and resources have been and will be.[3] The classification yields a fourfold typology of national budgetary processes: "Rich and certain environments lead to incremental budgeting; poverty and predictability generate revenue budgeting; unpredictability combined with poverty generates repetitive budgeting; and riches plus uncertainty produce alternating incremental and repetitive budgeting."[4] The combination of resource uncertainty and poverty drives poor country governments to budget repetitively, while uncertainty can nullify the margin of safety that wealth brings, thereby driving even rich countries to have their bouts with repetitive budgeting.[5] The typology implies that if a poor country with uncertain resource flows were suddenly to become rich and just as suddenly to become poor again, we should expect to see a cycle dominated by repetitive budgeting in the pre- and post-boom periods, though less so in the boom, when presumably incremental budgeting would also be (periodically) present.

Unfortunately, incremental budgeting alternating with repetitive budgeting in rich and uncertain countries has been found less in practice than theory would have us suppose. Repetitive budgeting by governments "has now become standard practice in relatively rich nations," as Wildavsky himself put it,[6] and features of year-round budgeting have been found in the U.S. federal budgetary process[7] and in some of the other Organization for Economic Cooperation and Development (OECD) countries.[8] Wildavsky and Caiden also identified considerable repetitive budgeting in the governments of poor countries after a decade or more of economic growth.[9] Thus, both theory and evidence would seem to support the hypothesis that repetitive budgeting dominates boom-and-bust cycles having the sequence of a pre-boom poor and uncertain country that becomes rich and uncertain during the boom only to become poor and uncertain after the boom.

Thus, although static, the Wildavsky typology remains useful in understanding what is described below as boom-and-bust budgeting. What we examine through case material are situations where the nature of resource uncertainty and wealth varies, thereby changing the nature of the government's repetitive budgetary process. Resource uncertainty remained in the boom-and-bust cycles, but there was the uncertainty that caused repetitive budgeting and the repetitive budgeting that caused additional uncertainty. Wealth also remained in the context of poverty, since the three countries concerned started out and ended up poor in the course of a boom and bust: there was the period when each went from poverty into what seemed to be riches and the period thereafter when the country went back once again into what seemed to many as poverty.

The Boom-and-Bust Budgeting Narrative

Empirically, the intersection of the two types of uncertainty—the uncertainty that caused repetitive budgeting and the uncertainty caused by repetitive budgeting—and the two types of wealth—the boom and the bust—combine into four situations that vary in terms of why government budgets are made and remade repetitively in many poor countries. These situations prove to be well-known and have offered up some of Third World's paradigmatic economic dilemmas. Government budgets are continuously revised in a poor country when: (1) domestic inflation has become uncontrollable, fueled by continuous government overspending in a period of rapid economic growth (read: budget-induced uncertainty during a boom); (2) efforts to exert expenditure control—such as budget cutting, expenditure "freezes," and lowering budget ceilings—are only partially effective and remain a continuing cause for concern during a period of economic decline (read: budget-induced uncertainty during a bust); (3) exogenous price increases in a country's main exports unexpectedly lift the budget's revenue constraint, thereby seeming to remove the cap on government expenditures for an indeterminate period of time (read: uncertainty-induced budgeting during a boom); and/or (4) the major importers of the country's products have themselves entered an indefinite period of stagnation or recession, leading in the process to an economic downturn of unknown duration and severity in the poor country (read: uncertainty-induced budgeting during a bust). In fact, the popular narrative of a poor country's boom and bust cycle has often conformed to the sequence of repetitive budgeting situations (3)—> (1)—> (4)—> (2), where the government budget is remade first by up to several years of buoyant export revenue that exceed original budget projections, then by rapidly rising government expenditures constrained less by the budget's printed estimates than by the country's capacity to absorb these expenditures, thereafter by an externally precipitated or accelerated economic downturn that renders budget projections once more obsolete, and lastly by government efforts to (re-)establish budget control, particularly through a series of expenditure- reduction stratagems.

These situations suggest it is important to distinguish three types of repetitive budgetary processes for the purposes of boom-and-bust budgeting—*a poor country government budgets repetitively as a way to exert control over its budget, or because it has no budget control, or due to exogenous factors unaffected by its budget control.* As just noted, the three types of repetitive budgeting can be causally related over a cycle of economic growth and decline. The pressure to exert

greater budget control during the bust by continually using the budget
to cut and scale down expenditures on development projects has in a
number of poor countries been due largely to the lack of budget control during the boom, when these uneconomic and unfeasible projects
were first added to a national budget continuously being revised upward by such additions.

The following case material from Ghana, Kenya, and Nigeria illustrates some of the principal features of the persistence, types, and
sequence of repetitive budgeting in three governments over their boom-
and- bust cycles. These cycles occurred at different times, but several
repetitive budgetary characteristics proved to be remarkably similar.
This chapter examines in detail the budgetary process of the federal
government of Nigeria during and after the 1970s oil price fluctuations. Government budgeting in Ghana and Kenya during and after
periods of agricultural price increases is first described in order to
introduce the reader to examples of repetitive budgetary processes
more fully detailed in the Nigeria case study. While sub-Saharan governments are known to have budgeted repetitively in the past,[10] no
claim is made below that all governments south of the Sahara do so
now, nor that all booms lead to busts, nor that boom-and-bust cycles
follow the sequence of repetitive budgeting outlined, nor that such
budgeting occurs only in sub-Saharan Africa. Rather, our argument is
that some of the different ways repetitive budgeting has been realized
during these cycles—in effect, the articulation of narratives of repetitive budgetary processes within a larger narrative of boom-and-bust
budgeting—are important to distinguish from the outset in discussions
of Except-Africa.

Bust in Ghana: A View from 1970[11]

At its Independence in 1957, Ghana very likely had the richest and
most educated population in all of black Africa, with an estimated
annual GDP growth rate of 5.9 percent between 1955–60 and an estimated 1960 per capita income of $500 (in 1980 dollars). Yet GNP per
capita declined by 0.7 percent yearly over the period of 1950–1980.
After the boom years of the 1950s with high cocoa prices, favorable
exchange rates, and relatively low inflation, the country's economy
began to sour in the early 1960s—and by 1966 Ghana suffered the
first coup of what would number nine different governments by early

1982. During this period, government budgets and plans were revised many times. An ambitious, then increasingly desperate, set of initiatives tried to guide national agricultural policy for the period up to 1982, e.g., the Five-Year Development Plan, the Second Development Plan, the Two-Year Development Plan, the One-Year Development Plan, Operation Feed Yourself, the Action Program for Agricultural Production, and the Urgent Action Program.[12]

Excerpts from summaries of interviews held with Ghanaian officials toward the end of 1970 capture a sense of the constant remaking of the national budget during the first three changes in government. That year was part of the stabilization and liberalization phase after the 1966 coup, a period better off on some economic measures than before the coup, but still far from the earlier economic boom. Information given in these 1970 interviews indicate that government budgets were revised during the post-boom period because expenditures had been out of control and as a way of bringing expenditures (back) under control.

An official in the planning unit of the Ministry of Education noted that then-recent capital estimates for the Ministry "were made on an ad hoc basis for one year." "[R]evisions in the recurrent budget are common and anticipated" as well, according to the summary of an interview with an official in the planning and coordination unit of the Ministry of Agriculture. Such revisions appear to have been in large part due to expenditure control efforts. In 1966–68, the Ministry of Finance and Economic Planning (F&EP) had tried to exert control by "their slashing of [capital] estimates submitted by the ministry [of Education] . . . Further, F&EP would lower the ceiling figures they had given to the ministry after estimate preparation." The Ministry's response to such cutting was predictable: "To protect their projects, they often inflated their estimates figures." Budget cutting was not restricted to the finance ministry and the Ministry of Education's capital budget. The interview summary with the Ministry of Agriculture official reported recent recurrent budget cuts experienced in and by his unit:

> About 50 percent was cut if you use the initial estimates prepared by [Ministry] divisions and sent to the [unit] as the base. But if you compare the budget submitted by [the unit] to Finance, the percentage loss is considerably reduced. The unit proposed a recurrent budget of 17–18 million cedis. The approved budget formally ran to the amount of 12 million, although in reality the 12 million figure can be

adjusted to 14 million as the ministry picked up some 2 million on below the line items.

Nor were all departments cut. The Ministry of Education official "was able to get 98 percent of the capital expenditures he asked for," though that had required constant follow-up by the official concerned: "He attributes this success to certain considerations . . . .He mentions he made it a point to establish frequent contact with people in F&EP, that some are now his close friends whom he sees every day or so . . . [M]ost discussions are informally arranged and informally conducted."

More drastic stratagems than budget cutting were tried in order to bring the budget under control. In 1968, according to the interview with an official in the planning section of F&EP, the country's Two Year Development Plan had sought to ensure that new "capital projects were prohibited across the board for every ministry; imports were severely curtailed; and no increases were allowed on personal emoluments." The Plan, however, had been difficult to implement and "[a]t the moment a one year plan is being prepared," notes the interview summary with this official. Government budgets were revised in other ways. Carry-overs from one financial year into the next complicated both budget preparation and execution, according to an interview with a capital budget officer in the economic planning division of the F&EP:

> [O]ne of the chronic headaches Economic Planning suffers is the problem of financial spillover, i.e., work completed but not paid for in the close of the previous fiscal year. They do not know until almost the close of the fourth quarter what the spillover rate will be . . . If Finance does not sign warrants for payment presented during [that] quarter because of work overload, Economic Planning has to work with a spillover that affects [the] capital budget in two ways: (1) part of the new fiscal year's budget will have to be used to meet last year's debts and (2) as a consequence *new* activities . . . will be financially constrained . . . The way the budgeting process is presently scheduled, it is almost inevitable that Finance will not be able to process all the warrants presented for payment by the close of the financial year [since that is when Finance is also involved in the estimates preparation exercise for the next financial year].

The budget preparation exercise had also been complicated by the F&EP being "late in issuing the circular for estimates preparation," the Ministry of Agriculture official was summarized as saying in his interview: "The circular allowed only three weeks between its receipt and the call for estimates preparation. Asked why such a short time period was allowed, he says the Ministry operates on the notion that spending ministries will wait until the last minute to prepare their estimates no matter how long they are given." In addition, economic guidelines for developing the plan and its budget continued to be vague, but this was "an unavoidable aftermath of the period of excessive spending that led to the [1966] coup," in the reported view of another official in the F&EP.

Although this evidence is anecdotal, it suggests the narrative of repetitive budgeting was popular among many Ghanaian government officials in 1970. Budgets had short-term time horizons, estimates were prepared at the last minute, and the budgetary process centered around cuts and lowered ceilings that were both many and frequent to those officials involved. Much (though by no means all) of this budget revision seems to have been the finance ministry's attempt to exert greater budget control than had been exhibited during past overspending. Indeed, earlier overspending and later efforts at expenditure control were related: the "microeconomic mismanagement" of the early years had led to "the proliferation of bad projects" and "white elephants" and their budgetary implications had now to be dealt with.[13]

Coffee Boom and Bust in Kenya after 1978

Repetitive budgeting when there is no budget control, for the purpose of greater control, and due to exogenous factors largely unrelated to that control are discernible in the government of Kenya (GoK) case material. The GoK's budgetary process in the mid-1980s exhibited clear features of repetitive budgeting with Treasury's heavy reliance on budget-cutting, setting ceilings, and repeated attempts at expenditure control counterpoised by the frequent efforts of the operating ministries to do otherwise. Repetitive budgeting also characterized the boom-and-bust cycle experienced by the government just prior to that period.

The boom in question was precipitated by production shortfalls in Brazilian coffee during the mid-1970s, which lead to substantially increased coffee revenues for Kenya for several years during and after. As Leonard, Cohen, and Pinckney put it, "the coffee-boom years of 1976–78 fueled expanding [GoK] budgets between [financial years] 1976–77 and 1981–82. During this 7–year period the overall budget trebled, rising from K£331, 188, 000 in 1975–76 to K£829,112,000 in 1981–82".[14] A number of government projects and activities were started during the coffee boom that were then and later considered uneconomic and largely unfeasible.[15]

The Kenya economy had entered a downturn by 1980. Using 1976 prices, GDP per capita had risen steadily from K£92.8 in 1976 to K£100.79 in 1979, only to decline to K£94.94 in 1980.[16] By 1981 the development and recurrent budgets (in constant prices) had declined by 15 percent and 4 percent respectively from those figures first proposed in the 1979–83 Development Plan.[17] The government expenditure situation worsened further in the 1982–83 financial year, with expenditure cuts and a "budget freeze" instituted by Treasury during that year.[18]

The best measure of the repetitive nature of GoK budgeting during this boom and bust cycle would be a chronology of its various official estimates as to what would be and what actually were the government's expenditures for the "bust" financial year of 1982–83. While government-wide data for that exercise are not available to us, it has been possible to construct the various figures for the GoK's 1982–83 agricultural expenditures in the development and recurrent budgets (the Ministry of Agriculture became the Ministry of Agriculture and the Ministry of Livestock Development after the 1979–80 financial year). The figures for development expenditures are set out in table 5.1 in their order of appearance and show that the budget in question was remade several times during this period, with an insistent gap between planned and actual expenditures.

While the GoK is no different than other governments in having fairly unreliable outer year estimates of expenditures, one can glimpse the heady days of the coffee boom reflected in the early forward budget estimates of the 1982–83 agricultural development budget. By late 1981 the proposed ceiling had been reduced considerably. This did not stop both the departments within the Ministries of Agriculture and Livestock Development as well as the Ministries themselves from adopting the usual operating-ministry practice of making requests considerably over the Treasury ceiling. The approved budget for that year was well over ceiling, though in the end subsequent budget cuts and underspending reduced actual agricultural expenditures to a level substantially below ceiling.

The available evidence for the Ministry of Agriculture (MoA) also shows a pattern of continuous changes in the recurrent budget for 1982–83 similar to those in the development budget. As summarized

TABLE 5.1
Chronology of Government of Kenya Figures for the 1982–83 Development Estimates for the Ministry of Agriculture (and Livestock Development)[19]

Description (Actual/Probable Date)	1982/83 Gross Development Estimates (K£)
1978/79-1983/84 Treasury Forward Budget Ceilings (December, 1977)	47,300,000
1979/83 Development Plan Ceilings (mid to late 1978)	70,000,000
1979/80-1982/83 Treasury Forward Budget Ceilings (January, 1980)	45,735,000
1980/81-1983/84 Treasury Forward Budget Ceilings (September, 1980)	47,850,000
1981/82-1984/85 Treasury Forward Budget Ceiling (August, 1981)	44,200,000
1982/83 Annual Estimates Ceiling from Treasury (late 1981)	41,976,000
Departmental Requests to Ministry (early 1982)	108,185,520
Ministry Submission to Treasury (early 1982)	81,134,190
Approved 1982/83 Estimates (mid-1982)	52,356,254
Actual Expenditures (figures released in 1984)	34,559,181

Sources: Republic of Kenya, "Forward Budget 1978/79-1983/84" circular in File No. EPD/SC 028, dated 7th December (Nairobi: 1977); Republic of Kenya, *Development Plan 1979-1983* (Nairobi: Government Printer, 1979); Office of the Vice-President and Ministry of Finance, "Forward Budget 1979/80-1982/83," in File No. ES 3/32/01, dated 22nd January (Nairobi: 1980); Treasury, "Programme Review and Forward Budget 1980/81-1983/84," ES 1/04 Treasury Circular No. 3, dated 5th September (Nairobi: 1980); Treasury, "Programme Review and Forward Budget 1981/82-1984/85," ES. 1/04 Treasury Circular Letter, dated 20 August (Nairobi: 1981); Thomas Pinckney, John Cohen, and David K. Leonard, "Microcomputers and Financial Management in Development Ministries: Experience from Kenya," Development Discussion Paper No. 137 (Cambridge, MA: Harvard Institute for International Development, 1982); Republic of Kenya, *Development Estimates for the Year 1982/83* (Nairobi: 1982); Controller and Auditor-General, *The Appropriation Accounts, Other Public Accounts, and the Accounts of the Funds for the Year 1982/83*, II (Nairobi: 1984). All figures are given as published.

in the minutes of the joint Ministry of Agriculture and Ministry of Livestock Development's Task Force on Budget and Financial Management Processes,

> [The Treasury] ceiling provided to the MoA in the 1980 forward budget was £36.15 million, which came to be reduced to £26.70 million in the 1981 forward budget circular. The [Ministry's] proposals for the recurrent forward budget amounted to £31.03 million and as a result of the discussions in [Treasury] the agreed forward budget for 1982–83 had an overall ceiling of £27.15

million . . . [Subsequent] division requests amounted to £90.62 million; while at the same time the forward budget ceiling of £27.15 million was further reduced to a fresh ceiling of £24.36 million . . . [The Ministry's actual 1982–83 request to Treasury] amount[ed] to £26.92 million, which was only £2.43 [million] more than the ceiling for the printed estimates. In the discussions that followed in [Treasury], the approved printed estimates were set at £25.46 million, which amounted to a small reduction (5.4 percent) of the ministry's request.[20]

Actual gross expenditure proved to be K£25.02 million for the 1982–83 recurrent budget in the Ministry of Agriculture.[21] Similar gaps between what was proposed and approved were also found for the GoK budget as a whole. Although the approved estimates for the 1982–83 GoK budget represented some K£1,025 million, "submissions by ministries to the Treasury for the 1982–83 Financial Year exceed the Forward Budget ceilings on the recurrent and development budgets by as much as K£200 million and K£300 million respectively".[22]

The Kenya government and ministry figures make more explicit some of the same features of the repetitive budgeting narrative found in Ghana: ceilings, budget cuts, and budget freezes were used as a way of trying to exercise greater control over expenditures, particularly after the boom. Loss of some control had occurred during the boom (e.g., when ceilings became inflated and unfeasible projects were approved), while expenditure control was stressed but never fully materialized during the bust (e.g., when departments and ministries persisted in coming in considerably over ceilings that were periodically being lowered by Treasury). Moreover, factors clearly unrelated to and independent of GoK budget control efforts, namely, shortfalls in coffee production elsewhere, precipitated the early series of budget revisions.

Boom-and-Bust Budgeting in Nigeria between 1970–1986[23]

The persistence, types, and sequence of repetitive budgeting over a boom-and-bust cycle are more fully illustrated by some two decades of Nigeria national budgeting. The rise and fall of oil prices had a profound effect on the federal government budget in Nigeria, an oil exporting country. In 1973, the Nigeria oil price index (1980=100) was at 11.2 and revenue from oil accounted for 59.9 percent of the federal government revenue. After the first oil price increase, the 1974 figures were 31.7 and 82.1 percent, respectively. A similar pattern accompanied the 1979 oil price rise: between 1978 and 1979, the price index changed from 39.5 to 58.5, while the revenue percentage moved from 63.1 percent to 81.4 percent. Oil prices declined, however, in the 1980s. After peaking at 108.4 in 1981, the oil price index fell to 83.3 in 1983, and oil revenue as a percentage of government revenue dropped from the 1979 high to 62.4 percent in 1981.[24]

The overall position of the Nigeria federal government revenue, Nigeria export earnings, and the government's foreign exchange position during the period 1970 to 1986 is set out in table 5.2. Three distinct periods can be observed in these data conforming to the oil boom and bust.

TABLE 5.2
Federal Government of Nigeria Revenue, Nigerian Export
Earnings and Opening Balance of Foreign Exchange 1970 to 1986

Year	Revenue	Export Earnings	Foreign Exchange Balance Jan. 1	Total Available Foreign Exchange
	Naira (million)	US$ (million)	US$ (million)	US$ (million)
(1)	(2)	(3)	(4)	(5) (= 3 + 4)
1. 1970	663	1,248	101	1,349
2. 1971	1,169	1,889	174	2,063
3. 1972	1,405	2,184	362	2,546
4. 1973	1,695	3,607	292	3,899
5. 1974	4,537	9,698	464	10,162
6. 1975	5,515	8,329	5,503	13,832
7. 1976	6,766	10,122	5,270	15,392
8. 1977	8,042	12,431	4,721	17,152
9. 1978	7,469	10,508	3,739	14,247
10. 1979	10,912	16,774	1,323	18,097
11. 1980	15,234	25,741	5,017	30,758
12. 1981	12,180	17,961	9,593	27,554
13. 1982	11,764	12,088	3,098	15,186
14. 1983	10,509	10,309	1,568	11,877
15. 1984	11,192	11,827	963	12,790
16. 1985	14,606	12,804	1,452	14,256
17. 1986	12,302	6,599	1,666	8,265

Sources: Central Bank of Nigeria and IMF, *International Financial Statistics Year Book 1987.*

The pre-boom period of 1970–73, prior to the first oil price increase, witnessed generally rising revenue, export earnings, and available foreign exchange. The boom between 1974 and 1979 saw these nominal figures increase by factors of up to five or more over the earlier period. After 1980 with the decline of oil wealth the figures worsen and by 1986 export earnings were about a quarter of the 1980 figure. The effect of this boom and post-boom cycle can be summarized by the changes in the Nigeria per capita GDP. In 1973 per capita income at market prices was estimated to be US$875. During the boom, the figure averaged US$1000 in 1976 and 1979. By 1982 the oil price bust had begun and per capita GDP had fallen below the 1973 estimate to US$824.[25] The real gross domestic product increased in Nigeria by 8 percent per annum between 1970–1979, thereafter declining by 2 percent per year between 1980 and 1983.[26]

As government revenues were doubling and doubling again, so were federal government expenditures. Table 5.3 shows that expenditure increases were substantial between 1970 and 1986, both in current price and real terms.

TABLE 5.3
Federal Government of Nigeria: Expenditure for the Calendar Years
1970–1986 and the Price Index During the Period

Year	Expenditure at Current Prices (million Naira)	Expenditure Index	Annual Percentage Change in Total Expenditure	Price Index 1970 = 100
1970	1,127	100	—	100
1971	997	88	−11.5	116
1972	1,464	130	46.8	119
1973	1,529	136	4.4	126
1974	3,067	276	100.6	142
1975	6,253	558	103.9	189
1976	8,057	715	28.9	232
1977	9,261	822	14.9	281
1978	9,865	875	6.5	342
1979	10,069	893	2.1	382
1980	17,513	1,554	73.4	420
1981	16,107	1,429	−8.0	508
1982	19,633	1,742	21.9	547
1983	15,800	1,402	−19.5	674
1984	15,882	1,409	0.5	940
1985	19,795	1,756	24.6	992
1986	21,106	1,873	6.6	1002

Sources: Central Bank of Nigeria, Economic & Financial Review and IMF International Financial Statistics Year Book 1987.

Unsurprisingly, inflation was a very severe problem in Nigeria during the boom-and-bust cycle. While there is no satisfactory price deflator for government expenditures, the magnitude of the price increases for government can be appreciated by examining the price changes witnessed in the private sector during the period (last column in table 5.3). Even after allowing for the declining value of the Nigerian naira, federal government expenditures increased substantially in real terms. Equally important as these increases were their volatility. The largest percentage changes in expenditures occurred in the years immediately following the 1973–74 and 1979 oil price shocks but were not sustained thereafter. Moreover, the pre-boom and post-boom periods recorded the only percentage declines in expenditures.

The Persistence of Repetitive Budgeting over the Oil Boom and Bust

What was the effect of these expenditure and revenue changes on the planned and actual federal budget in Nigeria? In each of the ten financial years between 1970–71 and 1979–80, actual government revenue was greater than planned revenue, as computed from the various Accountant General reports for these years. Some of the gap was due to the well-known strategy of finance ministries to underestimate revenue as a way of hedging against future demands and uncertainty.[27] Clearly, though, the unexpected rise in oil revenues had a major part to play in making this gap as wide as it was in some years, e.g., actual revenue was more than 50 percent above planned revenue in 1973–74 and 1974–75. Not unexpectedly, the start of the oil boom was perceived by federal officials as a lifting of the government's revenue constraint.

As for government expenditures, table 5.4 compares what the Nigerian federal ministries and departments planned to spend in terms of their recurrent and capital budgets versus what they actually spent during the financial years 1970–71 to 1986.[28]

Actual capital expenditures (in nominal terms) increased nearly sevenfold between the three financial years covering 1973–76, while actual recurrent expenditures increased some two and a half times during the same period. As in the Kenya case material, a gap between the proposed and realized budgets existed in the Nigeria federal government, and this gap varied over the pre-boom, boom, and post-boom period. Overall, the ratio of actual to planned expenditures is closer to

TABLE 5.4
Planned and Actual Recurrent and Capital Expenditures of Nigerian Federal Ministries/Departments 1970/71 to 1986

	RECURRENT EXPENDITURE			CAPITAL EXPENDITURE		
	Planned (in million) Naira	Actual (in million) Naira	Extent of Fulfilment of Plan Actual/Plan ×100 percent	Planned (in million) Naira	Actual (in million) Naira	Extent of Fulfilment of Plan Actual/Plan ×100 percent
	1	2	3	4	5	6
1. 1970/71	213.5	388.5	182.0	233.4	105.6	45.3
2. 1971/72	349.3	432.7	123.9	295.3	201.8	68.3
3. 1972/73	500.7	570.0	113.8	512.0	303.5	59.3
4. 1973/74	647.9	615.7	95.0	774.0	524.3	67.7
5. 1974/75	959.2	942.8	98.3	1890.3	1415.8	74.9
6. 1975/76	1695.6	1639.0	96.7	7062.9	3651.1	51.7
7. 1976/77	2218.3	1840.8	83.0	7116.6	4857.1	68.3
8. 1977/78	1965.5	1810.0	92.1	7379.8	5609.8	76.0
9. 1978/79	1629.7	1507.9	92.5	4996.1	3681.0	73.7
10. 1979/80	1894.4	2211.7	116.7	7563.8	5467.1	72.3
11. 1980	2300.2	2081.4	90.5	7256.9	5353.7	73.8
12. 1981	3529.8	3633.1	102.9	8919.2	5648.4	63.3
13. 1982	3473.0	3438.3	101.9	7507.6	4949.2	65.9
14. 1983	3833.6	3660.7	95.5	7489.5	4006.8	53.5
15. 1984	3180.0	3813.5	119.9	3166.0	1156.6	36.5
16. 1985	3541.8	4101.8	115.8	1385.8	2506.3	180.8
17. 1986	5574.0	4076.7	73.1	2485.9	1737.0	69.9

Source: Accountant-General Statement Numbers 3.2 and 4.

1 more often in the recurrent budget than it is in the capital budget, with the former budget having less of the repetitive budget gap between what is proposed and what is eventually realized. Nonetheless, the recurrent budget had years where planned and actual expenditures differed by more than 10 percent, though the boom period (roughly 1973/74–1979/80) had a lower proportion of these years than did the combined pre- and post-boom period. The boom also represented the period when actual recurrent expenditures started to be *less* than planned and the ratio only returned to greater than 1 after the boom. An absorptive capacity constraint on government expenditures may well have been operating during the boom, a point that becomes clearer when turning to allocations in the capital budget.

There was no financial year between 1970 and 1986 when the gap between planned and actual capital expenditures was not large. Indeed, except for 1985, considerable underspending took place in the capital budget throughout the other sixteen years under study. The mean allocation to programs funded in the capital budgets of the operating ministries was 63.6 percent of what was promised in the budget documents (table 5.5).

The effect of the oil boom on the capital budget and the nature of underspending in this budget can be better seen in table 5.5, which categorizes capital programs by percentage of their planned budget that they actually received. During the boom's flush of funds, a greater proportion of programs were likely to receive over 100 percent of the moneys they expected to receive than was the case before or after (excepting 1985). The absorptive capacity of government programs to use resources rather than these resources being too scarce seems to account for the capital budget underspending witnessed during these years of oil wealth. For example, at least 25 percent of the planned capital expenditures was not implemented in the financial years of 1971–72, 1973–74, and 1974–75, when actual revenue as a percentage of total expenditures was 111 percent, 115 percent and 138 percent, respectively. Still, excepting once again 1985, the top three years in terms of actual capital program allocations coming closest to what had been estimated in the budget for them were boom years. By the early 1980s, however, capital budget underspending had clearly become more a problem of insufficient resources than of insufficient capacity to absorb them. Between 1980 and 1986 export earnings dropped from

TABLE 5.5
Federal Government of Nigeria Breakdown of Budgetary Allocations on Capital Programmes for the Financial Years 1970/71 to 1986

ACTUAL ALLOCATIONS AS PERCENTAGE OF APPROVED BUDGET

Percentage of Programs affected each year	0-20	21-40	41-60	61-80	81-100	101-120	120 or more	Total Percentage	Mean Allocation to each Programme
1. 1970/71	53.3	33.3	0	6.7	0	0	6.7	100	27.6
2. 1971/72	20.0	6.7	19.9	6.7	33.3	6.7	6.7	100	68.4
3. 1972/73	6.7	0	26.6	53.3	6.7	6.7	0	100	62.3
4. 1973/74	6.3	12.5	18.7	50.0	12.5	0	0	100	60.7
5. 1974/75	0	18.7	6.2	31.3	31.3	0	12.5	100	78.1
6. 1975/76	11.5	34.6	30.8	15.4	7.7	0	0	100	44.2
7. 1976/77	23.1	7.7	23.1	23.1	19.2	0	3.8	100	57.6
8. 1977/78	0	15.4	19.2	30.8	11.5	15.4	7.7	100	77.7
9. 1978/79	8.3	16.7	12.5	20.8	20.8	16.7	4.2	100	71.3
10. 1979/80	0	7.7	15.4	19.2	38.5	11.5	7.7	100	84.3
11. 1980	3.7	11.1	18.5	44.5	14.8	3.7	3.7	100	68.4
12. 1981	12.9	9.7	19.4	35.5	16.1	3.2	3.2	100	62.9
13. 1982	6.2	6.2	34.4	18.8	18.8	9.4	6.2	100	68.3
14. 1983	6.1	15.2	51.5	15.2	12.0	0	0	100	52.9
15. 1984	9.7	25.8	16.1	29.0	6.5	3.2	9.7	100	59.7
16. 1985	0	3.6	0	0	3.6	3.6	89.2	100	335.3
17. 1986	3.2	3.2	19.4	29.0	29.0	13.0	3.2	100	73.8
Entire period apart from 1985	10.7	14.1	20.7	26.8	17.4	5.6	4.7	100	63.6

Source: Accountant-General's Statement No. 4.

US$25,741 million to US$6,559 million (table 5.2), while external debt payment as a percentage of export earnings increased from 2 percent to 43.3 percent.[29] External credit sources with which to purchase capital goods and services had begun to dry up by the mid-1980s.

In sum, while the planned budget was always a fairly unreliable predictor of the budget finally realized, the extent and nature of this predictive unreliability differed by type of expenditure (recurrent or capital) and by the period in which that expenditure was budgeted and spent during the boom-and-bust cycle. Repetitive budgeting persisted throughout the boom and bust cycle, but with some important differences along the way. These differences can best be illustrated by specific examples from the different periods. For instance, the fact that actual government revenue was more than 50 percent above planned revenue at the start of the boom represents an example of repetitive budgeting due to external factors largely beyond the control of the budget itself. What follow are examples of the other two types of repetitive budgeting.

Instances of How Repetitive Budgeting Proceeded during the Boom

Cases of uncontrolled expenditures abound from the boom. After the 1967–70 civil war, the problem arose over how to accommodate the army, which had increased from a prewar level of approximately 10,000 members to a postwar strength of some 250,000. The defense ministry embarked upon a massive importation of cement for barracks construction. The importation led to the widely reported port congestion of Lagos in 1975, which itself ultimately delayed or suspended implementation of even more government activities. The funds for this importation were not originally provided in the budget, and actual expenditures were ultimately debited against the wrong account. The total provision in the eventual barracks account was naira 55 million or equivalent at that time to some US$87.5 million for the two financial years covering 1974–76. By the end of June 1975, and with nine months to go in the 1975–76 financial year, a total sum equal to US$145.4 million had already been paid to the cement contractors alone, excluding the amount paid directly to the contractors handling the actual barracks construction. Moreover, outstanding government commitments to the cement contractors had burgeoned to US$847.77 million.[30]

Some attempts to exert expenditure control during the boom had the perverse effect of doing otherwise. By 1976 the upward revision of cost estimates had become the rule of the day and the Nigeria Federal Ministry of Finance felt compelled to request a meeting of Cabinet (called the Federal Executive Council) in order to prune and defer projects that were considered less essential in the Third National Development Plan (1975–1980). The Finance Minister later explained what happened during the council meeting:

It was that exercise that actually raised the capital expenditure plan from naira 30 billion to naira 43 billion. It was interesting to watch how the council was inexorably pursuing the *opposite* of what it *intended* just because every executive ministry was able to defend and argue for the crucial importance of its projects and to convincingly plead inflation to justify increased allocations. It did appear as though council deliberations were not being controlled by those around the table.[31]

This revision upward in the 1975–80 national development plan occurred even though the Plan had originally stated its initial estimates were the "maximum feasible" given absorptive capacity constraints.[32] This reversal also found its way into the annual estimates. The government produced a 1976–77 estimates document which on one page states the government's intention to limit actual expenditures to naira 5.5 billion on both recurrent and capital expenditures, while on a later page shows a total provision for naira 7.8 billion on capital expenditures alone.[33]

Instances of Repetitive Budgeting Proceeding before and after the Boom

The upward revision of budget estimates was a problem not only during the oil boom. As in the Kenya case, what was initially estimated in the national development plan frequently did not coincide with later estimates, e.g., in some instances the 1973 estimates for road construction were up to five times or more their original estimates in the 1970–74 national development plan.

In aggregate terms, the post-boom period witnessed a greater degree of budget cutting and government expenditure control than in the immediately preceding years. Government expenditures declined in real terms for several years after the boom (table 5.3) and the percentage share of the expenditure budget devoted to government goods and services (such as education, administration, social services) has decreased considerably from the boom years while the share allocated to debt servicing increased markedly (table 5.6).

After the boom, Treasury began to institute a series of expenditure control measures to delay the release of funds and staunch the flow of spending. For example, Treasury required spending ministries in 1983 to get its prior approval for cashing checks of over Naira 20,000. Similarly, that anomalous 1985 financial year in terms of capital expenditures represents just such an attempt to control expenditures through the use of budget ceilings, where planned expenditures in 1985 were set at less than half of what they were the year before in nominal terms (table 5.4).

But efforts to exercise greater expenditure control during the post-boom period were in large part necessitated by its continuing absence elsewhere in government. The upward revision of national development plan estimates found before the boom persisted after it. For example, the 1981–84 national development plan originally estimated total expenditures for Nigeria's river basin authorities to be Naira 1,822.7 million. By the end of 1983, over 90 percent of that sum had already been spent, leading to an increase in the planned expenditure estimate by two and a half times the original figure.[34] Even though Treasury tried to exert greater budget control after the boom, some operating ministries were able to circumvent these efforts. Ministries withdrew more funds from the Central Bank than their warrants permitted, delaying thereafter their submission of monthly expenditure statements to Treasury. Moreover, notwithstanding its 1985 efforts to reduce expenditures, the federal government reversed itself by allocating considerably more for capital expenditures than was planned (table 5.4). For instance, the National Universities Commission had been promised nothing for capital projects in the 1985 budget, only to receive Naira 46 million that year in capital project allocations.

Efforts to introduce planning, programming, and budgeting systems (PPBS)[35] and zero-based budgeting (ZBB) into the spending ministries by and large did little to reduce or stabilize their expenditures. Spending ministries did not always have complete control over matters ostensibly under their portfolio responsibilities. For instance, of the Naira 340 million budgeted for housing in 1982, only Naira 40 million was directly under the Ministry of Housing and Environment. The remaining 88 percent of the budget was controlled by appointees directly

TABLE 5.6
Functional Budget Shares of Nigerian Federal Government Expenditure for Selected Years 1970–1986

	1970	1972	1974	1975	1976	1978	1980	1982	1984	1985	1986	Average Share 1970-1986
Administration including defence and police	53.6	41.5	26.9	28.8	22.4	22.8	18.3	15.8	22.9	15.7	13.9	26.0
Economic Services	6.0	12.2	17.6	23.1	29.5	32.0	33.7	17.6	6.0	6.1	7.7	19.4
Education	0.6	2.0	6.4	13.6	13.0	8.3	7.1	4.7	4.7	4.2	4.2	5.6
Other Social and Community Services	1.2	2.9	8.4	5.8	6.0	8.1	5.1	6.5	1.6	7.4	3.0	5.2
Share of Expenditure on Goods and Serivces = A	61.4	58.6	59.3	71.3	70.9	71.2	64.2	44.6	35.2	33.4	28.8	56.2
Allocation to States and local government	23.8	22.6	21.0	16.8	20.4	18.0	21.1	21.7	26.4	25.1	20.5	23.5
Public Debt Servicing	11.4	6.4	4.4	3.0	4.2	7.9	4.8	19.3	19.7	25.7	42.2	11.0
Other Transfer Payments	3.2	12.4	15.3	8.9	4.5	2.9	9.9	14.4	18.7	15.8	8.5	9.3
Share of Transfer Payments = B	38.6	41.4	40.7	28.7	29.1	28.8	35.8	55.5	64.8	66.6	71.2	43.8
A + B	100.0	100.0	100.0	100.0	100.0	100.0	100.0	100.0	100.0	100.0	100.0	100.0
Total in million Naira	1127.0	1464.0	3067.0	6253.0	8057.0	9865.0	17513.0	19633.0	15882.0	19965.0	21100.0	—

Source: Central Bank of Nigeria, *Economic & Financiasl Review and Annual Report and Statement of Accounts, 1987.*

accountable to the president. The budget-cutting recommendations of the 1984 Onosode Committee, which relied the notion of ZBB in identifying what large-scale capital projects should be delayed or discontinued, were in large part repudiated in the government budget of the following financial year.

Federal government budgeting in Nigeria over the oil boom-and-bust cycle can be seen as the outcome of several forces which worked for or against each other and which balanced out differently in the boom and in the bust, but which singly and cumulatively resulted in the persistence of repetitive budgeting throughout the cycle. Again, at different periods in the cycle, government budgeting proceeded repetitively as a way to exert budget control, because there was no budget control, and/or due to external factors largely unaffected by budget control. Exogenous increases in the price of oil made necessary a considerable upward revision in the government's revenue estimates at the start of the boom. What efforts there were at budget control during the boom years were undermined by this revenue-induced pressure to spend as if revenues were no problem and absorptive capacity on expenditures were no constraint. Expenditures went out of control, at least for the many cost estimates in the recurrent and capital budgets that had to be constantly revised upward. Fueled by the spending, domestic inflation made it all the more difficult to reconcile planned and actual budget estimates. Exogenous factors eventually intervened again and led to a new series of budget revisions, this time downwards. When oil prices started to decline, published budgets continued to be a poor guide to what was actually spent, but now for additional reasons. In the post-boom era of fiscal stress and cutback management, expenditure control (such as the use of lowered 1985 budget ceilings) had become important, but by no means entirely successful. Inflation persisted and the budgetary implications of government activities approved during the boom often remained unavoidable in the bust. While the causes of repetitive budgeting thus varied over the boom-and-bust cycle, this budgeting dominated the cycle in the form of cost estimates that were often being revised and original budgets (particularly for capital expenditures) that were fairly unreliable predictors of final budgets.

Some Implications of the Boom-and-Bust Budgeting Narrative

It should be clear that the boom-and-bust budgeting narrative is not a mechanical sequence of repetitive budgeting without budget control followed by repetitive budgeting for increased budget control, each initiated by a period of repetitive budgeting due to factors largely independent of that control. Each of the three repetitive budgeting narratives is probably present throughout a boom-and-bust cycle, though the prominence of each varies at any point in that cycle. Instances of *repetitive budgeting for the purposes of greater budget control* occurred to varying degrees in the booms and the busts of Kenya and Nigeria, though such budgeting was more evident in the post-boom periods. Similarly, *repetitive budgeting without budget control* was also evident throughout the cycles, though more a feature of the boom's remaking of the government budget through overspending than afterwards. Finally, examples of *repetitive budgeting unrelated to budget control* appear less periodic than may first seem, when one realizes that boom and bust can be precipitated at the subnational level and by factors other than exogenously determined economic changes. Needless to say, ministries and departments can have their own boom-and-bust budgeting with differing magnitude, determinants and timing. The Ghanaian official who in a post-boom period was budgeted most of what he requested while others around him were being cut; the Kenya ministry which, unlike other ministries, prioritized its proposed cuts during a post-boom budget crisis; and those Nigerian projects which managed to have their estimates increased even during a post-boom cutback are all instances of repetitive budgeting behavior occurring on a subnational level, which were not in sync with the national boom-and-bust cycle. Because of such variation, Caiden's call for more country-specific descriptive studies of government budgeting in each country remains as relevant today as it was nearly twenty years ago.[36]

Indeed more detailed case studies of government budgeting in Nigeria, Kenya, and Ghana might better demonstrate just how repetitive budgeting is articulated over a boom and bust. For the distinction between repetitive budgeting undertaken in order to enhance expenditure control and repetitive budgeting that results when there is little or no such control is probably due in part to the different roles that finance and the operating ministries have in the budgetary process. As

Caiden and Wildavsky detailed,[37] a finance ministry often sees its role as guardian and conserver of the budget, where expenditure control is a major goal of its organizational charter; operating ministries just as frequently consider themselves to be advocates of increased spending and frequently do not regard revenues as fixed. The interaction and interdependence of these roles help to structure the budgetary process, though which role dominates varies over time, and presumably most visibly during a boom-and-bust cycle.

Such discriminations between repetitive budgeting modalities are crucial for policy reasons. First, these distinctions complicate the Except-Africa narrative.[38] Government budget control in African countries appears to be little different from that found in other countries, at least to the extent that such control diminishes in boom years and intensifies in bust years, according to the relative abundance or scarcity of funds in the government budget. It does well to be reminded that, as with many countries elsewhere, African governments cut their national or subnational budgets where the scissors of supply and demand pinch the hardest for government funds. Just as repetitive budgeting can be found in rich and poor countries alike, so too is boom-and-bust budgeting a feature of governments outside Africa.[39]

A second reason to insist on distinguishing differences in repetitive budgeting follows from Except-Africa's many "crises" are everywhere present and uniformly debilitating south of the Sahara.[40] Just as there is intragovernmental variation in budgeting, so too are there important differences between African governments, such as Nigeria and Kenya, in terms of how they budget and control expenditures over their boom-and-bust cycles.[41] Similarly, as in the past, so in the future will a number of African governments and/or their subunits undoubtedly go through more periods of boom and bust.[42] A continent whose governments have undergone price cycles associated with copper, uranium, coffee, cocoa, and diamonds, among other commodities, will not cease to have such cycles. Rather than acting as if Africa's future is an extended, pervasive "bust," donors and lenders must be better prepared to respond to the booms that are ahead for some of these governments, their ministries, or major departments.

Included in the preparation has to be a better understanding of the nature and implications of the boom-and-bust budgeting narrative. The literature sees repetitive budgeting as more the problem than a solution.[43] Yet, in the context of an economic boom-and-bust cycle, repetitive budgeting for the purposes of expenditure control becomes an important remedial tool. That is, if there were a way for *governments to treat their booms as if they were busts*, then repetitive budgeting for the purposes of expenditure control would be a distinct advantage over the comparative lack of expenditure control exhibited during the kind of booms described in this chapter. One incentive for encouraging a government to treat what is a boom as if it were not would for donors and lenders to leverage the debt they hold into a guarantee by the debtor nation to exercise more budget control as and when its boom becomes evident. Such action would encourage not only budgetary reform in some countries of sub-Saharan Africa, but also those forces for greater expenditure control already there.[44]

Finally, a more detailed exposition of the boom-and-bust budgeting narrative would have to address political factors left largely undiscussed in our three-country reconnaissance. It is tempting to treat such booms as politically destabilizing. Instead of creating complex redundancy, sudden changes in incomes often seem to increase uncertainty all the more, to return to the terminology of Caiden and Wildavsky. Yet busts should also be destabilizing for the same reason. It is unclear therefore to what extent political uncertainty is a conceptually unique factor in one period rather than the other. Empirically, political factors were at work in both the booms and the busts mentioned earlier, e.g., the budget freeze in the government of Kenya at the end of 1982 followed a coup attempt, while changes in the political leadership of the Nigeria federal government necessitated the budget reversals of 1976–77 and 1984–85. Yet we are struck by the similar pattern that boom-and-bust budgeting has across countries whose regime changes have varied considerably. Similar experiences in repetitive budgeting were observed in the three countries, even though Ghana's boom turned to bust under one regime, Kenya's boom witnessed the constitutional succession of a head of state by another, and Nigeria's boom took place during three unscheduled military governments and one scheduled civilian one. Since part of the Except-Africa narrative stems from the perception of disorder fostered by many regime changes, it is important to recognize some of the underlying regularity that government budget management and administration has during periods of extreme economic fluctuations. It is in this sense, then, that boom-and-bust budgeting in Africa, rather than supporting the Except-Africa narrative, contains the seeds of its own counternarrative.

Notes

1. For an earlier introduction to case material on boom-and-bust cycles, see Mats Lundahl (ed.) *The Primary Sector in Economic Development: Proceedings of the Seventh Arne Ryde Symposium* (New York: St. Martin's Press, 1985). A discussion of the fiscal management by governments of commodity boom-and-bust cycles can be found in The World Bank, *World Development Report 1988* (New York: Oxford University Press, 1988), pp. 71–74.
2. Naomi Caiden and Aaron Wildavsky, *Planning and Budgeting in Poor Countries*, New York, John Wiley and Sons, pp. 71–72 (1974).
3. Aaron Wildavsky, *Budgeting: A Comparative Theory of Budgetary Processes*, 2d rev. ed., New Brunswick, NJ, Transaction Books, p. 16 (1986).
4. Wildavsky, *Budgeting: A Comparative Theory of Budgetary Processes*, pp. 18–19.
5. Wildavsky, *Budgeting: A Comparative Theory of Budgetary Processes*, p. 18.
6. Aaron Wildavsky, *The New Politics of the Budgetary Process*, Glenview, IL, Scott, Foresman and Company, p. 399 (1988).
7. For example, Naomi Caiden, "The New Rules of the Federal Budget Game," in *Public Administration Review* (March–April 1984).
8. For example, Allen Schick, "Micro-Budgetary Adaptations to Fiscal Stress in Industrialized Democracies," in *Public Administration Review*, vol. 48, no.1 (1988).
9. Wildavsky, *Budgeting: A Comparative Theory of Budgetary Processes*, chapter 5. For what remains the most comprehensive introduction to the national budgetary systems of a variety of Third World countries, see A. Premchand and Jesse Burkhead (eds.), *Comparative International Budgeting and Finance*, New Brunswick, NJ, Transaction Publishers (1984).
10. See Emery Roe, "Counting on Comparative Budgeting in Africa," in *International Journal of Public Administration*, vol. 11, no. 3 (1988c).
11. Unless otherwise stated, we have relied heavily on the statistics and statements of Michael Roemer, "Ghana, 1950–80: Missed Opportunities," in Arnold Harberger (ed.) *World Economic Growth*, San Francisco, ICS Press (1984). We thank Aaron Wildavsky and Naomi Caiden for access to the summaries of Pat Anglim's interviews with senior Ghanaian officials during late 1970. The excerpts quoted in the text are Anglim's rendering of her discussions and not necessarily direct quotes of the interviewees. Spelling and punctuation in the excerpts have been silently corrected.
12. See Kodwo Ewusi, "The Relevance of the Lagos Plan of Action for Agricultural and Industrial Development in Ghana," paper presented at the Conference on Development Options for Africa in the 1980s and Beyond, Nairobi, Society of International Development (1983).
13. The terms are from Michael Roemer, "Ghana, 1950–80: Missed Opportunities," p. 211.
14. David Leonard, John Cohen, and Thomas Pinckney, "Budgeting and Financial Management in Kenya's Agricultural Ministries," in *Agricultural Administration*, vol. 14, p. 107 (1983).
15. See, for example, Republic of Kenya, *Report and Recommendations of the Working Party on Government Expenditures*, Nairobi, Government Printer (1982).
16. Republic of Kenya, *Economic Survey, 1980,* Nairobi: Central Bureau of Statistics, Ministry of Economic Planning and Development, p. 12 (1980); Republic of Kenya, *Economic Survey, 1981*, Nairobi, Central Bureau of Statistics, Ministry of

Economic Planning and Development, p. 14 (1980); Republic of Kenya, *Economic Survey, 1984*, Nairobi: Central Bureau of Statistics, Ministry of Finance and Planning, p. 17 (1984). See, for example, Republic of Kenya, *Report and Recommendations of the Working Party on Government Expenditures*, Nairobi, Government Printer (1982).

17. Leonard, Cohen, and Pinckney, "Budgeting and Financial Management in Kenya's Agricultural Ministries," p. 107.

18. Treasury Circular No. 10 of 1982 ("Reducing Voted Expenditure for 1982–83," ES 1–02 Treasury Circular No. 10, dated 8 December, Nairobi) called for budget reductions of at least K£36 million out of an overall development and recurrent budget approved by Parliament some five months previously at approximately K£1,025 million. Later a "budget freeze" on a wide range of expenditures came into force for the rest of the financial year (see Treasury Circular No.1 of 1983, "1982–83 Revised Estimates of Revenue and Expenditure: Recurrent and Development Estimates," dated 4 March 1983).

19. Sources: Republic of Kenya, "Forward Budget 1978–79 - 1983–84," circular in File No. EPD–SC 028, dated 7 December, Nairobi (1977) ; Republic of Kenya, *Development Plan 1979 - 1983*, Nairobi, Government Printer (1979); Office of the Vice-President and Ministry of Finance, "Forward Budget 1979–80 - 1982–83," in File No. ES 3–32–01, dated 22 January, Nairobi (1980); Treasury, "Programme Review and Forward Budget 1980–81 - 1983–84," ES 1–04 Treasury Circular No. 3, dated 5 September, Nairobi (1980); Treasury, "Programme Review and Forward Budget 1981–82 - 1984–85," ES. 1–04 Treasury Circular Letter, dated 20 August, Nairobi, (1981); Thomas Pinckney, John Cohen, and David K. Leonard, "Microcomputers and Financial Management in Development Ministries: Experience from Kenya," Development Discussion Paper No. 137, Cambridge, MA, Harvard Institute for International Development (1982); Republic of Kenya, *Development Estimates for the Year 1982–83* (Nairobi: 1982); Controller and Auditor-General, *The Appropriation Accounts, Other Public Accounts, and the Accounts of the Funds for the Year 1982–83*, volume 2, Nairobi (1984). All figures are given as published.

20. Task Force on Budget and Financial Management Processes, "Minutes of Workshop No.3, October 7–8, 1982," Nairobi, Ministry of Agriculture and Ministry of Livestock Development, p. 7 (1982).

21. Controller and Auditor-General, *The Appropriation Accounts, Other Public Accounts, and the Accounts of the Funds for the Year 1982–83*, volume II, p. 334. Underspending in the agricultural development budget had been a past problem, though the position improved by the 1981–82 financial year (compare Leonard, Cohen and Pinckney, "Budgeting and Financial Management in Kenya's Agricultural Ministries," p.107 with the Controller and Auditor-General, *The Appropriation Accounts, Other Public Accounts, and the Accounts of the Funds for the Year 1981–82* [Nairobi: 1983], pp. 813, 834). Moreover, the past trend up to 1981–82 was for actual GoK recurrent expenditure to exceed the figures estimated both in the annual estimates and in the ceilings for those estimates. Also, important differences in budgeting behavior can be found during this period between the Ministry of Agriculture and Ministry of Livestock Development, e.g., the latter undertook a very real effort to prioritize what activities should be cut during the budget minicrisis of 1981–82 (see David Leonard, *Individuals, Institutions and Interests in Kenya: The Public Management of Rural Development*, chapter 8 [Berkeley: Political Science Department, University of California, 1988], draft manuscript). For more information on the changing budget figures for agricultural expenditures

during this period in Kenya, see D.K. Ole Nasieku, Nils Isaksson, and S. Ramakrishnan, "Review of Present Budgetary Processes and Measures for Improvement," Task Force Paper No. 18, Task Force on Budget and Financial Management (Nairobi: Ministry of Agriculture and Livestock Development, 1984), especially table 2.

22. Republic of Kenya, *Report and Recommendations of the Working Party on Government Expenditures*, p. 16.
23. Facts and figures provided in this section are from Eddy Omolehinwa, *Government Budgeting Amidst Economic and Political Shocks: The Case of the Nigerian Federal Government*, unpublished Ph.D. thesis, University of Manchester (1986).
24. Computed from figures in International Monetary Fund, *International Financial Statistics Yearbook* , Washington,DC, pp. 481, 483 (1985) and Central Bank of Nigeria, *Economic & Financial Review and Annual Report and Statement of Accounts* (Lagos: various years).
25. International Monetary Fund, *International Financial Statistics, Supplement on Output Statistics*, Washington,DC, pp. 18–19 (1984).
26. Charles Andrain, *Political Change in the Third World*, Boston, Unwin Hyman, pp. 229, 238 (1988).
27. For a discussion of this conservative estimation practice, see Caiden and Wildavsky, *Planning and Budgeting in Poor Countries*, pp. 68ff.
28. Government expenditure estimates were not planned on the basis of the calendar year until the 1980 financial year. Unless otherwise stated, all figures are in nominal terms and were arrived at after deducting expenditures that were not direct allocations to government ministries and departments (e.g., consolidated revenue charges and external financial obligations).
29. Computed from figures in International Monetary Fund, *International Financial Statistics Yearbook* , Washington, DC, p. 527 (1987) and Central Bank of Nigeria, *Economic & Financial Review and Annual Report and Statement of Accounts* (Lagos: various years).
30. Federal Republic of Nigeria, *Report of Tribunal of Inquiry into the Importation of Cement by the Ministry of Defence*, Lagos, Federal Government Printers, p. 126 (1976).
31. A. E. Ekukinam, "The State of the Nation's Economics and Social Development," in *Management in Nigeria* (June), p. 18 (1980).
32. Federal Republic of Nigeria, *Third National Development Plan, 1975–1980*, vol. 1, Lagos, Federal Ministry of Economic Development, p. 366 (1975).
33. Federal Republic of Nigeria, *Approved Recurrent and Capital Estimates of the Government of Federal Republic of Nigeria 1976–77*, Lagos, Federal Ministry of Information, pp. xviii, xxxiv (1976). The 1976–77 planned capital expenditure figure in table 4 differs because it excludes non-direct capital allocations to the ministries. See footnote 28.
34. See Onosode Committee, "Report of the Review of Federal Capital Projects," mimeo (the report was never officially released).
35. For more on this topic, see Eddy Omolehinwa, "PPBS in Nigeria: Its Origin, Problems and Progress," in *Public Administration and Development* (forthcoming).
36. Naomi Caiden, "Budgeting in Poor Countries: Ten Common Assumptions Re-Examined," in *Public Administration Review* (January–February,1980).
37. Caiden and Wildavsky, *Planning and Budgeting in Poor Countries*, chapters 4 and 5.
38. See, for example, John Lewis, "Development Promotion: A Time for Regroup-

ing," in John P. Lewis and Valeriana Kallab (eds.) *Development Strategies Reconsidered*, New Brunswick, NJ, Transaction Publishers, pp. 23–25 (1986).

39. For a discussion of some aspects of boom-and-bust budgeting in the U.S., see Emery Roe, "Management Crisis in the New Class," in *Telos*, vol. 21, no. 2 (1988b).

40. See again Lewis, "Development Promotion: A Time for Regrouping," p. 17.

41. See also Roe, "Counting on Comparative Budgeting in Africa," for a discussion on inter-government budgeting differences. An example of intragovernment budgetary variation at the project level can be found in Emery Roe, "Getting and Spending: Some Observations on the Government of Kenya Budgetary Process," *Agriculture Administration Network Paper No. 19*, London, Overseas Development Institute (1984).

42. Consider for example a later article on Ghana's partial recovery, which claims in a headline "Ghana, Once 'Hopeless,' Finds Look of Success." See James Brooke, "In Western Eyes, Ghana Is Regarded As African Model," *New York Times,* 3 January 1989.

43. An exception is Caiden and Wildavsky, *Planning and Budgeting in Poor Countries*, pp. 316ff.

44. Some of the different ways to convert or reduce the debt burden are discussed in The World Bank, *World Development Report 1988*, pp. 34–35. This discussion, however, assumes, as does our chapter that strict control of expenditures in the recurrent and capital budgets is to be encouraged. It may be, though, that stronger budget control by a government is associated with a greater skewed distribution of income in the country concerned, while weaker control is associated with less skewedness. This topic deserves more attention in comparative budgeting. For a start, see Emery Roe, *Narrative Policy Analysis*, Durham, NC, Duke University Press (1994).

6

Decentralization, Rural Development, and Politics

Much of the development literature continues to give attention to government decentralization, the discussion of which is often cast in terms of a development narrative about the "politics of decentralization."[1] The government of Zimbabwe (GoZ) has embarked on a reform which is said as well to pivot on the politics of decentralizing rural development. Based on the early days of its implementation, the reform is not primarily about decentralization or politics or rural development. If its implementors are correct, the initiative is counter-narratively much more about reforming local government in a way that promotes economic development at the district level by capitalizing on the scarce administrative and technical skills within the local authorities.

Amalgamation and Its Background[2]

The reform in question is the consolidation (officially, the Amalgamation) of Zimbabwe's two rural local authorities, the rural councils (representing largely white, commercial farming interests) and the district councils (representing black, largely communal area residents). Some background on commercial and communal areas is necessary here.

Zimbabwe's total land area is approximately 39 million hectares, about 33.3 million (85 percent) of which has been set aside for agricultural purposes. This agricultural land has two dimensions of interest to this chapter, land tenure and agroecology. The main tenure categories in rural areas are: commercial (freehold), with commercial subdivided into large-scale commercial (mostly white farmers) and small-scale commercial (black farmers); communal land; and more recently, resettlement areas.[3] The country's agroecological zones are natural regions I-V, with region I being the best in terms of rainfall and soil conditions and region V the worst.

As of 1989, there were (in round numbers) 4,000 large-scale commercial farmers owning 11.2 million hectares; one million communal families holding 16.3 million; 10,000 small-scale commercial farmers on 1.4 million; and 52,000 resettlement farmers (that is, black Zimbabweans) on 3.3 million hectares. Thus, as of the early 1990s, a great deal of the agricultural land (a third of it) remained—and still remains—in the hands of the white farming population. Moreover, this land is in the better-off areas. Over half of the large-scale commercial farming land is in regions I, II, and III, while over three-quarters of the communal land is in regions IV and V. About 60 percent of the communal area population live in the arid and semiarid regions IV and V, the vast majority of whom have been small-holders in mixed crop and livestock enterprises.[4]

The land distribution is important because of the preeminent role large-scale farms play in the country's agricultural cash economy. The large-scale commercial farming sector has accounted for some 75 percent of the country's marketed agricultural output. Over 40 percent of the country's annual foreign exchange reserves has come from the agricultural industry, with some 85 percent of that due to products generated through large-scale farming. Large-scale farms also employ more than 25 percent of Zimbabwe's wage-earners. Still, it is estimated that six or seven out of every ten Zimbabweans obtain livelihood from communal lands agriculture. To give an indication what such figures mean at the household level, a sample survey in one of the districts visited for this chapter's research found that average annual household income among communal farmers was about Z$1,100, while the average annual household income in established commercial farming areas of the same district was over Z$400,000.[5]

With that background in hand, we can now turn to local government. Rural councils had been the local authorities for the commercial farming areas, while district councils had been the local authorities for the communal areas. District councils were themselves consolidated from the African councils of the pre-Independence era, while a number of rural councils traced their history back to roads committees established by colonial farmers. At Independence in 1980, small-scale commercial areas had a choice to join rural or district councils, and some chose to join the former, others the latter. Resettlement areas have been under the direct control of central government.

Amalgamation alters this local government set-up. At the time of writing, rural councils and district councils were in the process of being abolished and a new rural district council (RDC) established in their place. There would now be one local authority, the consolidated RDC, for each district (there are over fifty districts). The vast majority of councilors are to be elected from district wards (no more than 20 percent of all councilors can be appointed), and the wards would continue to follow land tenure categories found in the district prior to the creation of the amalgamated RDC. Depending on the district, there could be four basic types of rural wards within an RDC: commercial wards for the large-scale farming areas; commercial wards for its small-scale farming areas; communal wards; and resettlement wards. (Urban areas will have their own wards.) In brief, while Amalgamation is to change local government, it was not to change the land tenure distribution (though in the case of resettlement areas the change from central to local government could be considerable).

As a consequence, voting requirements for councilor elections were not planned to alter substantially after Amalgamation. Communal ward residents would still vote for their councilors according to universal franchise, while only ratepayers in the commercial wards (that is, property owners) have the right to vote for commercial ward councilors. Commercial area farm workers would continue not to have the right to vote for the councilor from the commercial ward in which they live and work. Farm workers would be expected to vote, if they vote at all, by registering in their communal wards of origin (which a number no longer have or ever had). Nonetheless, the new RDCs would have a majority of black councilors, if simply for the reason that communal, resettlement and small-scale commercial wards shall outnumber large-scale commercial wards.[6] Indeed, the number of black councilors should increase, as the GoZ land reform program increases its purchase and conversion of commercial farms into resettlement areas, a process to which President Mugabe has recently recommitted himself.

The Development Narrative of Amalgamation as Decentralization

Some readers may wonder why, after more than a decade of Independence, consolidation of the white and black councils began in earnest only in the 1990s. The answer most readily given in Zimbabwe is that President Mugabe wanted to tie up the countryside for his ruling party, the Zimbabwe African National Union (Patriotic Front) or ZANU(PF), prior to the 1995 elections. The rural areas have been a strong source of support for him, and if council elections were held before multipartyism took root in the countryside, all the better for the ruling party's future.

Politics of the countryside course through much of the literature on Amalgamation and its enacting legislation, the Rural District Councils Act of 1988. The

> desire [of rural councils] to preserve social and political institutions of the past is a central feature [of Amalgamation] and has to be tackled as a political problem . . . .Will [Amalgamation] result in distortion of the problem of rural underdevelopment and hence the need for agrarian change, or will it result in some form of redistribution (albeit in a limited form) of resources, particularly if District Councils have access to capital assets held by the Rural Councils?[7]

Another well-informed academic observes that "Amalgamation of the two forms of rural government has always been seen as a political priority," adding it "would do away with a last vestige of colonial government structure and it would enable the process of rural restructuring to continue."[8] "In spite of the post independence successes in decentralization, the future for effective decentralization depends crucially on the financial measures needed to complement the RDC Act," he argues. "Without these, the future of decentralized provision of local public goods and services and of rural local government is bleak."[9] "One of the most important dimensions of rural development policy in Zimbabwe since independence has been rural local government reform, in particular decentralization policy," concludes another long-time observer.[10] Decentralization has been an important topic in Zimbabwe's university circles, and Amalgamation has been discussed in two excellent books circulating there, *Decentralizing for Participatory Planning?* and *Limits to Decentralization in Zimbabwe.*[11]

Academics are not alone in holding these views. A ministry handbook for RDCs notes that changes brought about by Amalgamation "should be viewed from the broader context of Government's efforts to fundamentally restructure the administrative and economic dispensations of the rural communities and fashion them into a unified entity under a common management pursuing the goal of uplifting living standards for all in the countryside." The handbook then describes Amalgamation in distinctly decentralized terms, where it "ensures that people's needs are determined and planned for at the lowest level and not imposed from above. It is a way of bringing government closer to the people."[12]

Similar views are echoed in the donor community. A consultant's report on the GoZ and rural institutions concludes "Amalgamation can be used as the basis for devolving substantial power from central to local government" and recommends that "Amalgamation must be accompanied by a powerful vision of regenerated rural development through local accountability and participation with the new RDCs."[13]

This development narrative about Amalgamation-as-decentralization, while widespread and accurate as far as it goes, narrowed what Amalgamation was for those who were about to implement it. These latter views—many of which are invidious development narratives themselves, but some of which are counternarrative—are discussed in the remainder of this chapter.

Development Narratives from Below:
Amalgamation and Local Government Officials

The following findings are based on a study undertaken between May and July 1992, just as the Amalgamation process was beginning.[14] Six districts were visited, and in each district the major implementors of the Amalgamation exercise were interviewed, namely, the district administrator (who was responsible for overseeing and implementing Amalgamation in the district) and the two rural local government secretaries (the senior executive officer/district council and the chief executive officer/rural council). Other local officials were also questioned, including a rural council chair and vice chair, a district council finance committee, and several assistant district administrators. A total of thirty-eight people were interviewed in the districts.

Because of the provocative nature of some quotes,[15] two measures have been taken to ensure interviewee confidentiality. No names are given and in only one instance are positions mentioned. Interviewees have as well been grouped by their affiliated organization, that is, by district council (DC), rural council (RC) and district administration (DA). These three groupings over the six districts represent the core eighteen "respondents" referred to below. Only two instances were detected where interviewees within the same respondent group differed in their responses, and these differences are incidental to the findings of the following four subsections.[16]

First Pass Problems of Amalgamation

A quick survey of local official concerns over rural district councils would conclude Amalgamation has little chance of success. The most frequently mentioned objective given for Amalgamation is to unify the two local authorities into one, less fragmented whole (ten of the eighteen respondents said as much).[17] Yet the divide between district and rural councils appears, on initial inspection, too great to permit that. The two local governments seem locked into a zero-sum conflict, with district councils the winners only if rural councils are the losers.

During the interviews, development narratives were repeatedly resorted to about, on the one hand, communal areas, communal people, district councils, and district councilors, and on the other hand, commercial areas, commercial farmers, rural councils, and rural councilors. Whatever their factual merits, the important point is that *both black and white* interviewees agreed on the narratives. At least two among the three different types of respondents (i.e., district council, rural council, and district administration) said:

- Communal areas are not economically viable because they are abused and destroyed, while commercial areas are economically viable because they are conserved and managed;
- Communal people are occupiers of the land, non-commercial, and typically do not pay taxes, while commercial farmers are owners of the land, business-minded, and typically do pay taxes;
- District councils are highly subsidized, dependent on central government, and relatively inefficient, while rural councils are relatively self-supporting, independent of central government, and efficient;[18] and
- District councilors see themselves entitled to privileges, allowances, and a salaried position, while rural councilors see themselves volunteering their time for responsibilities that are more a burden than source of income.[19]

As one DA respondent put the divide: "Look at the two agendas [of rural and district council meetings] and you'll see how miles apart we are." A DC respondent is more philosophical: "Perhaps we've had too long history of separation" to make Amalgamation work. It is here that the many parallels between consolidating racially distinct local authorities in Zimbabwe and South Africa are their most patent.

From the divide said to separate Zimbabwe's rural local governments, many have found it fairly easy to conclude that district councils have everything to gain from Amalgamation and rural councils everything to lose:

- According to an RC respondent, "There is bound to be a deterioration in standards" in the commercial wards with Amalgamation, while a DC respondent in the same district says indeed there would be "some deterioration," though in the short-run only.
- An RC respondent worries that "district councils have the absolute minimum [of assets]" and that "district council will see [our road equipment] as a resource to use." A DC respondent in the same district basically agrees by saying that the "district council is poor, it has no equipment to do roads; rural council is much better equipped, so we will spread the equipment to the poorer areas."
- An RC respondent fears that communal ward councilors in the RDC will look over the fence and see the houses, cattle, and equipment on the commercial farms and then vote to raise commercial ward rates, while a DC respondent in another district sums up Amalgamation by saying it is "taking levies from the rich side [of the fence] and putting it to the poor side."
- A DA respondent worries that communal farmers will take Amalgamation to mean that commercial farms must now open their grazing to communal farmers, while a DC respondent in another district says that, unless Amalgamation is spelled out clearly, some villagers will see it as "repossession of their farms" taken by the whites.

"In a sense, their fears are valid," concludes a district council respondent of rural council concerns over Amalgamation. Eleven of the eighteen respondents see a very real conflict of interest and priorities—two called it a "tug of war"—developing after the local authorities are fully amalgamated. Here too the parallels between Zimbabwe and post-apartheid South Africa are palpable.

When asked what were the possible areas of cooperation between district and rural councils, four respondents mentioned roads, three agriculture, two water development or development planning, but by far the most common response was the pause, as respondents tried to think of an answer. Of the eleven respondents who expressed an opinion, six were pessimistic and five were uncertain about the prospects of Amalgamation. Three of those who were pessimistic and all who were uncertain are black.

Second Pass: The Overriding Problem of Financial Viability

Views in the preceding subsection are incomplete in important respects:

- For a start, not many rural people know of Amalgamation. One DC respondent thought less than 10 percent of his district residents knew about it, another DC respondent estimated the figure to be less than 30 percent for his area, and a third DC respondent even said only "three-quarters of [his] councillors knew what Amalgamation is, and one-quarter only can guess about it".[20]
- For some the divide between communal and commercial is bridgeable. Indeed, there are black interviewees who see a positive role for white leadership in addressing communal area problems. (It deserves stressing that their comments, like others in the chapter, were volunteered.) According to one DA respondent, Amalgamation would "reduce quality of debate for rural councillors, while increasing quality of debate for district councillors." A DC respondent thought that large-scale commercial farmers paying their high rates would "challenge" communal people to pay more. His point: if our commercial counterparts can pay cattle and grain taxes, why can't we do the same in the communal areas? Another DA respondent, who welcomed commercial wards as needed encouragement for privatizing communal land, basically asked: if they can have title deeds that side, why can't communal farmers have them this side?
- A final way in which the earlier views are incomplete is, however, the most instructive. A much more basic issue was found to preoccupy the eighteen respondents: *the financial viability of RDCs.*

The single most frequent problem volunteered by respondents about Amalgamation is the fact that the new rural district councils will be financially unworkable in terms of revenues meeting mandated duties. Thirteen of the respondents see ensuring the financial viability of the new local authority as an important, if not the central, challenge facing Amalgamation. The other five respondents are worried about the related issues of how rates and levies are to be set among the different types of wards and the need for central government to provide a greater share of tax revenue to the RDCs. Indeed, twelve respondents see setting rates and levies as a very real and urgent problem for the RDCs. The problem of rates was what, in the words of a DA respondent, "prolonged the Amalgamation exercise in the first place."

In short, *it was not clear to any respondent how the rural district councils were to be effectively financed and just who is to provide what by way of revenue to them.*[21] "The question of viability has not been answered," says an RC respondent. "Government hasn't come up with any meaningful ideas, not even a clue, on how to make RDCs viable" is how one DC respondent expressed it. "Politically they might be there, but practically they won't," said one black interviewee of the RDCs.

The uncertainty over RDC financial viability forces reconsideration of the earlier narratives. The DC respondent, who said problems will arise because communal farmers who "have never managed a Z$1,000" now become councilors "having to manage thousands more," is referring to a concrete financial management problem, not just to a divide separating communal from commercial. Worries about the attitudes of councilors toward allowances or about the length and number of council meetings are eminently legitimate when the starting point is financial viability. Inefficiency is a real—not racial—problem in these circumstances. Moreover, the concerns are unavoidable if one believes along with a DA respondent that "local authorities are finances, as far as I am concerned" or that finance "is the hub" of local government, as a DC respondent put it.

This central preoccupation with financial viability among local officials responsible for the implementation of Amalgamation was not something I had expected to find, given my reading of the Zimbabwe literature and my past familiarity with local authorities in other sub-Saharan countries. Like many readers, I was quite prepared to buy into the narrative of Amalgamation as the politics of decentralizing rural development. Such a politics is indeed there, but what I also found were local officials genuinely worried about the integrity of local government *qua* government, that is, officials who saw council more as organization and administration than as a vehicle for local politics and communal area (namely, rural) development.

Government decentralization typically means something like "the process through which government agencies or local organizations obtain the resources and authority for timely adaptations to locally specific conditions in the field."[22] Decentralization is thus understandably and necessarily about politics in the countryside, be it deconcentration—the delegation of some administrative responsibilities to rural units of the central government—or devolution—the establishment of rural governments with their own local powers and authority. Yet, the more the interviewees were probed, the more it became clear that, in addition to the politics of decentralizing rural development, Amalgamation was a local government reform that is more than deconcentration but not yet devolution, is much more than politics, and is not just about rural development within each district. Let us examine each briefly, for in these views are the counternarratives to Amalgamation-as-decentralization.

Decentralization

If the eighteen respondents are any indication, something much more durable than "deconcentration" is happening under Amalgamation. Local government is becoming entrenched.

Local government has been moving from the transitional to the permanent in Zimbabwe—or, more precisely, to the same kind of permanence that central government has. Even if district councils had been as financially viable as many rural councils were and as some African councils had been,[23] the three proved to be never more than transitory local governance. Independence and the liberation struggle ensured that. Amalgamated rural district councils are the first form of local government to arise in post-Independence Zimbabwe which no one views as "transitional" to anything other than local government. As one observer put it, "without an elimination of the pre-independence dualism, rural local government will not come to full fruition".[24] This is why financial viability is such a worry. It matters more than it ever did.

Moreover, the trend is toward a kind of devolution, that is, a local government that governs rather than just sets priorities in Zimbabwe. If the issue had been one simply of deconcentration, then the GoZ could have followed what Kenya had done or what its neighbor Malawi was thinking of doing, i.e., delegate to the district development committee (DDC)—not to the local authorities on the DDC—the responsibility to set important priorities for the line ministries operating in the district. Zimbabwe's RDC Act, in fact, does the reverse: not only is the DDC incorporated into RDC committee structure, but the Act allows RDC councilors to amend and modify the annual district development plan its DDC proposes. Other elements of devolution are promised in the RDC Act as well, e.g., central government resettlement areas are, as noted earlier, to become local government administrative wards.

Yet the road to devolution will not be an easy or certain one in Zimbabwe. It is difficult to describe any process that has, since Independence, consolidated over 200 African councils into 55 district councils, was at the time of writing amalgamating these 55 district councils and like number of rural councils into just under 60 rural district councils, and in between had transferred all land allocation powers of local chiefs and headmen to councils and all council responsibilities for primary education to the ministry of primary education as "decentralizing government" in any of the conventional senses.

Similarly, more immediate concerns work to undermine the implementation of devolution through Amalgamation. An artifact of the ministerial guideline that a rural district council should typically have no more than thirty councilors has been to increase the size of proposed wards in a number of districts. Half of the eighteen respondents noted that these district wards were now larger as a result of Amalgamation.[25] Several DC respondents said the wards would, as a result, be much more difficult to cover by councilors. For one respondent this meant that the ward he now represents with six village development committees would have more than three times as many, if Amalgamation proceeded as planned. Another ward is said to have become almost as large as a parliamentary constituency. Amalgamation, in effect, all but scraps an earlier prime minister's circular governing the decentralized structure of wards and villages.

What had happened up to the early 1990s is that the GoZ chose to merge local government units as a way of providing more services to more people rather than to expand the number of these units as a way of introducing more local autonomy to more places.[26] Regionalization of the local authorities rather than the decentralization of government to subdistrict authorities appears to be the road Zimbabwe has chosen for devolution.

Rural Development

Amalgamation is much more about *district* development than it is about rural (that is, communal area) development. Several reasons account for this.

In the first place, rural councils were something of a misnomer. They were also concerned very much with urban development. According to the 1986 Taxation Commission report, there were forty-one urban centers and twenty smaller urban areas within rural council boundaries (counterpart district council numbers are five and two respectively).[27] During the interviews, RC respondents took pride in pointing out the township developments fostered in their areas. Bringing rural councils into a rural district council format automatically makes RDCs "about" urban development in a very large way.

More compelling reasons explain why Amalgamation must be seen as not just about local government centered on improving rural development.[28] Bluntly, to base RDC financial viability on making the communal areas viable economically dooms RDCs from the start. "With that lot around our neck, we'll go under," said an RC respondent of what he saw as the broken-down communal areas. Nor is he alone in thinking this. If other respondents are the measure, few *black* officials see a future for themselves or others in the communal lands. To rapidly urbanizing black Zimbabweans, these areas are the Third World. They are the country's unofficial natural region VI said to be unsuitable for almost anything that is going on there. Whatever the reasons motivating the black elite who designed Amalgamation, one thing is clear: they are not doing it because they want to be better communal farmers.[29]

The bias against rural areas extends beyond the communal lands. No one interviewed had a good word to say about resettlement areas. As for small-scale commercial farming areas, one DC respondent felt they were little different from the communal areas in his district: "Our problems are almost the same," he said. As for large-scale commercial farming areas, no interviewee touted the commercial ranch or farm as a model for improving the economic viability of communal areas, nor did any interviewee argue that the rural development priority of the new RDCs should be the improvement of living conditions for the many disenfranchised commercial farm workers.

When one adds up the anticommunal, antiresettlement and

anticommercial narratives, they equal a markedly pro-urban bias on the part of black respondents. Not one interviewee—black or white—said anything negative about urbanization in the district or anywhere. While two respondents saw in villagization a possible answer to communal land problems, four promoted giving title to land as the way out, and three saw few, if any, "bankable ideas" for these areas, to this interviewer the answer clearly preferred by most respondents was, "Urbanize!" If attempts to modernize communal agriculture—the small-scale commercial farms, followed by resettlement areas, and more recently the communal area grazing schemes—have not worked, then the next best thing in this view is the growth machine of urbanization. Whatever the merits of the latter development narrative, it forces those interested in Amalgamation to look at the full canvas of economic development at the district level, and not just the rural background to that canvas.

Politics

Amalgamation is as much about administration and law as it is about politics. Unlike other parts of Africa,[30] in Zimbabwe there has been a profound tension between politics and administration, where bureaucrats at all levels of government use law and regulation to defend themselves against political interference, while politicians try to change law and regulation as a way of getting administrators to do what they, the politicians, want. The result is that bureaucrats seek to preserve their administrative and technical competence by becoming highly legalistic in orientation.[31]

The tension results in large part because policy is extremely politicized in Zimbabwe. As one senior-level administrator expressed it, the government bureaucrat who calls for new policies risks being seen as a politician and thus a critic of ZANU(PF). In this environment, it is not surprising that ministry departments continue to be organized around implementing legislation, not policy, and that ministry staff are preoccupied with planning and finances, that is, precisely those issues around which laws can be and have been made.[32]

All this is operating in the Amalgamation exercise. The armature of politics, administration, and the law is nicely illustrated by two consecutive interviews in one district. When I asked the district council's senior executive officer what were the aims of Amalgamation, he said that was hard to answer. It had come from the "top" as a "policy" conceived by central government in which they, the council staff, were just "actors." His counterpart, the rural council's chief executive officer, answered the same question by asking: "I expect you've read the Act . . . ?"

Other respondents expressed similar concerns when queried as to what were the aims of Amalgamation. "That one is a bit difficult," answered another DC respondent, "The whole thing was a political decision." Yet what was needed in the view of another DC respondent is to treat "the law as a guiding tool," by which he meant that each RDC's annual development plan should be gazetted into statute. This way RDC priorities could not be tampered with through political interference. But even the law can become politicized and a threat to competence and common sense. The "average person in Zimbabwe," according to a black interviewee, is "above the law" in that he or she knows "what is right," regardless of any ZANU(PF) legislation mandating otherwise. Some government administrators were embarrassed by the impracticality and expediency of proposals put forward by ministers and councilors with whom they have to work.

It is precisely in this sense, then, that the respondents' preoccupation with RDC financial viability must be understood: namely, what they see as the pivotal role of competence and common sense in making a piece of very important legislation less politicized. The RDC Act is politicized not because it is about the politics of decentralization or local government, but because it threatens to place further limitations upon the administrative competence and professionalism of its implementors. It gives politicians powers that would normally be reserved for bureaucrats in other times and places. In a piece of legislation that is some 200 pages long, reference is made on average at least once every page to the minister's or president's powers to amend, modify, or otherwise control RDC decisions.[33] To a professionally trained administrator such control is not centralization, it is worse. It is micromanagement by politicians of administrators who should be doing—by virtue of training, experience, and professionalism—that administration in the first place.

Just how key this concern is among bureaucrats to preserve and protect their own competence and areas of authority can be glimpsed in what respondents deem to be the necessary qualifications for an RDC's chief executive officer (CEO). All nine respondents who had an opinion on the issue saw as a matter of priority some mix of financial, administrative, and/or legal background on the part of the CEO. DA respondents provide the representative comments. According to one, the CEO has to be "someone strong in finance and administration." For another, an "administrative background" and "legal background" "would be quite useful." A third said the CEO "should be having an administrative and financial flair," and a fourth felt the CEO "should possess administrative, legal, and finance background." The DA views take on added credence, because district administrators and their assistants, who were seen by others as potential candidates for the CEO position, readily admit they often lack just such a background.

Conclusion

In sum, how Amalgamation is evaluated depends on what development narratives are used in parsing it. If one expects from Amalgamation improved rural development, but finds instead a polarized politics of decentralization cast against the continuing socioeconomic divide separating white from black, commercial from communal, rural rich from rural poor, and bureaucrats from the people, then there is little reason to be optimistic about the exercise or the exercise's usefulness as a model for other racially divided nations in Southern Africa.

If, however, other development narratives are engaged as above—that is, Amalgamation is much more about the nascent devolution of central government and reform of local government for the purpose of improved district-level development in a way that can maximize the utilization of scarce administrative and technical skills—then there is room for optimism and even excitement over the prospects for Amalgamation, even when initial implementation problems arise.

Optimism is at three levels, first for the future of government devolution and then communal area development, and lastly for the financial viability of the RDCs. If all three hold (and there are no guarantees here), they constitute a very real counternarrative to that narrative of Amalgamation-as-decentralization. In the first place, it makes sense within the Zimbabwe context to have a strong legal and administrative foundation at the national level for devolution. Practically, this means with Amalgamation and RDCs in place, people can start taking local government more seriously. Fortunately, the seeds for central government devolution of responsibilities to the RDC were there in the form of the RDC's incorporated district development committee.

Once local government is taken seriously, so too can communal area development. It is true that this development has been difficult to achieve in Africa's arid and semiarid lands (see preceding chapters). Nonetheless, there is just too great an inter-site heterogeneity in Zimbabwe and too high a level of local government administrative and technical competence to rule out that everywhere and at all times economic development of the communal areas cannot be undertaken effectively. One need only look at the expertise and skills large-scale commercial farmers bring to the new local authority to see this.

As for RDC financial viability, just how likely is it that RDCs can become more self-supporting financially? The chances may be favorable over the longer term, and the reason for some optimism is straightforward, though indirect. In a very real sense, rural district councils are functionally equivalent to central government parastatals.[34] Obviously, an RDC is not a commercial venture in the same way as is the average parastatal. Nonetheless, both are semiautonomous, legally mandated bodies working in the districts and having their own budgets and audits. The GoZ and parastatals have shown success in reducing parastatal subsidies and making some parastatals more viable. If the GoZ can rationalize and "free up" parastatals, then why is not the same thing possible for rural district councils?

Notes

1. See, as an example, Bienen, Kapur, Park, and Riedinger, pp. 63–64 (1990). As for other journals and at the time of writing, not a volume of *Public Administration and Development* had gone by since 1981 without at least one article (often more) on government decentralization, many of which centered as well around the politics of decentralized rural development.
2. Unless otherwise stated, figures and statements used in the next four paragraphs come from Takavarasha (1991). His paper has a wealth of information. Mr. Takavarasha has been a deputy secretary in Zimbabwe's Ministry of Lands, Agriculture and Rural Resettlement.
3. There are also state farms, national parks, and minor residual uses of stateland.
4. See, for example, Jayne, Chisvo, Hedden-Dunkhorst, and Chigume, pp. 46–47 (1990).
5. Wanmali, pp. 94–95 (1992). At the time of writing, US$1 = Z$5.
6. For more details on the information provided in this and the preceding paragraph, see Helmsing (1991).
7. de Valk and Wekwete, p. 96 (1990).

8. Helmsing, p. 97 (1991).
9. Helmsing, p. 145 (1991).
10. Mutizwa-Mangiza, p. 423 (1990).
11. See de Valk and Wekwete, eds. (1990) and Helmsing, Mutizwa-Mangiza, Gasper, Brand, and Wekwete (1991).
12. Ministry of Local Government Rural and Urban Development, p. 2 (1990).
13. Gunby, pp. 50, 43 (1992).
14. The study was commissioned by the Ford Foundation and undertaken for the unit coordinating the Amalgamation exercise within the Ministry of Local Government, Rural and Urban Development. The findings and conclusions do not necessarily reflect the views of the Ford Foundation, MLGRUD, or their staff. The following is a revised version of sections from Roe (1992a).
15. Interviews were not tape-recorded and interviewee quotes have in some cases been reconstructed from notes and recollection of what was said. No attempt was made to solicit the quotes or their specific phrasing. They are not verbatim extracts with all the pausing and starting over common to speech. In a few instances, coding interviewee responses required a judgment call on the author's part.
16. There are, of course, very real differences between bureaucrats and politicians within the same respondent group. Some of these tensions are discussed later in this chapter under the fifth subsection, "Politics."
17. The Trainer's Manual in Ministry of Local Government Rural and Urban Development (1990) states: "The general policy guiding the promulgation of the Rural District Councils Act No. 8 of 1988, was to change and revolutionize the Administrative, Social and Economic structures of rural Zimbabwe, by removing all colonial trappings of separatism based on racialism and its resultant economic imbalances between mainly the country's black and white communities" (chapter 1, p. 1). Background to this enterprise is given by Brand (1991): "The historical legacy of Zimbabwe makes the 'equalization of conditions' exceedingly difficult. Nonetheless, formal legal, political, and administrative equality rather than collective organization and participation is seen as the most effective way of realizing it" (p. 83). The significance of the legal, administrative and political is discussed later in the chapter.
18. RC respondents said about 80–90 percent of their Council budgets were funded through local rates and revenue. The 1986 Taxation Commission report records central government grants-in-aid to sample rural councils and district councils as 35.8 percent and 96.8 percent of their respective revenues (Government of Zimbabwe, 1986, p. 325.) Based on figures of Helmsing (1991), real per-capita central government grants as a percentage of real per-capita revenue for his sample of rural councils and district councils was under 45 percent and over 80 percent, respectively, for 1986/87 (Table 20, p. 128).
19. According to de Valk and Wekwete (1990): "Generally, the level of education of [district] councillors is lower than that of the officials with whom they have to deal" (p. 96).
20. An early phase of Amalgamation was to determine the district boundaries for the new RDCs. During one boundary commission, sixteen meetings were held with the public in that district's communal and resettlement areas. Attendance at these meetings was recorded as follows: "Nil" for three sites; "poor" for seven sites; "fair" for three sites; "good" for two sites; and "average" for one site. In the words of the commission's 1989 minute: "In all the areas where meetings were held, the question of rates was raised and was a burning issue."
21. Who pays what and when is as important an issue as how much the payment

contributes to RDC financial viability. As RC respondents pointed out, a council budget may be balanced, but only at the expense of raising commercial ward rates so revenues can equal expenditures.

22. David Leonard quoted in Uphoff, p. 221 (1986).

23. There is a view that African councils were not viable, i.e., their "small size undermined their financial viability and this together with low levels of efficiency caused poor service provision" (Helmsing and Wekwete 1987: 6). Three interviewees, two of them black, dissented, arguing that some African councils were much more viable than district councils.

24. Helmsing, p. 130 (1991).

25. Four respondents felt that districts were also too big. The Taxation Commission report (Government of Zimbabwe, 1986) says: " . . . existing district boundaries are large for local government purposes" (p. 318). One respondent felt thirty councilors was even too many.

26. The dominant focus on government as a service provider, even in the case of the RDCs, is reflected in the Taxation Commission report (Government of Zimbabwe, 1986): "With the amalgamation of rural and district councils . . . [i]t would be possible for the new rural local authorities to extend local services to the Communal Areas so that direct central government provision of local services in those areas would become unnecessary" (p. 321).

27. The urban figures are taken from p. 317 of the Taxation Commission report (Government of Zimbabwe, 1986).

28. Rural development has come in second to local government before in Zimbabwe, as illustrated by Gasper (1991): "The 1984–85 formation of provincial through to village level development committees contributed, for example, to the demise of the Ministry of Lands, Resettlement and Rural Development, which had been created in 1978, by splitting off sections of the former Ministry of Internal Affairs to be a development agency for the communal lands. A separate ministry for communal lands became incompatible with the new hierarchy of coordinating committees, which was linked instead to local government and administration" (p. 26).

29. It must be asked, What's wrong with the communal lands as they are? Zimbabwe needs places where the old, the young, and others can reside if they have nowhere else to go. Communal areas serve that function, and in a way that reproduces what many people there perceive as traditional life. I thank Peter Fry for pointing this out.

30. One well-known observer of comparative public administration (Montgomery 1987) speaks of the "relative calm surrounding the politics/ administration nexus in Africa" (p. 921).

31. In the Zimbabwe context, "competence" means a sense of professionalism and a commitment to mission on the part of the bureaucrat concerned. Clearly, not all central government and local government employees are competent. Some are corrupt, some politicized, and some have no sense of professionalism. The point is that many others want to do a good job and actually do so. This is illustrated from work on the study undertaken for this chapter. Although I frequently arrived unannounced, I was able to interview all the chief executive officers (CEOs), senior executive officers (SEOs) and district administrators (DAs) I wanted to interview. One DA took off from leave so that I could talk to him, and a SEO took time off from his weekend. Another SEO photocopied file material without my having to ask. All answered my questions, and some even asked me about Amalgamation. No DA made self-serving remarks about why he should stay on as

district administrator or become the new chief executive officer of the RDC. No DA, CEO, or SEO advanced the scenario I most expected to hear, namely, donors need have few worries about giving money to the RDCs as there were no real problems with Amalgamation. They all instead focused on RDC financial viability and related difficulties. Indeed, what would we have had to conclude about their competence had they not focused on such issues? For more on professionalism in African public administration, see Leonard (1991) and chapter 4.

32. Law and bureaucracy go together in Zimbabwe. Here is one observer's description of MLGRUD: "The most influential ministry in terms of administrative structures [for planning] is the Ministry of Local Government, Rural and Urban Development . . . which is directly responsible for local government. It is responsible for the Provincial Councils and Administration Act, Urban Councils Act, Rural Councils Act and District Councils Act" (Wekwete 1990: 47). Equating council operations to the law is served up in the first sentence from the first page of the draft Trainer's Manual in Ministry of Local Government Rural and Urban Development (1990): "Local authorities are the units or institutions with which local government law concerns itself" (p. i). The Manual's first chapter concludes with a note saying "The law is an ass, BUT IT KICKS!!!" (p. 20).

33. One respondent mentioned the minister's powers as a source of tension and conflict between MLGRUD headquarters and the RDC field staff. RDCs will not want the ministry, in his view, "to dictate" to them over staff and personnel matters, particularly over who RDCs can hire. The tangled link between power and politics in Zimbabwe and other African countries is examined in the conclusion.

34. My thanks to Brian Egner for this parallel. An outstanding primer on decentralization and local government in Africa can be found in Egner (1986).

Conclusion

The Power Narrative and Its Counternarrative, the Politics of Complexity

What has preceded are but a handful of the counternarratives that stand in contrast to an Except-Africa tumbling headlong into the abyss. As we have seen, there are multiple ways to read what is going on in Africa and to change popular conceptions about these goings on (introduction and chapter 1). What many see as a tragedy of the commons or common property resource management, for example, can be recast differently in terms of other conceptual frameworks (chapter 2). In fact, the very same literature developed to explain why rural people perform in the way they do can contain two (or more?) diametrically different models of that behavior (chapter 3). Rarely is the successful performance of rural development determined beforehand, but rather is the result of the highly contingent and provisional goodness of fit between the political and institutional context in which the rural development practitioner finds himself or herself and the professional values s/he brings to that context (chapter 4). That said, even in the worst of times and "busts," positive actions can and have improved policy and project performance (chapter 5). Moreover, the positive exists even when rural people themselves are most negative about where they live (chapter 6).

And all of this is possible because rural development is genuinely complex and thus open to multiple interpretations and interventions. To generalize a point in chapter 2, counternarratives are not only possible, they are *always* there to be developed and used. Why? Because rural Africa—like the world—is never just one way only. It is causally complex and changing in unpredictable ways that are never completely comprehensible to anyone, no matter how experienced s/he is.[1] Thus, rural development practitioners from the headquarters to the field are constantly surprised by the unexpected. Surprise and unpredictability, as organization theorists are fond of reminding us, are the principal features of the kind of complexity found in African rural development.

Repeat: surprise and unpredictability. Not power.

African studies, like African politics, is dominated by narratives of power. In his *Power in Africa: An Essay in Political Interpretation*, Patrick Chabal (1992) asks, What is politics?, and answers, "Politics is about power—in Africa as anywhere else." Chabal is certainly not alone in thinking this. Power is everywhere in the development literature. A review of articles published in *African Studies Review* (Sanders 1993) finds that "state power" shares the lead with "economic development" as that journal's numerically dominant topic. The "most frequent themes in *ASR* articles are politics and policy-making—influencing policy, setting agendas for policy analysis, and highlighting the centrality of politics."

But politics is no longer centered around power, but rather around complexity and uncertainty such as drive African rural development. While the conclusion focuses on the relevant Africa literature, its counternarrative of a politics of complexity, like the power narrative, is intended to apply more broadly.

***

In the African development literature, power and opposition go together. "Power, whatever its precise definition," in Chabal's view (1992), "is minimally about the balance between control and consent which governs the relation between ruler and ruled." As the relations between ruler and ruled are various, so too is power various. Moreover, the literature on African politics and development has been quite clear on insisting that the ruler-and-the-ruled is only one subset of the relations between the powerful and the powerless. For purposes of the conclusion, the varieties of power culled from the African development literature can be summarized into four polarized types—direct, indirect, artificial, and organic power.[2]

The starting pole, and the one which has received the greatest attention, is the direct power of those who govern. Read: the power of the postcolonial state, the colonial authorities, the power of patron over client, the hegemonic ideology. Arrayed around this pole are all those who have defined power as its opposite. First, direct power is subverted by its contrary, indirect power. For indirect power, read: local resistance, subversion, disseminated power, civil society, dissidence[3]— in short, all the terms popular in poststructuralism, culture critique, and cultural studies.

Then there are the contradictories of "both direct power and indirect power" and its contrary, "neither direct power nor indirect power." The former goes under various names—repressive tolerance, artificial negativity, the entrapment of ideology[4]—but all share the same theme: the government or dominant ideology needs opponents in order to rationalize its own existence; bureaucratic power perpetuates itself by ensuring there is sufficient indirect power around "in need of" government toleration or resolution. As for the "neither/nor" pole, it was the contradictory that galvanized many independence and nationalist movements—the dream of no-colonialism and no-government as unalienated people in homogeneous communities organically constituting a state that is truly its own people.

In case it needs saying, this four-poled power narrative of opposites, filled in as it is with local permutations and combinations, is the pattern in the carpet of contemporary African studies. Compare *International Security*, with its U.S.-expert view of Realpolitik, and *Critical Inquiry* with its poststructuralist privileging of Kulturkritik, and you stand in the midst of the same power grid of polarized opposites: the push and pull of always choosing sides, of defining oneself with respect to power. Even "Just what do you mean by 'power'?" ends up electrifying this grid further.

And the electricity is strong. The terms of power are *there*, truly there *in* reality, we repeatedly are told. "How can you *not* conceive of South Africa today without talking about power politics?" a South African asks me. It is inconceivable, he insists, to think of South Africa outside the power grid.

***

Of course, African politics can be rethought in terms other than power politics.

Return to the notion of tight and loose coupling introduced in chapter 1. More formally (Perrow 1984), a tightly coupled system is (1) highly time-dependent in not allowing for delays or unexpected contingencies; (2) fairly invariant in terms of the sequence of activities required (i.e., B depends upon A having happened first); (3) by and large inflexible in the way its objectives are achieved (not only is the sequence of specific activities restricted, but there is only one way to achieve the overall goal desired); and (4) characterized by little slack and resources available to tolerate delays, stoppages, and the unexpected when they do occur. In loosely coupled systems, delays are not only possible, but common; sequences of activities are by no means invariant (e.g., in a university it does not much matter when some course requirements are met before getting a degree); many ways to achieve a common goal are available; and sufficient slack exists to tolerate a degree of waste without imperiling system survival in the process. Both tightly and loosely coupled systems are, in turn, complexly or linearly interactive. Complexly interactive systems are those with unfamiliar, unplanned, or unexpected sequences of activities that often are not visible or comprehensible. The sequences in a linearly interactive system are by contrast much more familiar and expected and are quite visible and comprehensible, even if unplanned or unintended. The dimensions of coupling and interaction produces a typology of four cells:

		Interaction	
		Linear	*Complex*
	Tight	1	2
Coupling			
	Loose	3	4

Many of us—and not just in Africa—find ourselves more and more in cells 2 and 4 situations, thinking they really are or could be the good old days of cell 1. And there is no better example of cell 1 thinking in a cells 2 and 4 world than the linear, tightly coupled thinking that drives so much of the power narrative in African development. African rural development is a complexly interactive enterprise where cause and effect are not easily comprehensible nor predictable, yet you would never know this if you saw the world only through the lens of the tightly coupled, linear notions of direct power, artificial negativity, and organic power.

Such power surely does exist. The world is full of local-level cell 1 situations where the power narrative is most apposite, albeit fewer in number and far more site-specific than most in African studies would like to believe. More important for our purposes is understanding just how it is that power can exist even in cell 2 and 4 situations. Here the issue is not that power is complex, as in the case of indirect power, but rather that complexity itself creates power. In cells 2 and 4, power is better thought of as a "policy window," where policy is writ large to include projects and programs as well. In the terminology of Kingdon (1984), a policy window is created by the infrequent tangency of three streams that wend their way through the complexly interactive, variously coupled world of rural development. Kingdon's terminology is narrow, but his points general. These three streams—problems, policies, and politics—develop

> ... and operate largely independently of one another. Solutions are developed whether or not they respond to a problem. The political stream may change suddenly whether or not the policy community is ready or the problems facing the country have changed. The economy may go sour, affecting the budget constraint, which imposes a burden on both politicians and policy specialists that was not of their own making. The streams are not absolutely independent, however. The criteria for selecting ideas in the policy stream, for instance, are affected by specialists' anticipation of what the political or budgetary constraints might be ... Despite these hints of connections, the streams still are largely separate from one another, largely governed by different forces, different considerations and different styles . . . .Once we understand these streams taken separately, the key to understanding agenda and policy change is their coupling. The separate streams come together at critical times. A problem is recognized, a solution available, the political climate makes the time right for change, and the constraints do not prohibit action. Advocates develop their proposals and then wait for problems to come along to which they can attach their solutions, or for a development in the political stream like a change of administration that makes their proposals more likely to be adopted . . . I label an opportunity for pushing one's proposals a "policy window" . . . (Kingdon 1984: 93–94)

Within this framework, power arises out of those uncommon moments when rural development policies, problems, and politics converge so that the problems of the moment are tangent to the politics of the moment which in turn are tangent to the policies of the moment.[5] Depending on these tangencies, multinationals do have power, the president is powerful, the district councilor is far from powerless. But such instances of power are very much a matter of contingency. It could well have been otherwise and will be otherwise, when the streams meander off in their own directions and with great surprise and unpredictability, *as they inevitably will in cells 2 and 4 situations.* To say that something has "power" in a cells 2 and 4 world is simply to say the present is an alternate version of what could have happened instead. More concretely, contingent power arises, if it arises at all, in a world that is cells 2 and 4 precisely because many, if not most, parties to an issue, including the experts, are in the grip of many unknowns, frequent surprise, and little agreement there, where few involved know what really is in their best long-run interests, and where most everyone is playing it by ear, including the so-called power brokers.

Or to put it in narrative analytical terms: contingent power arises only when access to decision-making resources is articulated and differentiated through and by means of competing development (counter)narratives. Unequal power relations and power interests work themselves out across multiple sites and through the competition and opposition of development narratives that get people to change their own stories when conditions are complicated, full of unknowns, or divisive in the extreme. Indeed, competing narratives that change peoples' minds and end up "telling the better story" are the primary way we know that unequal access to resources really does matter when it comes to how any issue is perceived, communicated, and managed in situations of high interactive complexity.

Moreover, if we start with the oft-repeated insight that institutionalized relations of power are only really visible when they are already in decline,[6] then the corollary is that power relations are most effective when transparent, that is, when they are embodied in what we take as the unquestioned "givenness" of the world, in our common-sense understanding of reality. Thus, when one sets about to defamiliarize the givenness of reality through the kinds of strategies recommended in chapter 1 and throughout *Except-Africa*, s/he is confronting power, be it contingent or otherwise. Power is challenged intentionally or unintentionally, every time we generate a counternarrative whose claim to policy relevance is that it reconceives the development narratives of the day as if their time had passed, as if complexity itself creates plausible alternative readings of what we had taken for granted up until now. Such challenges are the key driver of rural development, because they represent the search for assumptions that stabilize and thereby legitimate decision making in the face of a genuinely complex development. Once again: there can be no development without alternatives. To return to where this book started: development in the absence of counternarratives is simply not possible.

***

If politics is not about power but first about complexity, then just what is this politics of complexity and what are its implications for the practice of rural development in Africa and elsewhere? Complexity has been defined in terms of three elements (e.g., Demchak 1991): the number of components in a system, the degree of differentiation in components, and the degree of interdependence among components. Since the problems of rural development are more numerous, varied, and interrelated than ever before, they are in this way more complex. In such instances, surprise and unintended consequences are never far behind because cause and effect in the system in which one is intervening is never fully apprehended, where the intervention itself frequently increases the complexity at issue. For example, when the local level is asked to do and involve more (e.g., increasing peoples' participation), its level of operational complexity increases enormously, other things being equal, especially as such interventions rarely entail a simultaneous reduction in other local operational tasks.

In order to better understand just what is meant by a politics of complexity, assume it is cast as a counternarrative of opposites just as the power narrative has been. That is to say, a politics of complexity will end up being articulated around opposites as was power, though the poles in this case center around "complex" and its oppositional variations of "simple," "neither complex nor simple, and "both complex and simple." We already see this underway. Some of the objection to direct power explanations of behavior has been a sense that what actually happens in Africa has been much more complicated. Moreover, even where things do prove to be relatively simple and straightforward, it is frequently said to be because of complex factors working to that end. Many would agree both that there have been relatively few, if any, successful large, donor-funded livestock projects in Africa and that this is because many of these projects have had multiple and inconsistent objectives, many constraints, often unwarranted design assumptions, multiple and conflicting evaluative criteria, and just too many unintended consequences.

What makes a politics of complexity more than the obvious, however, lies in the analytic purchase that comes from grappling with what it means to be those opposites, "neither complex nor simple" and "both complex and simple." The terms are not counterintuitive, as it might first seem, and with substantial effect. To understand what is neither complex nor simple, return to the three elements of complexity: the number of components, component differentiation, and the interdependence among components. Presumably, a relatively simple system is one with few components, little differentiation, and slight interdependence, whereas a system having more of each would be complex by comparison. What, in effect, is neither complex nor simple in this way? That is, what has no components, is undifferentiated, and exhibits no interdependence?

One obvious candidate is the immediacy of those epiphanies best conveyed by novelists and diarists. Leaving the bar and stumbling along the village path and drunk and pissing under the great globe of stars in the moonless night and knowing in an instant that it is all seamless, synesthetic, here in Botswana. Walking uphill to the government offices after a thunderstorm, pulling down a wet rose from the bush in front, and it is sky, raindrops, and the smell of rose and damp fused in a perfect counterpoint to my reach. Reading Sembene Ousmane's *God's Bits of Wood* in one sitting, through the night, under a hissing Coleman lamp, and the sensation that here it all is, in this book, a coherence, a frame of reference marking the dark beyond my lamplight as the place where struggle and family and purpose and experience have the single rush of wind. The old woman in Tsholotsho sitting under the thatch shade of her hut, legs straight out on the ground, hands folded on her lap, immobile, squinting into a blinding sunlight as white and hot as corrugated roofing sheets, a fly zigzagging across her cheek. The Motswana boy, having slashed about his eyes with a razor blade, his welts bleeding, screaming as he is dragged from my office, "I am you and you are me I am you and you are me I am you and you are me I . . . " This in-the-world of the lived moment becomes so elemental and immediate as to be beyond the flux of "complex" and "simple."

Terms are even less adequate when it comes to describing what is both complex and simple. Here I resort to analogy.

Many policy problems today have been described as both outlined and inlined (Riggs 1980). Say I have before me a sketch of a rowboat. The boat could be outlined as well as inlined. In the former, the shape was drawn as a boat; in the latter, a number of surrounding shapes have been drawn leaving behind, in the middle so to speak, the shape of a rowboat. In such examples, the shape's perimeter, as it were, mediates what the shape is taken to be—on one side of the line it is inlined, on the other side outlined. For example, the issue of homelessness is highly inlined because it is circumscribed by and takes its form from being a shelter problem, an income problem, a deinstitutionalization problem, a welfare problem, a race problem, and the like. Similarly, homelessness has its own configuration—it is a policy problem in its own right—because it is more than just a housing problem, income problem, race problem, and so on.

To return to the elements of complexity (components, differentiation, and interdependence), a policy issue is complex when it is highly inlined by a set of circumscribing and interrelated issues, while still being relatively simple in that it is its own issue with its own merits. A good example of these distinctions at work in African development studies has been the expatriate advisor discussed in chapter 4.

There we saw that the critics have found it easy enough to typecast expatriate advisors. These advisors exemplify direct power at its worst. If memory serves me right, Ousmane's film, *Xala*, has a scene where the colonial bureaucrats get up from the table and leave the room; black bureaucrats then file in and take their places at the table, and the whites re-enter now as advisors taking the chairs behind the blacks. Motivated by class and self-interest to secure long-term donor and employment prospects, these advisors are the ones who really make the decisions.

As we saw earlier, the problem is that this universalized narrative is wrong. The circumstances of expatriate advisors are far more complex and yet simpler than their outsider critics appreciate. They are more complex because what case material we have on advisors suggests that *in general terms* their effectiveness depends on an unpredictable, complex intersection of the advisor's background and the broader environment in which s/he works. That said, there is a sense in which being an expatriate advisor is simpler than even their critics suppose. While the effectiveness of an advisor depends generally on the tangency of complex conditions not altogether under his or her control, the effectiveness of any single advisor depends specifically on how s/he adapts to and exploits this tangency. *In specific terms* an effective advisor is one who is able to juggle multiple roles in government, e.g., s/he is an expert, manager, colleague, and expediter all rolled into one (see Roe 1987b). Moreover—and this is the important point—the juggling is most effective when it comes across as effortless and natural, straightforward and without deviousness, in short, simple and transparent. A good juggler is precisely what it takes to convince people that being a colleague and a manager at the same time does not involve contradictory mandates (especially if people believe that a colleague is someone who by definition does not act like a manager or expert).

Direct-power advocates would have us believe otherwise. The advocates (be they direct, indirect, artificial, or organic) simply cannot believe that the primary reason why advisors have to juggle roles is due to the multiple and unpredictable requirements of their task environment, where again, few people know what their real interests are or, when they do, they don't know how to promote those interests over time periods that matter to them. For many direct-power advocates, interests are clear and opposing; there is always an enemy or a difference that matters. Our foes or the differences may confuse us, but that they are our foes and that there are real differences never let us doubt. Uncertainty is a word that rarely passes the lips of the direct-power advocate. They persist in believing that cell 1 thinking is the only way to handle a cells 2 and 4 world.

***

To be fair, some advocates of the power narrative do believe they are complexifying power. Certainly, academics who are proponents of indirect power or artificial negativity are out to problematize direct power in fresh ways. Still, no social scientist who appeals to the complex interplay of power interests in Society, Culture, History, Politics, and Kapital to explain why the African Leader was doomed to fail could possibly subscribe to the belief that, while all that might be true, what also matters—*and matters equally*—is, quite simply, this Leader was an incompetent manager or politician. For power advocates to believe that would mean things were, well, too complex.

One night in Gweru, Zimbabwe, I was having supper when my table-mate burst out laughing, saying: "You shouldn't be in development, if you can't answer that!" "That" is the well-known conundrum: how can an Africa head of state, such as Nkrumah, Nyerere, de Klerk, or Mugabe, be personally and directly responsible for mucking things up in his respective country, when the fact of the matter is that the country he "leads" is not a command economy, but one whose many parts are more often than not loosely, rather than tightly, linked and unpredictably, rather than predictably, so? Isn't "leadership" simply cell 1 thinking in a cells 2 and 4 world?

The answer, at least in Robert Mugabe's case, is that the one thing he had "control" over—a highly politicized leadership style that transforms questions of national policy into questions about party performance—has independently undermined government policy-making and implementation, thereby adding even more uncertainty to an already complex economy. Mugabe may not have the control he would like others to believe he has, but he has politicized what control there is and to a very high degree (chapter 6). Before direct-power advocates take the preceding as support for their views, how Mugabe has juggled his way into this position remains unclear, highly complicated, and most certainly not reducible to "control = direct power" terms.

Subscribers to the four-poled power narrative do not see it this way. For them, Mugabe and the economy are ultimately marionettes, animated by those long chains of causality linked to the real sources of power, and it is these real sources of power which are working behind the scenes to ensure that Mugabe's intentions have no functionally independent role in explaining why he does what he does. Nothing could be further away from an economy that is loosely, rather than tightly, coupled and complexly, rather than predictably, interactive than these and all the other puppets that crowd contemporary African studies.

So the answer to my South African friend is: yes, there is politics, but it is the politics of complexity whose starting point is complexity, not power. Unlike the power narrative, this counternarrative, the politics of complexity, means you no longer know what side, if there is a side, you'll end up on when choosing who or what to be "against."

✳✳✳

I conclude by staking out some of the counternarrative territory of what it means to subscribe to a politics of complexity, one that takes complexity and its implications seriously, whether that politics is practiced in Africa or wherever.

First, we scarcely have a language to describe what could be called, for lack of a better term, the complexity counternarrative. Each pole—complex, simple, immediate, and mediating—turns out to be complex in its own way. What is simple, as we saw, often is so for complex reasons. What is complex depends on interdependence, of which we have no good measure. To describe the immediacy of an epiphany takes far more than the simple skills many of us have, and as for trying to grasp what might be both complex and simple in the same instant, that too, we have seen, is a complex undertaking. I can think of no greater challenge ahead in the study of politics than that of finding a language for the counternarrative that better articulates these poles of complexity along with their more subtle combinations and permutations.

Second, the conjunction of politics and complexity places up-front the core dilemma many power advocates have been happy to obscure. The social scientist or cultural theorist who finds, for example, that power is more complex than commonly supposed can leave the matter at that. No need to make anything like a practical recommendation about what real people with real problems in real time should do, now that things have been shown to be more complex. Their critique is policy relevant simply by virtue of being a critique of power, and what is more policy relevant than power, right?

Wrong. This trick won't work in a politics of complexity. Here you can't criticize your way to policy relevance. A politics that starts with complexity has always to ask: *how do we underwrite and stabilize the assumptions for policy-making in the face of that complexity? How can we make policy choices in the presence of recurrent surprise and persistent unpredictability?* Chapter 1 outlined six answers to the questions, while the bulk of *Except-Africa* has focused on one, the counternarrative option. Each option, however, shares the same implications. Each means avoiding the person who believes that the real objective of analysis is to critique and destabilize, without obligation to provide an alternative to that which is being criticized. Each means avoiding people who automatically assume their analysis is policy relevant, who wouldn't ever dirty their hands in such low-life things as having to choose the losers of a public policy, who in other words couldn't care less whether they had access to policymakers who treated their work seriously and used it in making decisions. Each means, finally, avoiding people who think that just because something can be criticized, something needs to be criticized. In short—and this is the sobering part—it means avoiding precisely many advocates of the polarized power narrative. Again: there can be no development without being committed to providing counternarratives.

The distaste that many power advocates in African studies have for working in or with government, a.k.a. the state, is palpable. Plucking up "development" between the tweezers of twin scare quotes is about as close as these critics want to get to something so power-saturated that it stinks from every direction. If government builds the road it planned, it is criticized for doing "development"; if it fails to build the road, it is criticized because its plans are based on wrong assumptions. In either case, government is not doing its job, because it can't have a job worth doing. Thus, the Wonderland of Permanent Critique identified in chapter 4: if a government policy actually succeeds, then it's a disaster or a misuse of power. The fact that a policy's implementation frequently falls short of what was originally planned is, however, never enough to make the failed policy a "success." In the critics' view, the real success would have been ensuring that government did not have the power to undertake the policy in the first place. Yet, if the criterion for success is government not undertaking a bad policy, then why aren't governments praised by critics for the many bad policies they have considered but not undertaken? But no critic wants to praise "state power," thank you very much! In their Wonderland, the critics' role is always to stand in opposition to the state, no matter if this stance raises nettlesome questions like, Just how does permanent critique determine when the future is better than the present, the present better than the past? But who needs alternatives, when you don't believe in "development" at all!

In contrast to the Wonderland, let me conclude by describing the very real counternarrative terrain we are led to in a politics of complexity. The classic method of stabilizing any system—biological, engineering, organizational—from a complexly turbulent environment is to decouple that system from that environment as best as one can. What would a politics of complexity look like if it were focused on such decoupling? There are no firm answers here, but available literature triangulates on the following (Roe 1998).

First, a politics of complexity would remind us that loose coupling itself is rational in a complex world, where system delays, reserves, and flexibility are not only required but desirable. It recommends decentralization if you are worried about coping with surprises in situations where delay and unpredictability are endemic. It implies that what works better is often a smaller scale of decision making, where information gatherers are as well the users of that information. It suggests that the fewer steps in implementation and the more conditional the probabilities (where success at one step enhances the chances of success at the next step), then the greater the chances for implementation as planned (precisely what is found in various localities and communities). It pulls us to the local level where those cell 1 notions we were brought up to believe in—power politics, learning curves, "getting the big picture"—have a better chance of being matched by cell 1 situations for which the notions are more appropriate. It maintains that some processes and systems are cases in their own right—when is policy a variable or a case?—and have to be analyzed as such. It argues fiercely against government micromanagement and for community-based management. It notes there are some important allocations systems—what Jon Elster calls local justice systems—which really are local and localized, that is, semi-decomposable from larger systems and must be treated as such. It resists a global analytic that scales up, rather than down, policy issues more effectively dealt with locally or regionally. It insists on distinguishing between insiders and outsiders to any local management system. It recognizes that no matter how interconnected the world is causally, people's stories about this world—their arguments and scenarios—are typically much less connected. Finally, it accepts the fact that sometimes the most useful analysis you can undertake is to use your own best judgment as to what are the merits of the case. This interdigitated landscape of loose coupling, decentralization, cases in their own right, communities, local justice, semi-decomposable subsystems, scaling downward, insiders and outsiders, cell 1 thinking only for cell 1 situations, locally conditional probabilities, and using your best judgment is the horizon, I believe, disclosed to us by a politics of complexity. Moreover, it is a landscape to which all of us are being driven, and not just in Africa. As the world becomes more complex and turbulent, one can expect more and more pressure to decouple from that world, particularly when that is the only way we have left to stabilize the assumptions for decision making in the face of a complexity and uncertainty that is out of our control. Once we have this landscape better in sight for Africa, we can see just how greatly advocates of the power narrative have muddled matters by claiming as anticolonialism, independence movements, nationalism, and the rise of civil society what really are the secessionist (decoupling) tendencies arising out of the politics of complexity.

What does this mean practically? It suggests, for example, that Rob Nixon in a *Transition* piece, "Of Balkans and Bantustans," got the analysis right but the conclusion terribly wrong when he conflated secessionist movements and nationalism . Yes, one can agree that Buthelezi and de Klerk were worse than contemptible. Yes, they manipulate "ethnic" identity for disgraceful ends. Yes, you can't talk about the "ethnicity" in South Africa without addressing, in Nixon's words, "the effects of chaotic urbanization, epidemic unemployment, economic recession, generational conflict, the legacy of migrant labor, and the attendant crises in masculinity." All that, and more, is true. Is it any wonder, then, that when confronted with expedient leaders, confused public management and economic uncertainty, many South Africans—with or without scare quotes around terms like "Zulu" or "Tswana"—will want to decouple themselves from this New South Africa as much as they did from the Old South Africa? Contrary to what Nixon's analysis says, his is a case for, not against, secessionist movements.

***

A final point for those of us who have made Africa into an object of our profession. In an important sense, the terms "territory," "terrain" and "landscape" of a politics of complexity are misnomers. Those who have taken complexity seriously will have been struck by how "at sea" they are. Indeed, "being at sea" has been the most tenacious leitmotif in Western literature for describing what to do in the face of high complexity (and, again, not just in Africa):[7]

> Descartes: The Meditation of yesterday filled my mind with so many doubts that it is no longer in my power to forget them. And yet, I do not see in what manner I can resolve them; and, just as if I had all of a sudden fallen into very deep water, I am so disconcerted that I can neither make certain of setting my feet on the bottom, nor can I swim and so support myself on the surface. I shall nevertheless make an effort . . .
>
> Michael Oakeshott: In political activity, then, men sail a boundless and bottomless sea; there is neither harbour for shelter nor floor for anchorage, neither start-

ing-place nor appointed destination. The enterprise is to keep afloat on an even keel; the sea is both friend and enemy; and the seamanship consists in using the resources of a traditional manner of behavior in order to make a friend of every hostile occasion . . .

Hans Magnus Enzenberger: The question whether it's best to swim with the current or against it seems to me out of date . . . The method of the yachtsman who tacks with the wind as well as against it seems more fruitful. Such a procedure applied to society demands stoic disbelief and the greatest attentiveness. Anyone who wants to reach even the nearest goal must expect, step by step, a thousand unpredictable variables and cannot put his trust in any of them.

Otto Neurath: Imagine sailors who, far out at sea, transform the shape of their vessel . . . They make use of some drifting timber, besides the timber of the old structure, to modify the skeleton and the hull of their vessel. But they cannot put the ship in dock in order to start from scratch. During the work they stay on the old structure and deal with heavy gales and thundering waves. In transforming their ship they take care that dangerous leakages do not occur. A new ship grows out of the old one, step by step—and while they are still building, the sailors may already be thinking of a new structure, and they will not always agree with one another. The whole business will go on in a way we cannot even anticipate today . . . .That is our fate.

G.L.S. Shackle: [We] are like a ship's crew who have been wrecked in a swirling tide-race. Often a man will hear nothing but the roar of the waters in his ears, see nothing but the dim green light. But as he strikes out, his head will come sometimes well above the water, where for the moment he can see clear about him. At that moment he has the right to shout directions to his fellows, to point the way to safety, even though he may feel sure that next moment he will be again submerged and may then doubt whether after all he has his bearings.

Many of us, men and women alike, from Africa and beyond, are indeed in turbulent seas, our ship is taking on water, and the task is to rebuild it with whatever is at hand. We do so with what we have, as going back to port is no longer an option. The task ahead is difficult and complicated, which is why we must act now. And should we eventually find ourselves in the broil of Shackle's tide-race, the first thing we do is shout out advice to our mates, since that is the best, the absolute very best, we can do.

Complexity and uncertainty in politics are, to summarize, the reason why we act, not our excuse for inaction. But then again, as power advocates in African studies are always fond of telling us, only "power" can account for inaction.

If we act now, we can keep African studies afloat with the debris of real life floating all around us, these odds and ends and surprises left behind by the very peoples we set out to know. But to do that we must first pull our gaze away from the mirage on the horizon toward which we have been navigating. In truth, there is no navigation chart for where we are. No lantern on the stern or backward-facing angel can tell us where we are, let alone what's up ahead. In the far distance, the shore of that continent promised by the mirage may well only be the overlapping shorelines of many different islands, each inhabited in its own right and all variously connected, if connected at all.

Whatever, our powerful dreams have drawn us into uncharted, changeable waters that are, at least for now, the only home African studies has.

Notes

1. In case it needs saying, the argument here is not that everything in a complex world is equally subject to change all the time. There are, for examples, models in evolutionary biology and population genetics that suggest increasing complexity can give rise to some relatively stable characteristics, e.g., the fixing of the vertebral column in the vertebrates as distinct from the less complex invertebrates (Wagner 1998).
2. What follows is a reading off of the opposing positions on a Greimassian semiotic square, whose defining pole is "direct power." For an introduction to the square, see again Schleifer (1987).
3. See Chabal (1992).
4. See Marcuse (1965); Roe (1990); and Sinfield (1992).
5. In such circumstances, the question, "'Who *really* makes the decision?'. . .is meaningless," according to Nobel Laureate, Herbert Simon; "a complex decision is like a great river, drawing from many of its tributaries the innumerable component premises of which it is constituted. Many individuals and organization units contribute to every large decision. . ." (1976). His colleague and another organization theorist, James March, put it this way: power occurs in decision making when "different parts of the system contribute to different decisions in different ways at different times" (1966).
6. Instances of this insight are commonplace. Zygmunt Bauman notes that the term intellectual arose during the Dreyfus scandal, precisely at the moment the homogeneity and cohesiveness of intellectuals as a group was in decline. Michael Hamburger notes that terms, like culture, gain increasing importance and popularity, precisely at the moment things like culture are in disarray and shambles. See Zygmunt Bauman, *Legislators and Interpreters: On Modernity, Post-Modernity and Intellectuals*, Polity Press, Oxford, p. 21 (1987). See also Michael Hamburger, *Testimonies: Selected Shorter Prose, 1950–1987*, Carcanet, Great Britain, p. 50 (1989). For the general principle involved, see John Myles's review in *Contemporary Sociology*, vol. 18, no. 2, p. 219 (1989).
7. The quotes are from: Descartes in Charles Simic, *Wonderful Words, Silent Truth: Essays on Poetry and a Memoir*, University of Michigan Press, Ann Arbor, p. 56 (1990); Michael Oakeshott, "Political Education," in Timothy Fuller (ed.)*The Voice of Liberal Learning: Michael Oakeshott on Education*, Yale University Press, New Haven, pp. 149–150 (1989); Hans Magnus Enzenberger, *Mediocrity*

and Delusion: Collected Diversions (Martin Chalmers, tr.), Verso, London, pp. 161–162 (1992); Otto Neurath, *Foundations of the Social Sciences*, vol. 2, no. 1, International Encyclopedia of Unified Science, The University of Chicago Press, Chicago (1944); G.L.S. Shackle, *Uncertainty in Economics and Other Reflections*, Cambridge University Press, Cambridge, p. 239–240 (1955).

Selected Bibliography

Aaron, Henry, in *The Journal of Human Resources*, vol. 25, no. 2, (1990).

Abercrombie, Frank D., *Range Development and Management in Africa* (Washington, DC: Office of Development Services, Bureau for Africa, United States Agency for International Development, 1974).

Agrawal, Arun, "The Grass Is Greener on the Other Side: A Study of Raikas, Migrant Pastoralists of Rajasthan" (London: IIED Drylands Issue Paper, 1992).

Animal Production Research Unit, *Beef Production and Range Management in Botswana* (Gaborone, Botswana: Ministry of Agriculture, 1980).

Bailey, Charles, *Cattle Husbandry in the Communal Areas of Eastern Botswana*, Ph.D. dissertation (Ithaca, NY: Cornell University, 1982).

Barber, William, "Land Reform and Economic Change Among African Farmers in Kenya," *Economic Development and Cultural Change*, vol. 19, no. 1 (Oct. 1970), pp. 6–24.

Behnke, Roy H., Ian Scoones, and Carol Kerven, *Range Ecology at Disequilibrium.* (London, England: Overseas Development Institute, 1993).

Bekure, Solomon and Neville Dyson-Hudson, *The Operation and Viability of the Second Livestock Development Project (1497–BT): Selected Issues.* Report (Gaborone, Botswana: Ministry of Agriculture, 1982).

Bernard, Frank, *East of Mount Kenya: Meru Agriculture in Transition* (Munich: Weltforum Verlag, 1972).

Bienen, Henry, Devesh Kapur, James Park, and Jeffrey Riedinger, "Decentralization in Nepal," *World Development*, vol. 18, no. 1 (1990).

Blaikie, Piers and Harold Brookfield, *Land Degradation and Society* (London: Methuen, 1987).

Boffey, Philip M., "Spread of Deserts Seen as Catastrophe Underlying Famine," *New York Times* (8 Jan. 1985).

Bonte, Pierre, "Ecological and Economic Factors in the Determination of Pastoral Specialization," in John Galaty and Philip Carl Salzman, *Change and Development in Nomadic and Pastoral Societies* (Leiden, The Netherlands: E.J. Brill Publishers, 1981).

Brand, Coenraad, "Will Decentralization Enhance Local Participation?" in A.H.J. Helmsing, N.D. Mutizwa-Mangiza, D.R. Gasper, C.M. Brand, and K.H. Wekwete (eds.), *Limits to Decentralization in Zimbabwe* (Harare: University of Zimbabwe, 1991).

Brokensha, David and E.H.N. Njeru, "Some Consequences of Land Adjudication in Mbere Division, Embu," Working Paper no. 320 (Nairobi: Institute of Development Studies, University of Nairobi, 1977).

Caiden, Naomi, "The New Rules of the Federal Budget Game," *Public Administration Review*, vol. 44, no. 2 (Mar./Apr. 1984).

Caiden, Naomi and Aaron Wildavsky, *Planning and Budgeting in Poor Countries* (New York: John Wiley and Sons, 1974).

Caro, Deborah A., "The Socioeconomic and Cultural Context of Andean Pastoralism," in Corinne Valdivia, *Sustainable Crop-Livestock Systems for the Bolivian Highlands* (Columbia, MS: University of Missouri, 1992).

Chabal, Patrick, *Power in Africa* (New York: St. Martin's Press, 1992).

Chambers, Robert, *Challenging the Professions: Frontiers for Rural Development* (London: Intermediate Technology Publications, 1993).

Chambers, Robert, *Rural Development: Putting the Last First* (London: Longman, 1983).

Chambers, Robert, *Managing Rural Development: Ideas and Experience from East Africa* (Uppsala, Sweden: The Scandinavian Institute of African Studies, 1974).

Cohen, David and Janet Weiss, "Social Science and Social Policy: Schools and Race," in Carol Weiss (ed.) *Using Social Research in Public Policy Making* (Toronto: Lexington Books, 1977).

Cohen, John, *Integrated Rural Development: The Ethiopian Experience and the Debate* (Uppsala, Sweden: The Scandinavian Institute of African Studies, 1987).

Cohen, John and David Lewis, "Role of Government in Combatting Food Shortages: Lessons from Kenya 1984–85," in Michael Glantz (ed.), *Drought and Hunger in Africa* (Cambridge: Cambridge University Press, 1987).

Colclough, Christopher and Stephen McCarthy, *The Political Economy of Botswana: A Study of Growth and Distribution* (Oxford: Oxford University Press, 1980).

Coldham, Simon, "Land-Tenure Reform in Kenya: The Limits of the Law," *The Journal of Modern African Studies*, vol. 17, no. 4 (Dec. 1979).

Colony and Protectorate of Kenya, *A Plan to Intensify the Development of African Agriculture in Kenya,* compiled by R.J.M. Swynnerton (Nairobi: Government Printer, 1954).

Dahl, Gudrun, and Anders Hjort, *Pastoral Change and the Role of Drought*, SAREC Report R2 (Sweden: Swedish Agency for Research Cooperation with Developing Countries, 1979).

Dahl, Gudrun, and Anders Hjort, *Having Herds* (Stockholm, Sweden: University of Stockholm, 1976).

De Boer, A. John, James A. Yazman, and Ned S. Raun, *Animal Agriculture in Developing Countries: Technology Dimensions*, Development Studies Paper Series (Morrilton, AR: Winrock International Institute for Agricultural Development, Feb. 1994).

de Haan, Cornelis, "An Overview of the World Bank's Involvement in Pastoral Development," Pastoral Development Network Paper 36b (London: Overseas Development Institute, 1994).

Demchak, Chris, *Military Organizations, Complex Machines* (Ithaca, NY: Cornell University Press, 1991).

Demchak, Chris, "Tailored Precision Armies in Fully Networked Battlespace: High Reliability Organizational Dilemmas in the 'Information Age,'" *Journal of Contingencies and Crisis Management*, vol. 4, no. 2 (June 1996).

de Valk, P. and K. Wekwete, "Challenges for Local Government in Zimbabwe," in P. de Valk and K. Wekwete (eds.), *Decentralizing for Participatory Planning?* (Aldershot, Great Britain: Gower Publishing Company, 1990).

de Valk, P. and K. Wekwete, eds., *Decentralizing for Participatory Planning?* (Aldershot, Great Britain: Gower Publishing Company, 1990).

Doggett, Clinton, *The Vihiga Project: A Development Experience in Africa* (Nairobi: USAID/Kenya, 1973).

Doig, Jameson W. and Erwin Hargrove, eds., *Leadership and Innovation: A Biographical Perspective on Entrepreneurs in Government* (Baltimore: Johns Hopkins University Press,
1987).

Dyson-Hudson, Rada, "Ecology of Nomadic Turkana Pastoralists: A Discussion," in Whitehead, Emily et al, *Arid Lands Today and Tomorrow*, the proceedings of a conference (20 Oct. 1985), held in Tucson, Arizona (Boulder, CO: Westview Press, 1988).

Dyson-Hudson, Rada, and Neville Dyson-Hudson, "Nomadic Pastoralism," *Annual Review of Anthropology*, no. 9 (1980).

Egner, Brian, *The District Councils and Decentralisation, 1978–1986*, Report to SIDA (Gaborone, Botswana, 1986).

Ellis, Frank, *Peasant Economics* (2d ed., Cambridge, Great Britain: Cambridge University Press, 1993).

El Wakeel, Ahmed, and Mohamed Azim Abu Sabah, "Relevance of Mobility to Rangeland Utilization," *Nomadic Peoples*, no. 32 (1993).

Enzenberger, Hans Magnus, *Mediocrity and Delusion: Collected Diversions*, trans. Martin Chalmers (Verso: London, 1992).

Fairhead, J. and M. Leach, "False Forest History, Complicit Social Analysis—Rethinking Some West African Environmental Narratives," in *World Development*, vol. 23, no. 6 (June 1995).

Fleuret, Anne, "Some Consequences of Tenure and Agrarian Reform in Taita, Kenya," in R. E. Downs and S.P. Renya (eds.), *Land and Society in Contemporary Africa* (Hanover, NH: University Press of New England, 1988).

Fortmann, Louise, "Peasant and Official Views of Rangeland Use in Botswana: Fifty Years of Devastation?" in *Land Use Policy* (July 1989).

Fortmann, Louise, and Emery Roe, *The Water Points Survey,* Report (Gaborone, Botswana: Ministry of Agriculture and center for International Studies, Cornell University, 1981).

Fortmann, Louise and Emery Roe, "Common Property Management of Water in Botswana," in *Proceedings of the Conference on Common Property Resource Management* (Washington, DC: National Academy Press, 1986).

Galaty, John G., and Douglas L. Johnson, eds., *The World of Pastoralism* (New York: Guilford Press, 1990).

Galaty, John and Dan Aronson, "Research Priorities and Pastoralist Development: What is to be Done?," in John Galaty, Dan Aronson, Philip Salzman, and Amy Chouinard (eds.), *The Future of Pastoral Peoples: Proceedings of a Conference Held in Nairobi, Kenya, 4–8 August, 1980* (Ottawa: International Development Research Center, 1981).

Gasper, D.R., "Decentralization of Planning and Administration in Zimbabwe: International Perspectives and 1980s Experiences," in A.H.J. Helmsing, N.D. Mutizwa-Mangiza, D.R. Gasper, C.M. Brand, and K.H. Wekwete (eds.), *Limits to Decentralization in Zimbabwe* (Harare, Zimbabwe: University of Zimbabwe, 1991).

Gasper, Des and Raymond Apthorpe, "Introduction: Discourse Analysis and Policy Discourse," *The European Journal of Development Research*, vol. 8, no. 1 (1996).

Gefu, Jerome O., and Jere L. Gilles, "Pastoralists, Ranchers and the State in Nigeria and North America," *Nomadic Peoples*, no. 25–27 (1990).

Gilles, Jere, "The World Bank and Pastoral Development," Pastoral Development Network Paper, no. 36b (London, England: Overseas Development Institute, 1994).

Gilles, Jere, and Cornelis de Haan, "Recent Trends in World Bank Pastoral Development Projects: A Review of 13 Bank Projects in Light of the 'New Pastoral Ecology,'" Pastoral Development Network Paper, no. 36b (London, England: Overseas Development Institute, 1994).

Government of Botswana, Ministry of Agriculture, *Botswana's Agricultural Policy: Critical Sectoral Issues and Future Strategy for Development* (Gaborone, Botswana, 1991).

Government of Zimbabwe, *Report of the Commission of Inquiry Into Taxation* (Harare, Zimbabwe: Government Printer, 1986).

Gray, Nancy, "Acceptance of Land Adjudication Among the Digo," Discussion Paper no. 37 (Nairobi: Institute of African Studies, 1972).

Green, Joy, "Evaluating the Impact of Consolidation of Holdings, Individualization of Tenure, and Registration of Title: Lessons from Kenya," LTC Paper no. 129 (Madison: Land Tenure Center, University of Wisconsin, 1985).

Gunby, D.S., "Government and Rural Institutions," Consultant's Paper prepared for the National Action Committee for Rural Water Supply and Sanitation (Harare, Zimbabwe: Ministry of Local Government Rural and Urban Development in association with the World Bank, 1992).

Hahn, F., *Equilibrium and Macroeconomics* (Basil Blackwell: Oxford, 1992).

Hardin, Garrett, "The Tragedy of the Commons," in Garrett Hardin and John Baden (eds.), *Managing the Commons* (San Francisco: W.H. Freeman and Company, [1968] 1977).

Hardin, Garrett, "Denial and Disguise" and "An Operational Analysis of 'Responsibility,'" in Garrett Hardin and John Baden (eds.), *Managing the Commons* (San Francisco, 1977).

Haugerud, Angelique, "Development and Household Economy in Two Eco-Zones of Embu District," Working Paper no. 382 (Nairobi: Institute of Development Studies, University of Nairobi, 1981).

Haugerud, Angelique, "The Consequences of Land Tenure Reform among Smallholders in the Kenya Highlands," *Rural Africana*, nos. 15–16 (Winter 1983).

Haugerud, Angelique, "Land Tenure and Agrarian Change in Kenya," *Africa*, vol. 59, no. 1 (1989).

Helmsing, A.H.J., "Rural Local Government Finance—Past Trends and Future Options," in A.H.J. Helmsing, N.D. Mutizwa-Mangiza, D.R. Gasper, C.M. Brand, and K.H. Wekwete (eds.), *Limits to Decentralization in Zimbabwe* (Harare, Zimbabwe: University of Zimbabwe, 1991).

Helmsing, A.H.J., N.D. Mutizwa-Mangiza, D.R. Gasper, C.M. Brand and K.H. Wekwete, eds., *Limits to Decentralization in Zimbabwe* (Harare, Zimbabwe: University of Zimbabwe, 1991).

Helmsing, A.H.J. and K. Wekwete, "Financing District Councils: Local Taxes and Central Allocations," RUP Occasional Paper no. 9 (Harare, Zimbabwe: Department of Rural and Urban Planning, University of Zimbabwe, 1987).

Heussler, Robert, *Yesterday's Rulers* (Syracuse, NY: Syracuse University Press, 1963).

Heyer, Judith and J.K. Waweru, "The Development of the Small Farm Areas," in

Judith Heyer, J.K. Maitha, and W.M. Senga (eds.), *Agricultural Development in Kenya: An Economic Assessment* (Nairobi: Oxford University Press, 1976).

Hitchcock, R.K. and T. Nkwe, "Social and Environmental Impacts of Agrarian Reform in Rural Botswana," in J.W. Arntzen, L.D. Ngcongco, and S.D. Turner (eds.), *Land Policy and Agriculture in Eastern and Southern Africa* (Tokyo: The United Nations University, 1986).

Hjort, Anders, "Herds, Trade, and Grain: Pastoralism in a Regional Perspective," in John Galaty, Dan Aronson, Philip Salzman, and Amy Chouinard (eds.), *The Future of Pastoral Peoples: Proceedings of a Conference Held in Nairobi, Kenya, 4–8 August, 1980* (Ottawa: International Development Research Center, 1981).

Hobbs, Joseph, *Bedouin Life in the Egyptian Wilderness* (Austin, TX: University of Texas Press, 1989).

Holm, John, "The State, Social Class and Rural Development in Botswana," in Louis Picard (ed.), *The Evolution of Modern Botswana* (London and Lincoln: Rex Collings and University of Nebraska Press, 1985).

Hunt, Diana, *The Impending Crisis in Kenya: The Case for Land Reform* (Aldershot, England: Gower Publishing Company, 1984).

Huntington, Samuel P., "Why International Primacy Matters," in *International Security*, vol. 17, no. 4 (1993).

Hyden, Goren, *No Shortcuts to Progress: African Development Management in Perspective* (Berkeley: University of California Press, 1983).

IFAD/UNDP, "Historical Perspective, Existing ASAL Programmes and Institutional Analysis," Technical Paper no. 3 written by Dr. Gideon Cyrus Mutiso, in *Republic of Kenya—Arid and Semi-Arid Lands (ASAL) Development Programme: Summary of Technical Reports on the Strategy, Policy and ASAL Development Programme 1989–1993* (Nairobi, n.p.: 1988)

International Labour Office, *Employment, Incomes and Equality: A Strategy for Increasing Productive Employment in Kenya* (Geneva: International Labour Organization, 1972).

Isaac, Jeffrey, "The End of Power," *Transition* 64 (1994).

Jayne, T.S., M. Chisvo, B. Hedden-Dunkhorst, and S. Chigume, "Unravelling Zimbabwe's Food Insecurity Paradox: Implications for Grain Marketing Reform," in *Integrating Food, Nutrition and Agricultural Policy in Zimbabwe*, UZ/MSU Food Security Project, 1990 Proceedings of the First National Consultative Workshop (Harare, Zimbabwe: University of Zimbabwe, 1990).

Johnson, Douglas L., "Nomadism and Desertification in Africa and the Middle East," *Geojournal*, no. 31.1 (Sept. 1993).

Johnston, Bruce and William Clark, *Redesigning Rural Development: A Strategic Perspective* (Baltimore, MD: The Johns Hopkins University Press, 1982).

Kawamura, Itsuo, "Summary and Conclusions," in Dominick Salvatore (ed.), *African Development Prospects: A Policy Modeling Approach* (New York: Taylor and Francis on behalf of the United Nations, 1989).

Kennedy, Paul, *Preparing for the Twenty-first Century* (New York: Random House, 1993).

Kenya Times, "Focus on 1989 Nakuru Show—Rift Valley: Land of Plenty," Newspaper article prepared by Mr. Yusuf Haji, the Rift Valley Provincial Commissioner (Nairobi: 29 June 1989).

Kingdon, J.W., *Agendas, Alternatives, and Public Policies* (Little/Brown: Boston, 1984).

Korten, David, "Community Organization and Rural Development: A Learning Process Approach," *Public Administration Review*, vol. 40, no. 5 (Sept./Oct. 1980).

Kuznar, Lawrence, "Transhumant Goat Pastoralism in the High Sierra of the South Central Andes: Human Responses to Environmental and Social Uncertainty," *Nomadic Peoples*, no. 28 (1991).

Lamb, David, *The Africans* (New York: Vintage, 1984).

Lancaster, William, and Fidelity Lancaster, "The Concept of Territory Among the Rwala Bedouin," *Nomadic Peoples*, no. 20 (Mar. 1986).

La Porte, Todd, "High Reliability Organizations: Unlikely, Demanding, and At Risk," *Journal of Contingencies and Crisis Management*, vol. 4, no. 2 (June 1996).

La Porte, Todd, "'Organization and Safety in Large Scale Technical Organizations': Lessons from High Reliability Organizations Research and Task Force on 'Institutional Trustworthiness," paper prepared for a seminar on Man-Technology-Organization in Nuclear Power Plants, Finnish Centre for Radiation and Nuclear Safety, Technical Research Center of Finland, Olkiluoto, Finland (14–15 June 1993).

La Porte, Todd and Paula Consolini, "Working in Practice But Not in Theory: Theoretical Challenges of 'High Reliability Organizations,'" *Journal of Public Administration Research and Theory*, vol. 1, no. 1 (1991).

Leach, James, "Administrative Coordination in African Rural Development," *Agricultural Administration II*, vol. 11, no. 4 (1982).

Leach, James, "Managing Rural Development in Botswana," *Public Administration and Development*, vol. 1, no. 4 (1981).

Leach, James, "Rural Development, Botswana: Project Findings and Recommendations" (United Nations, TC/BOT-72–028/1, 1980).

Leach, James, "The Kenya Special Rural Development Programme," *Journal of Administration Overseas*, vol. 13, no. 2 (1974).

Lele, Uma, *The Design of Rural Development: Lessons from Africa* (Baltimore and London: The Johns Hopkins University Press, 1975).

Leonard, David, *African Successes: Four Public Managers of Kenyan Rural Development* (Berkeley: University of California Press, 1991).

Leonard, David, "Disintegrating Agricultural Development," *Food Research Institute Studies*, vol. 19, no. 2 (1984).

Lewis, John P., "Overview: Development Promotion: A Time for Regrouping, " in John P. Lewis and Valeriana Kallab (eds.), *Development Strategies Reconsidered*, U.S.-Third World Policy Perspectives no. 5 (Washington, DC: Overseas Development Council, 1986).

Loabsy, B., *Equilibrium and Evolution* (Manchester University Press: Manchester and New York, 1991).

Ludwig, Donald, Ray Hilborn, and Carl Walters, "Uncertainty, Resource Exploitation, and Conservation: Lessons from History," *Science*, vol. 260 (2 Apr. 1993).

Mace, Ruth, "Pastoralist Herd Compositions in Unpredictable Environments: A Comparison of Model Predictions and Data from Camel-Keeping Groups," *Agricultural Systems*, no. 33 (1990).

Manger, Leif, "Managing Pastoral Adaptation in the Red Sea Hills of the Sudan: Challenges and Dilemmas, "Dryland Networks Programme Issues Paper, no. 52 (London: International Institute for Environment and Development, Sept. 1994).

Mannarelli, Thomas, Karlene Roberts and Robert Bea, "Learning How Organizations Mitigate Risk," *Journal of Contingencies and Crisis Management*, vol. 4, no. 2 (June 1996).

March, James G., "Power of Power," in D. Easton (ed.) *Varieties of Political Theory* (Englewood Cliffs, NJ: Prentice-Hall, 1966).

March, James and Johan Olsen, "The New Institutionalism: Organizational Factors in Political Life," *American Political Science Review*, vol. 78, no. 3 (1984).

Marcuse, Herbert, "Repressive Tolerance," in Robert Paul Wolff, Barrington Moore, Jr, and Herbert Marcuse, *A Critique of Pure Tolerance* (Boston: Beacon Press, 1965).

McCay, Bonnie and James Acheson, eds., *The Question of the Commons: The Culture and Ecology of Communal Resources* (Tucson: The University of Arizona Press, 1987).

Merafe, Yvonne, "Social and Economic Effects of the Tribal Grazing Land Policy in Botswana with Particular Reference to Livestock Production," in *Botswana— Education, Culture, and Politics: Seminar Proceedings no. 29*, Proceedings of a conference held 15–16 December 1988 (Edinburgh: Center for African Studies, University of Edinburgh).

Merton, Robert, "Insiders and Outsiders: A Chapter in the Sociology of Knowledge," *American Journal of Sociology*, vol. 78, no. 1 (1972).

Ministry of Lands and Settlement, "Programme of Work and Performance Targets for the Year 1988," Memo numbered MLS 2/001 vol. II/(16) (Nairobi: Jan. 1988).

Ministry of Local Government Rural and Urban Development, *Rural District Council's Accounting Handbook: Trainer's Manual*, First Draft (Harare, Zimbabwe: Government of Zimbabwe, 1990).

Molomo, Mpho, "The Bureaucracy and Democracy in Botswana," in John Holm and Patrick Molutsi (eds.), *Democracy in Botswana* (Athens, OH: The Botswana Society, the University of Botswana, and Ohio University Press, 1989).

Molomo, Mpho, "Land Reform and the Tragedy of the Commons in Botswana," *Pula: Botswana Journal of African Studies*, vol. 6, no. 2 (1989a).

Molutsi, P.P., "The Ruling Class and Democracy in Botswana," in John Holm and Patrick Molutsi (eds.), *Democracy in Botswana* (Athens, OH: The Botswana Society, the University of Botswana, and Ohio University Press, 1989).

Montgomery, John D., "Probing Managerial Behavior: Image and Reality in Southern Africa," *World Development*, vol. 15, no. 7 (1987).

Moris, Jon, *Managing Induced Rural Development* (Bloomington: International Development Institute, Indiana University, 1981).

Moris, Jon and Derrick Thom, *African Irrigation Overview: Main Report*, Water Management Synthesis Report 37 (Logan: Utah State University, 1987).

Mutizwa-Mangiza, N.D., "Decentralization and District Development Planning in Zimbabwe," *Public Administration and Development*, vol. 10, no. 4 (1990).

Nellis, J.R., "Report on the Special Rural Development Programme: Calendar Year 1971" (Nairobi: Institute of Development Studies, University of Nairobi, 1972).

Neurath, Otto, *Foundations of the Social Sciences*, vol. 2, no. 1, International Encyclopedia of Unified Science (Chicago: University of Chicago Press, 1944).

Njeru, E.H.N., "Land Adjudication and its Implications for the Social Organization of the Mbere," Research Paper no. 73 (Madison: Land Tenure Center, University of Wisconsin, 1978).

Oakeshott, Michael, "Political Education," in Timothy Fuller (ed.)*The Voice of Liberal Learning: Michael Oakeshott on Education* (New Haven, CT: Yale University Press, 1989).

Oba, Gufu, "Perception of Environment Among Kenyan Pastoralists: Implications for Development," *Nomadic Peoples*, no. 19 (Sept. 1985).

Odell, Malcolm and Marcia Odell, "Communal Area Livestock Development in Botswana: Lessons for the World Bank's Third Livestock Development Project," Paper presented to the World Bank (Amesbury, MA: Synergy International, 1986).

Odingo, Richard, "The Dynamics of Land Tenure Reform and of Agrarian Systems in

Africa: Land Tenure Study in the Nakuru, Kericho and Machakos Areas of the Kenya Highlands" (Rome: FAO, 1985), cited in Green (1985).

Oluoch-Kosura, Willis in collaboration with S.E. Migot-Adholla, A World Bank-sponsored study on the effect of land registration in four localities from two districts in Kenya (Nairobi: forthcoming).

Panel on Common Property Resource Management, *Proceedings of the Conference on Common Property Resource Management* (Washington, DC: National Academy Press on behalf of the Board on Science and Technology for International Development, Office of International Affairs, National Research Council, 1986).

Parson, Jack, *Botswana: Liberal Democracy and the Labor Reserve in Southern Africa* (Boulder, CO and London: Westview Press, 1984).

Parson, Jack, "Cattle, Class and State in Rural Botswana," *Journal of Southern African Studies*, vol. 7, no. 2 (1981).

Perrow, Charles, *Normal Accidents: Living with High Risk Technologies* (New York: Basic Books, 1984).

Perrow, Charles, "The Limits of Safety: The Enhancement of a Theory of Accidents," *Journal of Contingencies and Crisis Management*, vol. 2., no. 4 (Dec., 1994).

Peters, Pauline, "Embedded Systems and Rooted Models: The Grazing Lands of Botswana and the 'Commons' Debate," in Bonnie McCay and James Acheson (eds.), *The Question of the Commons* (Tucson: The University of Arizona Press, 1987).

Peterson, Stephen, "Microcomputers and Institutional Development: Emerging Lessons from Kenya," Paper prepared for the Harvard Institute of International Development Conference on Economic Reform, Marrakech, Morocco, October 1988 (Nairobi, 1988).

Picard, Louis, *The Politics of Development in Botswana: A Model for Success?* (Boulder, CO and London: Lynne Rienner Publishers, 1987).

Picard, Louis, "Bureaucrats, Cattle, and Public Policy: Land Tenure Changes in Botswana," *Comparative Political Studies*, vol. 13, no. 3 (1980).

Pinckney, Thomas, John Cohen, and David Leonard, "Microcomputers and Financial Management in Development Ministries: Experience from Kenya," *Agricultural Administration*, vol. 14, no. 3 (1983).

Prince, Gerald, *A Dictionary of Narratology* (Lincoln: University of Nebraska Press, 1987).

Ragin, C., "Introduction: Cases of 'What is a case?'," in C. Ragin and H. Becker, eds., *What Is a Case: Exploring the Foundations of Social Inquiry* (Cambridge: Cambridge University Press, 1992).

Ramakrishnan, Subramaniam, "Issues in Budgeting and Fiscal Management in Sub-Saharan Africa," Discussion paper prepared for the Workshop on Economic Reform in Africa sponsored by the University of Michigan's Center for Research on Economic Development and USAID(Nairobi: July 1989).

Reckers, Ute, "Learning from the Nomads: resource and Risk Management of Nomadic Pastoralists," *U.N. Desertification Control Bulletin*, no. 24 (1994).

Republic of Botswana, *White Paper of 1975: National Policy on Tribal Grazing Land* (Gaborone, Botswana: Government Printer, 1975).

Riggs, Fred, "The Ecology and Context of Public Administration: A Comparative Perspective," *Public Adminsitration Review*, vol. 40, no. 2 (1980).

Roberts, Karlene, "Some Characteristics of High Reliability Organizations," School of Business Administration, University of California at Berkeley (Feb. 1988).

Rochlin, Gene, "Reliable Organizations: Present Research and Future Directions," *Journal of Contingencies and Crisis Management*, vol. 4, no. 2 (June 1996).

Rochlin, Gene, "Defining 'High Reliability' Organizations in Practice: A Taxonomic Prologue," in Karlene Roberts, *New Challenges to Understanding Organizations* (New York, NY: Macmillan Publishing Company, 1993).

Roe, Emery, *Taking Complexity Seriously: Policy Analysis, Triangulation and Sustainable Development* (Kluwer Academic Publishers, 1998).

Roe, Emery, "On Rangeland Carrying Capacity," *Journal of Range Management*, vol. 50, no. 5 (Sept. 1997).

Roe, Emery, *Narrative Policy Analysis* (Durham, NC: Duke University Press, 1994).

Roe, Emery, "Against Power, For the Politics of Complexity," in *Transition* 62 (1994a).

Roe, Emery, "Global Warming as Analytic Tip," in David Feldman (ed.), *Global Climate Change and Public Policy* (Chicago: Nelson-Hall, 1994b).

Roe, Emery, "Global Warming as Analytic Tip," *Critical Review*, vol. 6, nos. 2–3 (1993).

Roe, Emery, "Report on the Amalgamation of District Councils and Rural Councils," CASS Occasional Paper NMR: 7/1992 (Harare, Zimbabwe: Center for Applied Social Science Research, University of Zimbabwe, 1992a).

Roe, Emery, "Government has no coherent policy on communal area development," *The Financial Gazette* (Harare, Zimbabwe: 23 July 1992b).

Roe, Emery, "Intertextual Evaluation, Conflicting Evaluative Criteria, and the Controversy over Native American Burial Remains," *Evaluation and Program Planning*, vol. 15, no. 4 (1992b).

Roe, Emery, "Artificial Negativity and University Affirmative Action," *Telos*, no. 86 (1990).

Roe, Emery, "Six Myths About Livestock Rangeland Development South of the Sahara," *Rangelands*, vol. 11, no. 2 (October 1989).

Roe, Emery, "Folktale Development," *American Journal of Semiotics*, vol. 6, no. 2 (1989b).

Roe, Emery, *Uncommon Grounds for Commons Management: Making Sense of Livestock Rangeland Projects South of the Sahara*, unpublished Ph.D. dissertation, University of California, Berkeley (1988).

Roe, Emery, "The Expatriate Advisor as Senior Policy Analyst," *Policy Studies Review*, vol. 7, no. 3 (1988a).

Roe, Emery, "Management Crisis in the New Class," *Telos*, no. 76 (Summer 1988b).

Roe, Emery, "Counting on Comparative Budgeting in Africa," *International Journal of Public Administration*, vol. 11, no. 3 (May 1988c).

Roe, Emery, "Individualism and Community in Africa?: The Case of Botswana," *The Journal of Modern African Studies*, vol. 26, no. 2 (June 1988d).

Roe, Emery, "Last Chance at the African Kraal: Reviving Livestock Projects in Africa," in J.T. O'Rourke (ed.), *Proceedings of the 1987 International Rangeland Development Symposium* (Morrilton, AZ: Winrock International Institute for Agricultural Development, 1987a).

Roe, Emery, "Lantern on the Stern: Policy Analysis, Historical Research, and Pax Britannica in Africa," *African Studies Review*, vol. 30, no. 1 (March 1987b).

Roe, Emery, "The Ceiling as Base: National Budgeting in Kenya," *Public Budgeting and Finance*, vol. 6, no. 2 (Summer 1986).

Roe, Emery, "Project Appraisal: A Venture Capitalist Approach," *Development Policy Review*, vol. 3, no. 2 (Nov. 1985).

Roe, Emery, "Range Conditions around Water Sources in Botswana and Kenya," *Rangelands*, vol. 6, no. 6 (Dec. 1984).

Roe, Emery, "Who Brews Traditional Beer in Rural Botswana?: A Review of the Literature and Policy Analysis," in *Botswana Notes and Records*, vol. 13 (1981).

Roe, Emery, Lynn Huntsinger, and Keith Labnow (forthcoming), "High Reliability Pastoralism," *Journal of Arid Environments*.

Roe, Emery and Louise Fortmann, *Allocation of Water Points at the Lands* (Gaborone, Botswana: Ministry of Local Government and Lands and the Center for International Studies, Cornell University, 1981).

Roe, Emery and Louise Fortmann, *Season and Strategy: The Changing Organization of the Rural Water Sector in Botswana*, Special Series in Rural Development (Ithaca, NY: Rural Development Committee, Cornell University, 1982).

Rosenau, J. and M. Durfee, *Thinking Theory Thoroughly* (Boulder, CO: Westview Press, 1995).

Roth, Paul, "How Narratives Explain," *Social Research*, vol. 56, no. 2 (Summer 1989).

Sagan, Scott, *The Limits of Safety: Organizations, Accidents, and Nuclear Weapons* (Princeton, NJ: Princeton University Press, 1993).

Sanders, Rickie, "The Last Decade: A Content Analysis of the *African Studies Review*, 1982–91," *African Studies Review*, vol. 36, no. 1 (Apr. 1993).

Sandford, Stephen, *Management of Pastoral Development in the Third World* (Chichester, England: Wiley, 1983a).

Sandford, Stephen, *Organisation and Management of Water Supplies in Tropical Africa*, (Addis Ababa, Ethiopia: International Livestock Center for Africa, 1983b).

Sax, Joseph , "Property Rights and the Economy of Nature: Understanding *Lucas v. South Carolina Coastal Council*," *Stanford Law Review*, vol. 45 (May 1993).

Schick, Allen, "Microbudgetary Adaptations to Fiscal Stress in Industralized Democracies," *Public Administration Review*, vol. 48, no. 1 (Jan./Feb. 1988).

Schleifer, Ronald, *A.J. Greimas and the Nature of Meaning: Linguistics, Semiotics and Discourse Theory* (Lincoln: University of Nebraska Press, 1987).

Schulman, Paul, "Heroes, Organizations and High Reliability," *Journal of Contingencies and Crisis Management*, vol. 4, no. 2 (June 1996).

Schulman, Paul, "The Analysis of High Reliability Organizations: A Comparative Framework," in Karlene Roberts, *New Challenges to Understanding Organizations* (New York, NY: Macmillan Publishing Company, 1993).

Scoones, I., *Living with Uncertainty: New Directions for Pastoral Development in Africa*. Overview Paper prepared for the Workshop on New Directions in African Range Management and Policy, Woburn, UK, June 1993 (International Institute for Environment and Development, London, 1994).

Shanmugaratnam, Nadarajah, Trond Vedeld, Anne Mossige, and Mette Bovin, "Resource Management and Pastoral Institution Building in the West African Sahel," Discussion Paper no. 175 (Washington, DC: The World Bank, 1992).

Shackle, G.L.S., *Uncertainty in Economics and Other Reflections* (Cambridge: Cambridge University Press, 1955).

Shipton, Parker, *Land, Credit and Crop Transactions in Kenya: The Luo Response to Directed Development in Nyanza Province*, Ph.D. diss. (Cambridge: University of Cambridge, 1985).

Sidahmed, Ahmed and L. Koong, "Application of Systems Analysis to Nomadic Livestock Production in the Sudan," in James Simpson and Phylo Evangelou (eds.), *Livestock Development in Subsaharan Africa: Constraints, Prospects, Policy* (Boulder, CO: Westview Press, 1984).

Simic, Charles, *Wonderful Words, Silent Truth: Essays on Poetry and a Memoir* (Ann Arbor, MI: University of Michigan Press, 1990).

Simon, Herbert, *Administrative Behavior*, 3d ed. (New York: The Free Press, 1976).

Sinfield, Alan, *Faultlines: Cultural Materialism and the Politics of Dissident Reading* (Berkeley: University of California Press, 1992).

Sorrenson, M.P.K., *Land Reform in the Kikuyu Country: A Study in Government Policy* (Nairobi and London: Oxford University Press, 1967).

Sperling, Louise, and John Galaty, "Cattle, Culture, and Economy: Dynamics in East African Pastoralism," in John Galaty and Douglas Johnson, *The World of Pastoralism* (New York: Guilford Press, 1990).

Spooner, Brian, "The Cultural Ecology of Pastoral Nomads," *Addison-Wesley Modules in Anthropology,* no. 45 (Reading, MA: Addison-Wesley, 1973).

Stevens, William K., "Threat of Encroaching Deserts May Be More Myth Than Fact," *New York Times* (18 Jan. 1994).

Stoddart, L., A. Smith, and T. Box, *Range Management* (New York: McGraw-Hill, 1975).

Sullivan, Timothy, "Knowledge and Method in the Study of Public Management," Paper prepared at the Graduate School of Public Policy (Berkeley and Los Angeles: University of California, 1987).

Swallow, Brent, "The Role of Mobility within Risk Management Strategies of Pastoralists and Agropastoralists," in Gatekeeper Series, no. 47 (London: International Institute for Environment and Development, 1994).

Takavarasha, T., "An Analysis of Zimbabwe's Agricultural Price Policy Since Independence," Paper prepared for the Conference on Zimbabwe's Agricultural Revolution: Implications for Southern Africa (Victoria Falls, Zimbabwe: July 1991).

Tandon, Y., "Technical Assistance Administration and High-Level Manpower Requirements in Uganda," in Y. Tandon (ed.), *Technical Assistance Administration in East Africa* (Stockholm: The Dag Hammarskjold Foundation, Almqvist and Wicksell, 1973).

The Economist, "Emerging-Market Indicators," vol. 330, no. 7849 (5 Feb. 1994).

The Economist, "The World This Week: Business and Finance," vol. 328, no. 7821 (24 July 1993).

Tiffen, M., M. Mortimore, and F. Gichuki, *More People, Less Erosion*. (New York: J. Wiley, 1994).

United Nations Development Program, "Pastoral Natural Resource Management and Policy," (New York: UNDP, 1994).

United Nations Economic Commission for Africa, *African Alternative Framework to Structural Adjustment Programmes for Socio-Economic Recovery and Transformation*, E/ECA/CM.15/6/Rev.3 (New York?: 1989).

Uphoff, Norman, *Local Institutional Development: An Analytical Sourcebook with Cases* (West Hartford, CN: Kumarian Press, 1986).

USAID, "Suggestions for the Improvement of Rangeland Livestock Projects in Africa: A Panel Report" (Washington, DC: 1985).

Vedeld, Trond, "Procedural Law: Land Tenure Reforms as a Long-Term Political Process," Pastoral Development Network Paper, no. 36b (London: Overseas Development Institute, July 1994).

Viscusi, W. Kip, *Fatal Tradeoffs* (New York and Cambridge: Oxford University Press, 1992).

Wagner, Gunther, "Complexity Matters," *Science*, vol. 279, no. 5354 (20 Feb. 1998).

Walker, Brian H., "Rangeland Ecology: Understanding and Managing Change'" *Ambio*, vol. 22, no. 2–3 (May 1993).

Wangari, Esther, PhD dissertation on land registration in Lower Embu District (New York: New School for Social Research, forthcoming).

Wanmali, Sudhir "Patterns of Household Consumption and Production in Gazaland District," in S. Wanmali and J.M. Zamchiya (eds.), *Service Provision and its Impact on Agricultural and Rural Development in Zimbabwe: A Case Study of Gazaland District* (Washington, DC: Department of Physical Planning, Ministry of Local Government Rural and Urban Development, Government of Zimbabwe and International Food Policy Research Institute, 1992).

Wekwete, K.H, "Constraints to Planning for Socialism in Zimbabwe," in P. de Valk and K. Wekwete (eds.), *Decentralizing for Participatory Planning?* (Aldershot, Great Britain: Gower Publishing Company, 1990).

Wescott, Clay, "Microcomputers for Improved Budgeting by the Kenya Government," Development Discussion Paper no. 227 (Cambridge, MA: Harvard Institute for International Development, 1986).

Western, David, and Thomas Dunne, "Environmental Aspects of Settlement Site Decisions Among Pastoral Maasai." *Human Ecology*, vol. 7, no. 1 (1979).

Westoby, Mark, Brian Walker, and Imanuel Noy-Meir, "Opportunistic Management for Rangelands Not at Equilibrium," *Journal of Range Management*, vol. 42, no. 4 (July 1989).

Wildavsky, Aaron, *The Politics of the Budgetary Process*, 4th ed. (Boston: Little, Brown and Company, 1984).

Williams, Raymond, *The Country and the City* (London: The Hogarth Press, [1973] 1985).

Wilson, James Q., *Bureaucracy: What Government Agencies Do and Why They Do It* (New York: Basic Books, 1989).

Wilson, Rodney, "The Economic Implications of Land Registration in Kenya's Smallholder Areas," Staff Working Paper no. 91 (Nairobi: Institute of Development Studies, University of Nairobi, 1971).

World Bank, *Kenya: Agricultural Credit Policy Review*, Report no. 5619–KE (Washington, DC: August 1985).

World Bank, *World Development Report 1988* (New York: Oxford University Press, 1988).

World Bank, Economics and Policy Division, Department of Agriculture and Rural Development, *Livestock Strategy Paper*, draft (Washington, DC: World Bank, 1987).

World Bank, *Botswana National Land Management and Livestock Project: Staff Appraisal Report* (Washington, DC: Report no. 5471–BT, Eastern and Southern Africa Projects, Southern Agriculture Division, 1985).

Zolo, Danilo, *Democracy and Complexity* (University Park: Pennsylvania State University Press, 1992).

Index